FISH STICKS

*The Fall and Rise of the
New York Islanders*

Peter Botte
and
Alan Hahn

Sports Publishing L.L.C.
www.sportspublishingllc.com

Director of production: Susan M. Moyer
Developmental editor: Mark E. Zulauf
Copy editor: Cindy McNew
Dust jacket design: Kerri Baker

ISBN:1-58261-664-7

Printed in the United States of America

Sports Publishing L.L.C.
www.sportspublishingllc.com

Contents

Acknowledgments

The authors would like to thank their respective families for their love, support and patience throughout this project.

We also collectively need to thank the New York Islanders, who despite years of losing still managed to provide years of wildly entertaining stories—some of which might have been wild but not so entertaining at the time. And they still found a way to come up with a happy ending.

Also, thanks to Mike Milbury, who had nothing to do with this book and had serious reservations about it from the minute he heard we were working on it, but who opted to let two sportswriters tell their unbiased stories. We'd like to thank Stan Fischler, the dean of American hockey writers, who guided us to Sports Publishing L.L.C. and gave us encouragement along the way.

And finally, a special thanks to the many people who provided us with information for this book and the laughs we shared along the way. Like Patrick Flatley, who, when he heard we were working on a book about the Islanders, replied, "What is it, one of those truth-is-stranger-than-fiction stories?"

Exactly. You can't make this stuff up.

1

A Season on the Brink

And so erupted Mike Milbury in deliciously typical fashion one evening in a dimly lit, lacquered-wood bar at a posh Adirondack resort in upstate New York. He was telling the funniest, most ruthless and craziest hockey stories he knew and showing his intense passion and love for a sport that for some reason refused to equally love him back. He swung his tragically proper trademark after-dinner sambuca through the electrified air. The rest were drinking scotch, single malt, with a double shot of biting one-liners. And each Milbury crack drew more wide eyes and laughter.

This is the man at his finest, as he has been so many times over the years. Unbridled, unfettered and unflinching, and so damned charming that you never wanted that bottle of scotch to run dry. You never wanted the sun to come up over Whiteface Mountain, which slept in the distance of a crisp early autumn night sky over Lake Placid. You never wanted to run out of logs to toss on the fire. You didn't care what Islander legend he dared to label "a fucking asshole." He was on a roll. And when Mike Milbury's on a roll, you let him roll.

For many seasons as general manager of the shipwreck that was the New York Islanders, this was all the team had to keep it from being less than a blip on the screen. It was also all Milbury had to keep himself sane, and at times, even that was up for debate. Things were so bad for this franchise that he couldn't even hang himself with poor job performance. So for six straight losing seasons after he joined the organization in 1995, the irrepressible Milbury was the one constant—well, along with losing.

As quickly as they arrived on the scene as an expansion team in the early 1970s, the once-proud Islanders, who claimed four consecutive Stanley Cups in the early 1980s, had become the National Hockey League's punching bag. Milbury was the stuffing, and, oh, how they loved to try kicking the stuffing out of that franchise. The contentious Canadian hockey media had a field day with this American-born wise-ass who couldn't help himself when given the opportunity to sound off. And the legends of the fading glory years took their shots as from afar they watched the foundering franchise sink to the depths of the NHL.

For many years, one man was truly an island. How he stayed afloat is one of the greatest wonders, and stories, in sports history. How the franchise survived is equally amazing. And on this evening, surrounded by entranced amanuenses lost in his engaging presence and entertaining spin, Milbury was a bundle of nerves. He was overcome by anticipation and trepidation, which are the usual emotions a general manager feels at the start of every season after a summer spent building a team with the intent of winning hockey games.

For Milbury and the Islanders, however, this wasn't just a season. This was a comeback, one he dreamed he might live to see during those rare nights over the past six years when he actually did sleep. This was vindication, not just for him, but for an organization that was on life support only two seasons earlier under a miserly ownership that ran the franchise into near financial ruin. For an under-manned, unstable team that went through more hockey players than a Montreal puck bunny and was many times pronounced dead on arrival hardly a month into the season. For a masochistically loyal fan base that, no matter how bizarre things got with their team—from the ridiculous logo change to the nationally embarrassing news about their fraudulent new owner that was one of four ownership changes in a five-year span to the debilitating salary purge and perpetual last-place finishes—never gave up hope that one day those glory years would return.

But, deep down inside, it had to be mostly for him: a 49-year-old former lunch-pail defenseman from East Walpole, Massachusetts, who all of his life was haunted by a need to prove himself. Who, for six years on Long Island, had to deal with daily dysfunction that would put Jerry Springer to shame along with the echoes of fans chanting "Mike Must Go!" ringing in his head as the overmatched teams he would construct and destruct with impulsive fury were buried under the Nassau Coliseum ice.

Here was the stuffing's chance to finally kick back.

The rebirth of the franchise began on April 26, 2000, when billionaire computer magnate Charles Wang and his partner, Sanjay Kumar, bought the team and rescued it—and Milbury—from oblivion for one simple purpose: keeping both on Long Island. Between the two of them, Wang and Kumar had been to three hockey games in their lives, and all of them were Rangers games at Madison Square Garden. This was not a purchase of passion; it was one of philanthropy.

This was a challenge.

They walked in carrying a copy of the book *Hockey for Dummies.* After a transition season in 2000–01, they closed the book, opened their wallets and gave Milbury the green light to pursue star-quality players such as Alexei Yashin and Michael Peca, who both just happened to be available because of contract disputes with their former teams.

And just like that, the Islanders, who in 1999–2000 had the lowest payroll in the league at a sparse $15 million, had a far more workable budget that hovered around the league average.

"We're back in business," Milbury declared at the end of that eventful summer.

For the Islanders, it was as if the planets aligned and fortune, which seemed to defiantly avoid the franchise over the past decade, finally showed them some favor. Two high-quality centermen, players with a pedigree that teams look to build upon, were the cornerstones. And the mortar came in the form of Stanley Cup championship goalie Chris Osgood, who was left unprotected by the Detroit Red Wings in the preseason waiver draft. It was a draft for which the Islanders, thanks to a last-place finish the season before, sat first in line.

In hindsight, the debacle that was the highly disappointing 2000–01 season became a blessing. With Yashin, Peca and Osgood headlining a revamped roster that suddenly compared favorably against most of the NHL, the Islanders exploded out of the gates in October with 11 wins in their first 14 games and no losses in regulation. For the rest of the season, they never fell below seventh in the Eastern Conference, in which the top eight teams make the playoffs. And with the arrival of April, a month that had become relief only because it meant another depressing season was thankfully coming to an end, the Islanders had finally put an end to the misery. After seven long years, the longest current drought of any team in the NHL, the Islanders were back in the playoffs.

And Milbury had indeed lived to see the day.

In the end, you couldn't help but cheer for a team that made it through hockey hell and back. But you also had to applaud the resilient man who somehow survived the ride, survived himself and was front and center in the most bizarre era any sports franchise has ever endured.

2

Humiliation, Disintegration and Don Maloney

As one curse ended, another began.

It was fitting that the New York Rangers, the hated city rivals who for many years found themselves in the shadow of the great Islanders teams of the 1980s, delivered in April of 1994 the knockout blow, sending the Islanders reeling. It came only a year after the Rangers missed the playoffs and gasped as the Islanders made an inspiring run to the Stanley Cup semifinals in an attempt to add a fifth championship before the Rangers could muster just one in the time since the Islanders arrived on the scene in 1972.

That was the spring of 1993, when the Islanders were again the darlings of the New York hockey scene. They rolled through two playoff rounds and knocked off Mario Lemieux and the two-time defending champion Pittsburgh Penguins in a thrilling seven-game series before losing to the Montreal Canadiens, the eventual champion, one step before the Finals.

But in 1993–94, the Rangers became the toast of the town and the NHL and were determined to end the widely publicized 54-year curse. Led by fiery coach Mike Keenan and lion-hearted captain Mark Messier, the Rangers took the President's Trophy as the top team in the NHL during the regular season and then, in the first round of the playoffs, faced off against the Islanders, who earned a playoff berth in the second to last game of the season.

It was the eighth time the teams had met in the postseason since 1975, and the Islanders held a commanding 5-2 historical advantage. The Rangers, however, were a dominant force that quickly and easily disposed of their overmatched rivals in a four-game sweep without a single close game and a 22-3 aggregate score that included a pair of 6-0 shutouts at Madison Square Garden to open the series.

But what Islanders fans and Rangers fans alike remember most is how that series ended, with the Rangers celebrating the first-round walkover on the Coliseum ice while their fans filled the enemy's building with thunderous chants of "Let's Go Rangers!"

Islanders fans, who came to both games at the Coliseum with confidence, optimism and, of course, that needling "19-40!" chant that reminded Rangers fans how long it had been since the Rangers' last Cup, were long gone at that point. They sat in their cars in stunned silence along Hempstead Turnpike and the Meadowbrook Parkway, roads that at that time of year after a playoff game were usually turned into postgame block parties.

The playoffs, no matter if it was or wasn't a struggle to get there during the regular season, were always their time. They had witnessed so many magical moments: the amazing run in their first-ever playoff appearance in 1975, which saw a first-round win over these same Rangers and two improbable three-games-to-none comebacks in the next two rounds against the Pittsburgh Penguins and Philadelphia Flyers; the Easter Epic of 1987, which saw Pat LaFontaine score in quadruple overtime to eliminate the Washington Capitals in Game 7 of the first-round series; and the intoxicating miracle run just a year before. Not to mention the four straight Cups and 19 straight playoff series wins from 1980 to 1984, a record that will, in all likelihood, never be challenged.

They have had quick playoff exits before, but this one stung a bit more. And while disappointments from the past were usually forgotten in achievements that followed, the 1994 sweep by the Rangers was a pain that only got worse over time. It was a trickle of blood that became a gaping, almost fatal wound.

The dismantling was so thorough, so humiliating, that most people associated with the Islanders considered it the lowest moment in franchise history. While Messier, Keenan, Mike Richter, Brian Leetch, Stephane Matteau and the Rangers continued on a path to their cursed organization's only Stanley Cup title since 1940, the Islanders had no idea how low "low" could get.

Who would have believed it would be eight years before the team would see another playoff game? Who could have fathomed what would take place over that time?

The demise of that Islanders team actually began before the 1993–94 season, when newly appointed general manager Don Maloney, a former Ranger who signed with the Islanders in 1989 and played two seasons before retiring to the front office under the tutelage of Hall of Fame architect Bill Torrey, began to tear apart the '92–93 semifinal squad. In truth, though, the poor personnel decisions were simply a continuation of nearly a decade of laurel-resting and penny-pinching that belied the Islanders' reputation as the league's model franchise, one that built through strong drafting and shrewd trades in an unprecedented ascent from expansion team to champion.

It began with the breakup of one of the sport's last legitimate dynasties, which boasted five eventual Hall of Fame players—consummate two-way center Bryan Trottier, legendary goal hound Mike Bossy, premier defenseman Denis Potvin, swashbuckling big-game goaltender Bill Smith, and revolutionary power winger Clark Gillies—as well as one of the winningest and most respected coaches in NHL history, Al Arbour. It was a team whose so-called second-tier players—Bob Nystrom, Brent Sutter, John Tonelli and Butch Goring, to name just a few—were stars in their own right. It was a team that couldn't be assembled in the 21st-century NHL, not in a sport punctuated by spiraling finances which would have pushed that team's overall payroll to unprecedented levels likely to make even the big-city, bigger-spending Rangers blush.

Those Islanders upset the Philadelphia Flyers, the legendary Broad Street Bullies, winning their first Stanley Cup on Nystrom's redirection goal at 7:11 of overtime in Game 6 on May 24, 1980. The Minnesota North Stars went down in five games in 1981, the Vancouver Canucks were swept in 1982, and the Edmonton Oilers (the sport's next dynasty, winning five of the next seven Stanley Cups) were swept in 1983 with defensive-minded defenseman Ken Morrow scoring more goals than The Great Gretzky.

The sad truth, though, was that those Islanders were simply a team that then-ownership either couldn't or didn't want to afford. Owner John O. Pickett decided sipping margaritas poolside in Florida was a more favorable way to conclude his stewardship of the organization he had been credited with rescuing from potential financial ruin at the start of its Cup run.

While Torrey's scouting staff endured a brutal stretch of failed amateur drafts unable to replenish the aging talent base, the dynasty quickly fractured like an imitation Ming vase soon after the younger, faster and just plain better Edmonton Oilers of Messier and Gretzky ended the Islanders' Cup string by overpowering the weary four-time champions with a five-game victory in the 1984 Stanley Cup Finals.

Goring, a feisty two-way center considered the final piece of the Cup teams and someone who later returned as one of the more tragic figures in franchise history, was gone via waivers in the next year. Gillies, the prototypical Power Islander before anyone's kids ever heard of the Power Rangers, was also lost on waivers. Tonelli, who scored enough huge goals to remain prominent on the team's highlight reels in the new century, was traded away for two mediocre and entirely forgettable players, forward Rich Kromm and defenseman Steve Konroyd.

As for the biggest guns, Bossy's dominance was cut short by a debilitating back injury. He was forced to retire with 573 goals in just 10 seasons in 1987. Potvin and Smith also soon arrived at the twilight of their storied careers.

Perhaps the best example of the organization's drafting failures came in 1990, when they qualified for the postseason on the final day of the regular season despite a substandard 31-38-11 record. Choosing sixth overall in the entry draft that summer, the Islanders selected Saskatoon forward Scott Scissons, who would wind up appearing in just two games for them over four seasons in the organization. The Scissons failure stood out because the first five players chosen in that draft—Owen Nolan, Petr Nedved, Keith Primeau, Mike Ricci and Jaromir Jagr (a five-time NHL scoring leader as of 2001–02)—all reached 30 goals in one season at least once in their NHL careers.

Still, it was the way Trottier's playing days as an Islander ended—in a messy financial dispute that eventually landed him in bankruptcy after he concluded his playing career (including two more Stanley Cup titles with the Pittsburgh Penguins)—that signaled the true underlying problems with the Islanders, ones they were unable to shake until Wang and Kumar arrived more than a decade later: marketing and, of course, money.

Pickett eventually remarried and moved to Florida, initially leaving the Islanders under the stewardship of two of his trusted lieutenants.

Bill Skehan was the team's general counsel and an original Islander employee from the 1972–73 expansion season under their first owner,

Roy Boe. He was remembered by one former coworker mostly because "he never wore socks on the three days a week he showed up at the office." And Art McCarthy was hired in 1985 as the team's chief financial officer, a title he retained as of 2002 under current ownership.

"There was just no leadership, no planning, no vision. And no commitment," another former employee said. "Some of the people working there at the time, I wouldn't leave responsible for the cash cup at a lemonade stand."

Despite a landmark cable television deal that, with a $13 million annual payout, remains one of the most lucrative in the NHL, the Islanders began to play financial hardball with several of their players, including young American center and teen idol Pat LaFontaine, a new breed of superstar who was supposed to help the transition from the dynasty years. He ultimately was driven away because of an ugly contract impasse.

Still, the frugality wasn't reserved to the team itself. Pickett's financial decision makers purportedly chose the company's health insurance carrier one year because that company bought a luxury suite at Nassau Coliseum for the season. Employees worked without the promise of pensions or other amenities until the early 1990s.

On the ice, there were few shining moments until the spring of 1993, when a squad led by the players acquired in separate deals for LaFontaine, Sutter and others, such as Pierre Turgeon, Steve Thomas and Ray Ferraro, recaptured some of the magic that had been missing in the decade since the final championship banner had been raised by embarking on an unlikely run to the Wales Conference championship round.

By that time, Pickett had sold 10 percent of his share in the team— and, in an unheard-of move, control of the day-to-day hockey operations— to a four-man group of well-intentioned but ultimately overmatched local investors.

Like Pickett, Torrey also was moving on to Florida, but not to retire or to polish his championship rings. He was named president and general manager of an NHL expansion franchise based in south Florida, the Florida Panthers. While Torrey remained with the Islanders briefly as a consultant, the teasingly labeled "Gang of Four" management team—Robert Rosenthal, Stephen Walsh, Ralph Palleschi and Dr. Paul Greenwood— and new team president Jerome Grossman named the 34-year-old Maloney, Torrey's assistant for one and a half years, as the second of three general managers in franchise history and the youngest ever in the NHL.

"His record speaks for itself," Maloney said of Torrey on the afternoon Maloney's promotion was announced.

"My goal," he then dared to add, "is to eclipse his accomplishments."

Maloney was a hard-working winger known for his affable personality and his ability to maximize his hockey talent in carving out a 13-year career in the NHL, which included 214 goals and a designation as the most valuable player in the NHL All-Star Game in 1984. He also spent most of his career as a Ranger, and regardless of the immediate success the Isles enjoyed in his first season at the helm, that's what he always would remain for the majority of the team's fan base.

"Plus, Al was still there," one former player said about Arbour remaining behind the bench despite Torrey's departure. "There was no way Al, with everything he had accomplished, wanted to report to anyone, especially a young guy like Donnie."

Of the 64 players who convened for training camp in September of 1992, 63 of them (all but former Ranger Brian Mullen) had been drafted, signed or acquired by Torrey. Arbour and his coaching staff—former Islanders Smith, Lorne Henning and Rick Green—were Torrey's guys. Even former players Morrow and Darcy Regier—brought in by Torrey as the director of pro scouting and the assistant general manager, respectively— were not chosen by Maloney.

"It did enter my mind to quit," Arbour said at the time. "Then I said it's part of the business, always has been and always will . . . Hey, we've got a young group here and they're going to be entertaining."

While the team Torrey left behind had some flaws, completing the regular season with a middling record of 40-37-7, and while Arbour was the only remaining holdover from the Cup years, there was a unique chemistry forged among that collection of players.

No one expected much from them during the 1993 playoffs, except perhaps themselves. Arbour likened them to his formative Islanders teams before the Cup dynasty began.

His 1974–75 squad, in just the third year of the franchise's existence, had defeated the established Rangers in overtime of the final game of a best-of-three first-round series on J. P. Parise's unforgettable goal, the first of many clutch tallies in the franchise's young but storied history. In the following round against the Pittsburgh Penguins, the Isles became only the second team in North American professional sports history to overcome a 3-0 deficit to win a seven-game series. They nearly duplicated that feat in the Stanley Cup semifinals that season—again storming back from a three-game hole against Philadelphia, only to lose in Game 7.

If nothing else, the 1992–93 team showed similar qualities of character and perseverance throughout its unlikely playoff march. It relied on both stars and foot soldiers, it boasted emerging leaders and precocious youngsters, and it received contributions from all corners of the locker room.

Turgeon, the signature player obtained from the Buffalo Sabres in the 1991 deal for LaFontaine, had developed into a viable star center that season, producing 132 points and a whopping 58 goals. It was a goal total only Bossy previously had surpassed (albeit five times) in franchise history. Turgeon also copped the NHL's Lady Byng Trophy for sportsmanship and gentlemanly play.

Forwards such as Thomas, Benoit Hogue and Derek King joined Turgeon in shouldering much of the regular-season scoring load. But it was Ferraro, a fiery if undersized center, who nearly matched his regular-season offensive totals by leading the club in playoff scoring. And it was unheralded players such as Mullen, David Volek, Tom Fitzgerald and others, as so often is the case, who made names for themselves along the way.

Glenn Healy, by all rights, was a journeyman goaltender with not much of a track record to suggest the remarkable playoff ride he would take with the Islanders in 1993. But with the legendary Smith serving as the team's goaltending consultant, Healy's confidence increased with every spring victory.

And there were others. Russian defenseman Vladimir Malakhov, for instance, also was named to the NHL's All-Rookie team after he'd totaled 14 goals and 38 assists for an impressive 52 points in his first professional season.

But it was another rookie defenseman with Soviet roots, an agitating Lithuanian named Darius Kasparaitis, who immediately endeared himself to Islanders faithful with a hard-hitting and often reckless approach to defense and a cocky demeanor that was only accentuated by his quirky command of the English language. Kasparaitis's mauling and flustering of Lemieux in the '93 playoffs were considered among the most important factors in the Isles' shocking ouster of the two-time defending champion Penguins in the second round.

The Isles stole that series in seven games, with Volek, a little-used winger who was often booed at Nassau Coliseum, notching the overtime winner in the clinching game.

But they also won it without the services of Turgeon, who had been violently cross-checked from behind by Washington's Dale Hunter following a late insurance goal in the Isles' six-game elimination of the Capitals in the opening playoff round, which included three overtime victories. Hunter was suspended for 21 games by the NHL for that transgression, starting the following season. While Turgeon returned for the Wales Conference semifinals against the Montreal Canadiens, the eventual Stanley Cup champions, he was barely a factor as the Isles were ousted in five games in the best-of-seven series.

"We thought we could've won the Cup if 'Pete' was right," one former teammate said of Turgeon, who earned the nickname "Sneaky Pete" for his quiet ability to dominate a game offensively. "But he wasn't. There's no denying that."

Maloney and the Islanders worried that Turgeon never would be the same player after the incident, although the affable French Canadian did lead the team in scoring with 94 points despite missing 15 games to injury the following season. And he continued to produce into the next decade.

One thing was for sure, however. The Islanders were never the same team.

With one or two notable exceptions, Maloney actually kept most of the magical group intact to start the 1993–94 season. Some of the clubhouse chemistry was fractured, though, when an integral part such as Fitzgerald, a respected leader and penalty-killing forward, was left unprotected in favor of mediocre tough guy Mick Vukota and underwhelming forward Brad Dalgarno, a disappointing former first-round draft pick who would be out of the NHL within a few years. Fitzgerald was snapped up by Torrey's Florida Panthers in the expansion draft.

Still, fans always have love affairs with goaltenders, and many of them never forgave Maloney for also exposing Healy to that draft. He was chosen by the new Mighty Ducks of Anaheim and then by the Tampa Bay Lightning in Phase II of the expansion draft. Before the start of the season, Healy was traded to—gasp!—the Rangers. He served as Richter's backup goaltender during the Rangers' humiliating sweep of the Islanders in the 1994 first round and on their march to the Stanley Cup title. And Healy maintained a bitterness toward the organization ever after.

For Healy's replacement, Maloney imported veteran goaltender Ron Hextall from the Quebec Nordiques, a team that later relocated to become the Colorado Avalanche. Hextall, a former Philadelphia Flyer who never was able to endear himself to Islanders fans, was terrible in the playoffs against the Rangers (0–3 with a 6.08 goals-against average) and was gone one year later. Healy's departure, in fact, set off a revolving door within the Islanders that included 15 goaltenders before two-time Cup-winning veteran Chris Osgood arrived in 2001.

Arbour, who had taken a two-year sabbatical from coaching before returning to his post behind the bench in 1988, retired for good following the Rangers' sweep. But again, Maloney didn't conduct much of a coaching search. Arbour, who was named the team's vice president of hockey operations, basically handpicked Henning as his replacement.

Maloney, meanwhile, started small, but continued to break up the core of the 1993 team.

He ostensibly traded dependable defenseman Uwe Krupp for the rights to draft 18-year-old junior forward Brett Lindros, the younger brother of emerging Flyers star center Eric Lindros. One year earlier, with a few of the Islanders' defensemen injured, Maloney had killed a deal that would've sent Krupp to the Detroit Red Wings for promising center Keith Primeau, who would go on to become one of the top power forwards in the NHL.

While Maloney would forever be haunted by his claim that the Isles had just acquired "the better Lindros," he quickly compounded the ridicule by awarding the unproven project winger a five-year contract worth $7.5 million at the end of the 18-year-old's first training camp—and at a time when several players who had contributed to the team's success in previous seasons, such as Ferraro and Thomas, fought for every penny during their negotiations.

"That contract was a killer for Maloney," one NHL executive told Newsday. "After that, it was like he was afraid to make another mistake."

Not that it prevented him from making them.

Soon after, the NHL locked out its players in a labor dispute that lasted more than three months and shortened the regular season to 48 games when it resumed in late January.

Maloney was quoted during the lockout as saying the Lindros contract, "quite frankly, is a horse-shit deal." He admitted he felt pressured to sign him because the Islanders were desperate for a marquee name. But it wouldn't be Lindros, who scored two goals in 51 NHL games before he was forced to retire following a series of concussions after the 1995–96 season. He was 21 years old.

The opportunity Henning had trained his eye on for years didn't turn out to be much of an opportunity at all. He was the player who started the rush that led to Nystrom's overtime winner that clinched the Islanders' first Stanley Cup title in 1980. He also had been the head coach of the Minnesota North Stars in 1985-86 and that year was named a finalist for the Jack Adams Award before he was fired during the following season.

"He might not have been ready then," Arbour said at Henning's introductory press conference as his replacement, "but he's ready now."

Henning, an original Islander, had returned as one of Arbour's assistants in 1989, a position he retained until the Hall of Famer retired to the front office following the '94 playoffs as the NHL's second winningest coach ever, with 739 of his 781 victories over 22 seasons coming with the Islanders.

While Arbour pushed strongly for the team to choose his successor from inside the organization, Maloney continued to contemplate changes to shake up a roster of players he believed had grown stagnant the previous season.

"I don't think we can put the same team on the ice that finished the fourth game against the Rangers," Maloney said.

He insisted there were "very, very few" Islanders he wouldn't consider trading. Asked if there were, in fact, any untouchables, he said, "Quite frankly, no."

He wasn't kidding. The two most significant decisions of Maloney's four-year tenure as the second general manager in team history were still to come.

On April 5, the first of the two sent shockwaves throughout Long Island when he traded Turgeon and Malakhov, who never duplicated his rookie success, to the Montreal Canadiens for three players. The most notable of those coming in return was a gritty center named Kirk Muller whom Maloney expected to lead his wavering team back to prominence.

The second was his decision to can the coaching staff after the Isles had completed the abridged 1994–95 season with a 15-28-5 record, the first of what would become seven straight years of playoff misses (and 10 in 13 years) following a 14-year qualifying streak.

Maloney's first true search for his own coach ultimately led him to a franchise-altering choice as Henning's successor—and ultimately his own. Maloney pursued and hired blustery former Boston Bruins coach Mike Milbury as the sixth bench boss in team history in the summer of 1995.

3

Fish Sticks and the Great Kirk Muller

Kirk Muller popped into the home dressing room at Nassau Coliseum on a sunny June afternoon during the Stanley Cup Finals in 1995. This was the big debut of the Islanders' new uniforms, the first glimpse of what many fans and media members immediately crowed was a blasphemous move by management to make a final break from the team's storied past.

"I think it's awesome," Muller said of the new jerseys. The truth was, he never wanted to wear one, and it had nothing to do with the ill-advised fisherman someone thought was a good idea to affix on the front of it. In fact, Muller never wanted to wear any jersey with any Islanders logo on it.

The public relations fiasco that would be known as the Islanders' 1995–96 hockey season actually started near the end of the previous campaign, when Don Maloney committed the signature sin of what would be a short tenure in the general manager's office. He traded his best player, Pierre Turgeon, in a five-player deal for Muller, a widely respected leader who simply wanted no part of leading the Islanders back to the playoffs after they had failed to qualify during the lockout-abridged 1994–95 season.

If Maloney's worst crime was his misguided belief that his first blockbuster move would benefit the Islanders on the ice, the four-pronged management group's decision to drastically alter the team's fashion sense only accelerated their transformation into league laughingstocks.

"We never intended to strip the team of its tradition," Islanders cochairman Bob Rosenthal said. "But we made a mistake. We did not read the signals correctly. We misunderstood the underlying passion of the fans."

The team's dwindling yet impassioned fan base never forgave Maloney for the Turgeon trade, not even after Maloney and Muller were both mercifully expunged from the organization over the next nine months. But the logo fiasco served as a rallying point for a segment of fed-up paying customers who suddenly found themselves forming activist groups and organizing protest rallies rather than worrying about the power play or the Stanley Cup playoffs.

The infamous Gang of Four management group assumed operating control from Pickett in early August, just before the start of the 1992–93 season. They were nice guys. They were longtime season ticket holders. They were highly successful local businessmen.

And they were totally in over their heads from the wacky day they were introduced to the New York media. On the eve of the foursome's official announcement that they would be allowed to run the team in exchange for a $10-million loan to Pickett—with an understanding that the loan could be converted and augmented up to a 50-percent ownership stake over five years—Cablevision Systems chairman Charles Dolan also announced that he had negotiated a complicated deal with Pickett to purchase 99 percent of the team.

At the Gang of Four's introductory August 17 press conference at the Garden City Hotel, longtime *Newsday* columnist Steve Jacobsen raised his hand and asked the first question. It was straight out of the classic hockey movie *Slapshot*.

"So," Jacobsen asked, "Who own da Chiefs?"

Who, indeed.

According to Pickett's complex agreement with Dolan, Dolan was to assume responsibility for the Islanders' $32-million debt—$22 million in bank debt and the $10 million in the form of the convertible loan made by Long Island businessmen Stephen Walsh, Robert Rosenthal, Ralph Palleschi and Dr. Paul Greenwood. Pickett was to retain just a one-percent interest in the team, which was to be run by the Gang of Four.

"We both saw it as sort of an inevitable transaction," said Dolan, who claimed the management group was aware of his interest when it made its loan on August 7. "For 10 years we had discussed it, on and off.

But our positions are different now and it is perhaps more possible now for Cablevision to do it, for me to do it, than it was then."

Cablevision owned half of SportsChannel, which broadcast Islanders games. Pickett and Dolan had struck a 30-year broadcast contract in 1982, during the middle of the Stanley Cup run. It was extraordinarily lucrative to Pickett, bringing him between $10 million and $15 million per year.

Pickett had assumed control of the Islanders when they were on the verge of bankruptcy in 1978 before moving to Florida to count Dolan's cable cash shortly after the team's four-year Cup reign ended.

"One of the problems we had was that the franchise had lost touch with Long Island," Pickett told *Newsday.* "Here I was, the owner of the team and I live in Florida. I didn't know anybody in the community, didn't know the businesses we were dealing with. We never had to sell tickets before. It was a no-brainer. And then, all of a sudden, we had to go out and sell a product and we had no idea who we were dealing with, what we had to do to sell it, and it hurt us.

"We could have sold the team faster. We could have sold it to Joe Blow from Illinois, could have sold it to a group from Alabama. But there is more to it than just owning a franchise on Long Island. Owning the Rangers is different. Anybody can own the Rangers. But Long Island is still a community. We needed someone local."

Dolan, for more than 40 years a Long Island resident, was thought to be that person. But Pickett's agreement to sell his controlling interest in the team to Dolan fell through under the weight of complexity in July of 1993. And Dolan ultimately formed a partnership that bought Madison Square Garden—and, of course, the Islanders' chief rivals, the Rangers.

In the aftermath, Pickett's deal with the Gang of Four remained in place, and they converted their $10 million loan into a 10-percent equity stake in the franchise shortly thereafter. They had been running the team for Pickett in the months after he had failed to close his deal with Dolan, with Rosenthal and Walsh serving as cochairmen and Palleschi as executive vice president. Jerome Grossman was installed as president, with Torrey forced out and replaced as general manager by his assistant, Maloney, in August of 1992.

Torrey, who was involved at every level of the organization and who helped mold the 1980s dynasty, would continue to be a consultant for a brief time, although he wasn't present at the press conference because he was on a golfing vacation in Scotland.

"After 21 years it was time for a change," Torrey said in a statement.

Upheaval was more like it. And it had only just begun.

When the Walsh and Rosenthal group assumed control of the day-to-day operation of the Islanders in August of 1992, they found a team whose attendance had dropped precipitously with its fortunes on the ice, to barely 10,000 fans per game. Even the team's surprising run to the Stanley Cup semifinals in the spring of 1993 did little to rectify the emerging cash-flow problems.

"We believed that many of the people who had followed the team in the late seventies and eighties had moved off the Island," Rosenthal said. "Their kids had grown, and maybe they moved away as well. The season ticket base, which had been 13,000 to 14,000 at its peak, had dropped to 5,000, so we not only were looking to improve our play on the ice, we started looking for ways to attract new fans."

In retrospect, they probably should've found another way.

For the first 23 years of their existence, the Islanders' uniforms were adorned with a simple logo, a circled crest of Long Island that also included an "NY" with the "y" appearing in the form of a hockey stick. It was designed on just three days' notice by John Alogna, who owned a Garden City ad agency, in 1971, and it quickly became synonymous with the Islanders as they ascended from expansion franchise to NHL champions.

Still, after the 1993–94 season ended in a disgraceful first-round playoff sweep by the Rangers, Islanders management "began to feel that younger fans were starting to think about the old logo in terms of the futility of the previous years, not the four Stanley Cups," according to Rosenthal.

The NHL, buoyed by the marketing and sales success of merchandise adorned with logos of new franchises such as the Mighty Ducks of Anaheim and the San Jose Sharks, encouraged the Islanders to consider making a change, more in line with other cutting-edge sports fashions. The league recommended SME Design in Manhattan, which had modernized the uniforms of the St. Louis Blues and also designed the logo of the expansion Florida Panthers and other pro and college teams.

Initially, Walsh and vice president of communications Pat Calabria served as the point men for ownership.

"The Islanders were living in the shadow of the Rangers," designer Ed O'Hara told *Newsday*'s Steve Zipay in 1997. "We all agreed that a strengthened tie to Long Island was important, to keep the heritage of the Island and amplify it. Savvy marketers will tell you to think locally."

As New Coke and Pepsi Clear showed, sometimes it's better to leave well enough alone.

Walsh, who allowed his children's opinions to influence his decision, had a vision of a maritime theme. SME submitted a proposal to the Islanders with three to five concepts. In April, designs with various colors and logos of a lighthouse, a bearded grimacing mariner and the steering wheel of a fishing boat were offered.

"Everyone agreed that the bayman was the one, although the entire process was a huge concern. There was always self-doubt," O'Hara said. The NHL approved the entire concept in early fall of 1994 for implementation during the 1995–96 season.

Beat writer Colin Stephenson of the *Daily News* was the first to report the changes and updated colors, remarking how the chosen logo resembled frozen-food advertising icon the Gorton's fisherman. In a photograph accompanying the story, former captain Denis Potvin was pictured hoisting the Stanley Cup while wearing a computer-generated uniform adorned with the new logo and deeper color schemes. SportsChannel announcer Stan Fischler was cited as bearing a remarkable resemblance to the logo fisherman.

Barely one week after the official introduction on June 22, 1995, 78 percent of 1,006 respondents to a *Newsday* poll asking for responses panned the new logo. To prove there's no accounting for the taste of the consumer public, *Team Licensing Business*, a publication that tracks purchases of sports apparel, reported as of March 31, 1996, that the Islanders had moved up to No. 17 of the 26 clubs in jersey sales. According to the NHL, that was three or four slots higher than the previous season.

Still, the Islanders fans deplored the blasphemous changes, with many comparing it to the Gorton's fisherman. That comparison prompted Rangers fans to mockingly chant, "We want fish sticks!" when the Islanders visited Madison Square Garden for the first time that season.

Petitions were drawn up and signatures gathered. The Gang of Four was chided mercilessly at Nassau Coliseum, including an ugly incident in which Palleschi's teenaged daughter was booed while singing the National Anthem before one game. A small but vocal contingent of disgruntled fans even formed a group that initially was spawned in protest of the logo. It soon would be known as the Save the Islanders Coalition (STIC), which proved to be a thorn in management's side concerning several other consumer-related gaffes and injustices over the next half-decade.

"With change comes risk; with change comes unhappy fans," Rosenthal said. "As the team continued to lose, fans needed something to cling to and homed in on the logo. We began to realize it was not dying down. In the final analysis, we didn't want our fans or players to be subjected to ridicule for something other than our play."

To be sure, there was plenty of room to mock all aspects of the operation. Ultimately, the one thing that all sides agreed on was that the fisherman logo became the lightning rod for all of the team's misfortunes and the focal point of fan frustration. "There's no doubt it was the scapegoat. But winning would have helped," O'Hara said.

On April 11, 1996—a few games before the end of another disastrous season—the Islanders announced plans to restore the old logo for 1997–98 while retaining the new colors and wavy designs.

"Good," Islanders defenseman Darius Kasparaitis told reporters after he was informed of the reversal back to the original logo. "We looked like idiots."

That Muller was present the first day the Islanders introduced the ill-fated fisherman was probably the fishiest aspect of the whole sordid affair.

Muller was the key player Maloney had acquired on April 5, 1995, for marquee center Pierre Turgeon in a deal that also sent defenseman Vladimir Malakhov to Montreal in exchange for defenseman Mathieu Schneider and forward prospect Craig Darby.

The Islanders believed Turgeon, a 58-goal scorer in 1992–93, never was the same player after he was crushed in the back of the head by Washington's Dale Hunter during the 1993 playoff run. Muller had led the fabled Canadiens to the Stanley Cup title that spring, including a five-game ouster of the Islanders in the Wales Conference finals. He also had established a bulletproof reputation as a leader and an unselfish team player. Or so it seemed.

"I did it for all the right reasons," Maloney said eight months later, when his failure to rectify the mess surrounding Muller ultimately cost him his job. "You have to get competitors, people who want to sacrifice and win."

Ironically, Muller, who also had captained the New Jersey Devils earlier in his career, was expected to bring grit and leadership in exchange for Turgeon's goal-scoring touch. Only Muller never had any desire to lead the downtrodden Islanders.

The Islanders' first game following the trade was at Madison Square Garden three days later. Muller was a no-show, still in Montreal, devastated that Canadiens GM Serge Savard had told him just prior to the trade deadline that Montreal had no plans to deal its captain. He also believed he had paid his dues on struggling Devils teams in the 1980s and quickly asked the Islanders to trade him again to a contending club.

When asked whether he was aware of Muller's disposition before the deal, Maloney made a comment that now seems ironic and telling, "I'm not Kreskin."

"At the time," Maloney said, "he was distraught. He was the king of Montreal and he was upset. The deal was done at one o'clock. I called him at 1:30. He was going to get on a flight at five o'clock but somebody convinced him not to. It was a continual battle after that. . . . I just said 'Come to Long Island and give us a chance.'"

Maloney eventually convinced Muller to report, but only after assuring him he would try to move him over the summer. Muller and Maloney also both engaged publicly in a charade that the sides were discussing a renegotiation of Muller's Canadian-based contract to U.S. dollars, when Muller had virtually no intention of signing on for an extended stay.

"The easy thing for me to do would have been to take the offer, spend five years with the Islanders helping the younger kids, have no pressure. I won my Cup," Muller said. "I never told anybody that I wouldn't play there or that I had to have a new contract. But people are going to believe what they want.

"After I thought about everything, I wanted a chance to play for one more Stanley Cup, and I didn't think the Islanders were on my timetable."

In truth, Muller's heart didn't accompany him to Long Island; a career point-per-game player, he posted seven goals and eight assists in 27 games with the Isles over parts of two seasons. The situation finally deteriorated to the point that first-year coach Mike Milbury thought Muller's presence was becoming too much of a distraction in his dressing room. His reputation sullied, Muller was banished to await a trade on November 12, 1996.

"Any player that doesn't want to play for us, we'll get them out of here as soon as possible," Maloney said that day.

"I never threatened them or told them I wouldn't report," Muller says years later. "I had been in a rebuilding situation in New Jersey, and when I was traded to the Islanders I was honest with Donnie. I told him at that stage in my career I didn't want to be part of another rebuilding process. The only thing I was guilty of, if anything, was I asked to be traded."

If anything, Muller's banishment only lessened his trade value and hamstrung Maloney's ability to get anything close to market value for a player whom he had just traded his marquee center (Turgeon) to obtain.

When Islanders management determined Maloney was unable to resolve the Muller situation, Rosenthal admitted that was the final factor that triggered Maloney's firing on December 2, 1995.

"I have no problem with Don Maloney. You never like to see anyone lose their job," Muller said. "But I did everything he asked me to. I came from Montreal because he asked me to give the team a chance.

"I came to training camp [the following season] because he asked me to. I did agree that it would be best for everybody if I played and got off to a good start rather than play hardball and hold out. . . . But Donnie was not able to live up to our agreement, which was to trade me to a team that was playing for today and not rebuilding for tomorrow."

Shortly after Milbury replaced Maloney as GM, he ordered Muller to return from ex-Isle, er, exile. Muller refused to report and was suspended; at least the Isles were no longer obligated to pay him.

On January 23, 1996—more than nine months after he became a reluctant Islander—Muller was traded to Toronto in a three-team, multiplayer deal that brought the Islanders defenseman Bryan Berard and forwards Martin Straka and Ken Belanger.

The following Halloween, Muller returned with the Maple Leafs to Nassau Coliseum. He fittingly was booed every time he touched the puck, with the costume-decked crowd chanting "We hate Muller!" throughout.

While Muller acknowledged, "I didn't expect to be applauded," and, "Obviously, I'm not a fan favorite here," he was perturbed by how he suddenly was perceived as another greedy, selfish athlete only out for himself.

"Why didn't Donnie just say, 'No. You know what? You're an Islander. No promises.' That would have been a lot easier for everybody," Muller said. "I never walked out. I was there to play even though I was told I would be moved in June.

"If they would have said, 'No, you come to play, do your thing and if the time is right, we'll move you,' so be it. "But when you're told, 'Try it, and if you don't like it, we'll move you in the summer,' that's different.

"People forget that I played for the Islanders," Muller added. "There were never any threats on my part. I was told that if I left it would speed up a trade, but 80 percent of the people think I walked away on that team. And I'm looked upon as the bad guy."

But Muller was right the first time. He's more of a forgotten figure in the history of the franchise. In fact, his departure barely overlapped the arrival of the man who would become the most notorious figure in the team's mercurial history.

4

Enter Mad Mike

Anyone who has followed hockey over the past 20 years knows about the famous shoe incident at Madison Square Garden. It was Milbury's first appearance on the New York sports scene—a legend that grows with time and a story that never gets worn out.

Milbury, who is the lead character in the story, tells it better than anyone. And, with some prodding, a few glasses of wine and a full belly, he'll offer a sheepish grin and roll his eyes before finally giving in.

The Bruins had just completed a 4-3 come-from-behind win over the Rangers at the Garden on December 23, 1979, the last game before the Christmas break. After the final horn sounded, Rangers goalie John Davidson skated the length of the ice to chase down Bruins forward Al Secord, whom Davidson said "suckered" Rangers center Ulf Nilsson as the game ended.

Players from both teams jostled by the zamboni entrance at the end of the Garden ice, and the scrum got close to the sideboards, which, in those days, had shorter plexiglass than in modern rinks. A Rangers fan reached over the glass and pulled away the stick of Bruin Stan Jonathon, who was subsequently cut by the stick as the fan swung it over the group of players. Boston tough guy Terry O'Reilly spotted this and immediately climbed up and over the boards to chase the fan. A few other Bruins teammates followed as Rangers players watched in shock.

Remember that scene in the movie *Slapshot?*

Wait, it gets better.

While all this was going on, an oblivious Milbury had already walked into the tunnel toward the Boston locker room in the bowels of the Garden—coincidentally right underneath the developing mayhem—put his stick in the rack, taken off his gloves and started to light up a postgame cigarette.

Goalie Gerry Cheevers wandered in with a beer in hand, and Milbury noticed Cheevers had no one behind him.

"Where is everybody?" he asked.

"I don't know," Cheevers shrugged with typical apathy. "Something's going on out there."

So Milbury wandered back out the tunnel to the zamboni entrance, where he was faced with, as he describes it, "bedlam."

He saw some of his teammates, most notably O'Reilly and Peter McNabb, in the stands. A few others were climbing up over the glass. Milbury, still wearing his skates, headed to a set of steps that lead to the lower section of seats.

"I have no idea why I'm going anywhere," is how he explains it over 20 years later. "It was because my teammates and friends were there. I was heading toward the melee."

About 10 or 12 rows up was McNabb, who'd pulled a fan over one of the seats. Milbury raced up to them.

"You okay?" he asked McNabb, who had the fan jammed almost upside-down over the back of the seat. When the fan saw Milbury, he started kicking him.

Milbury put his guard up and barked at the fan.

"You're in no position to be doing any of this shit," he yelled as his heart raced. He had no idea why he was there, why his team was in the stands at Madison Square Garden, fighting fans two days before Christmas. He had no idea why he wasn't still in the locker room, having a beer with Cheevers.

Then the fan kicked him again, and the switch was thrown.

"Fuck off," Milbury snarled. "Don't do that again."

Another kick. And now the adrenaline level was off the chart.

Milbury grabbed at the fan's flailing legs and his hand slipped to the fan's shoe, which Milbury described to reporters afterward as "a cheap penny loafer." It came off in his hand, and his first instinct was to throw it on the ice. But first he whacked the fan with it in the thigh. He then whacked him a few more times in the thigh before tossing it onto the ice.

Satisfied, he walked down the steps and back to the Bruins locker room, where Cheevers was waiting with, of course, a beer.

Harry Sinden, who was general manager of the Bruins at the time, was standing at the foot of the steps near the zamboni tunnel and witnessed the events.

"I thought it was comical," Sinden says. "I really did."

Sinden also said that Milbury's willingness to race into the stands to assist his teammates was typical of his personality. "That's the way he played," Sinden said. "To me, he was a real teammate."

And his teammates loved to give him hell about it. If during a game an opposing player was getting the better of Milbury, someone would shout, "Hit 'em with your shoe, Mike!"

Television cameras caught the entire bizarre incident, but newscasts all around the country showed only one clip: Milbury whacking the fan with the shoe. It became an image that then-NHL president John Ziegler would call "a black mark" on the sport. It was also one that haunted Milbury throughout the rest of his career.

"There actually was a study," he said when recently discussing the incident. "Somebody wrote to me about it. 'How many times did he hit the guy with the shoe and where did he hit him? He hit him three times in the head. He hit him in the chest and shoulders.'

"But it is what it is," he continued. "I was there to be with my buddies more for moral support than anything, but the perception out of that was 'He's the guy that jumped into the stands and went nuts.' Actually, I was the first guy off the ice and into the locker room. . . . But I guess it sort of floats into the rest of the things that I've done."

Naturally.

The public image of Milbury has always been of this self-labeled character he calls "Mad Mike," which the press gleefully wore out in Calgary after he turned the 2000 NHL Draft on its ear by trading away blue-chip goalie prospect Roberto Luongo to the Florida Panthers and then drafting unproven college freshman goalie Rick DiPietro with the first overall pick.

"There is the very real chance that Mad Mike will end up looking like an idiot," Stephen Harris of the *Boston Herald* wrote of the events in Calgary. "Probably an unemployed one."

And that is where Milbury had all of us fooled.

The middle child of seven siblings in a Polish-Irish family, Michael James Milbury was born into an ultra-competitive environment.

"The motto was, 'He who yells loudest oftentimes wins,'" younger sister Lynne once explained in a *Newsday* interview.

His father, Roy, worked in a factory most of his life and later attended night school to become a lawyer. Mike was 19 years old when Roy died of a heart attack at the age of 48 while playing in a pickup basketball game. Mike, who turned 50 on June 17, 2002, is only the fourth oldest male in the clan, yet he progressively took over as head of the family. His mother, Marion, remained the matriarch until she passed away in 2001. She was his biggest fan and would scold critical fans when she attended his games during his Bruins playing days.

Milbury, despite his arrival as a self-made, blue-collar type who carved out a solid 11-season NHL career, wasn't entirely a fan favorite, even at the old Boston Garden. One fan was on a crowded Garden elevator after a game, viciously ripping Milbury's performance. When the elevator doors opened and people filed out, the fan felt a hand grab his shirt and pull him back in just as the doors closed.

It was Milbury.

A few seconds later, the doors again opened and the fan, his face now beet-red, quietly cowered away.

During games, his family would often find themselves defending his honor. In the final game of his playing career, the fourth game of a four-game first-round sweep to the Montreal Canadiens on April 12, 1987, the Garden fans were jeering Milbury as the Bruins fell in a 4-2 loss.

"Get off the ice!" one screamed.

"You suck!" said other.

Lynne was there with her brothers, all of them trying hard to swallow their anger. But little sister could only keep her temper for so long, and the Milbury ire was up.

Oldest brother Roy Jr. quickly grabbed her arm.

"Look," he said, "after 15 years and with a little bit of luck, Mike's gonna walk off that ice today with every one of his own teeth. And if you think I'm gonna lose some of mine defending him in the stands with you, you're crazy!"

They did their best to save him from his critics, but it was impossible to save him from himself. Mike was Mike; he spoke his mind and stuck to his guns. After his playing career ended and Mike moved into coaching and management, his public persona began to develop even more.

His first post-playing career job was in 1987–88 as head coach and general manager of the Bruins' American Hockey League affiliate in Maine.

He earned AHL Coach of the Year honors in his first season, and in the following season he also garnered dubious attention for once again leaving the confines of the playing area when he charged after an organist during a road game in Quebec.

As at Madison Square Garden some eight years before, Milbury was defending one of his own.

Maine's captain that season was Steve Tsujiura, who was Japanese-Canadian. The arena organist in Sherbrooke, Quebec, a man named Mario Gosselin, thought it was funny to play cartoonish, Oriental-sounding music each time Tsujiura was knocked down or took a penalty.

So Milbury complained to an official at the arena after the second period. When the organist kept it up in the third period, Milbury snapped and headed directly for the organist's perch in the high reaches of the tiny arena. Alert and somewhat shocked security guards stopped him just short of the organist.

His players from the bench saw the scuffle between Milbury and security, and some tried to hurdle the glass to assist their coach. He was given a game misconduct and tossed out of the game, which his team lost, 5-1.

"It's sort of demeaning and has some racial overtones," Milbury said of the organist's teasing ditty. "Steve doesn't deserve that."

When questioned about inciting violence off the ice—and people quickly made reference to the shoe incident—Milbury played it off.

"Aw," he moaned, "I was just trying to keep the guys loose. Show biz."

Nevertheless, Milbury had a successful rookie campaign with the Mariners as he led them to a Northern Division title and semifinal appearance in 1987–88. The following year, however, the team dropped to fifth place and didn't make the playoffs. Sinden had been monitoring Milbury's progress over that time, and in the spring of 1989, he hired a 36-year-old Milbury to replace a burned-out O'Reilly as head coach of the Bruins. Milbury brought from Maine his longtime friend, Gordie Clark, to assist him on the bench.

Over the next two seasons, Milbury won a pair of Adams Division titles; both teams were tops in the East (then known as the Prince of Wales Conference) with 101 and 100 points, respectively. In 1989–90, two national publications—*The Sporting News* and *The Hockey News*—named him their Coach of the Year. But the Jack Adams Award went to Bob Murdoch of the Winnipeg Jets by a narrow 128–123 vote. Murdoch directed the Jets to a 21-point improvement in the power-packed Smythe Division, which boasted the Stanley Cup champion Edmonton Oilers, the defending champion Calgary Flames and the Wayne Gretzky-led Los Angeles Kings.

While Murdoch didn't have much at his disposal in Winnipeg (Dale Hawerchuk was his lone star), Milbury's lineup was laden with burgeoning superstar talents Ray Bourque and Cam Neely, who had a breakout season with 55 goals and 92 points.

Sinden continued to play the role of mentor during Milbury's first season behind the bench of a team that had intriguing potential. The Bruins for years had been trying to finally catch their Original Six rival Montreal Canadiens, who had won six Cups in the time since the Bs' last championship in 1971–72 and had finished ahead of them in the division standings every season since 1984–85.

That streak would end in 1989–90, when the Bruins not only won the Adams Division, they also took the Wales Trophy and made their first appearance in the Stanley Cup Finals since 1977–78.

With all of the success that season, rookie NHL coach Milbury was still learning on the job. In February, the Bruins were to embark on a grueling six-game road trip that included five games out west. They dropped the first game, 3-2, at Winnipeg but then ripped off three straight blowout wins over Vancouver, Calgary and Chicago before pulling out a 3-2 victory in Minnesota.

The team headed back east to close out the road trip in New York against the Rangers, who that season were the top team in a moderately weak Patrick Division. Milbury was feeling good about his team, which was riding a four-game winning streak and a 21-7-2 run since late December. So when they arrived in Manhattan on February 25, Milbury took the team out to dinner to show his appreciation for their effort.

He called Sinden to update him on things and let him know about the dinner.

"We had such a good trip," a giddy Milbury told his boss.

Sinden frowned.

"Well," the crusty GM then replied, "it won't be so good after you play the Rangers."

"Why do you say that?" Milbury asked.

"Because," Sinden grumbled, "by taking them out to dinner, you told them they've done enough and they don't have to do any more."

Sure enough, the next night the Rangers scored five second-period goals and blew out the Bruins in a 6-1 whitewash. It's a lesson Milbury will never forget.

"I think we caught them at a good time," then-Rangers coach Roger Neilson said of the win.

An interesting side note to that game was Milbury's comments earlier in the season that the Rangers' slow-down, grinding style—a precursor to the arrival of the neutral zone trap—was "boring." Garden fans taunted Milbury with chants of "Bo-ring! Bo-ring!" as the home team dominated the Bruins.

Afterward, Milbury, in typical fashion, provided a parting shot.

"They dominated us from start to finish," he said of the Rangers' performance, "and that makes it all the more sad when they play that boring way."

Then he chuckled along with the entertained gathering of postgame media.

"I'm obnoxious," he said, "aren't I?"

Some Bruins from that era might have a better example of Milbury at his obnoxious best.

It came the following season in the playoffs, when he ordered the team to meet him at a fleabag motel somewhere north of Boston—the newspapers dubbed it "Hotel No-tell" because no one outside the team was allowed to know about it—before Game 5 of the Adams Division finals against the hated Canadiens.

The Bruins had taken a 2-0 lead in the series but dropped the next two in Montreal, including an ugly 6-2 drubbing in Game 4.

"This is what you deserve," he told his team during a meeting at the motel that night.

Milbury, like many old-time Bruins, has a lifelong disdain for the Montreal Canadiens. As a player, he twice lost to them in the Stanley Cup Finals (1977 and '78) and he's never forgotten it.

Anyway, following a night at the Hotel No-tell, the Bruins smoked the Habs, 4-1, and eventually won the series in seven games. In the conference finals against the Pittsburgh Penguins, they again took a 2-0 series lead before losing two in Pittsburgh. The Boston media cracked that the team perhaps needed another dose of Hotel No-tell.

"I don't think we'll be in any hotels," Gordie Clark said before the eventual champion Pens blew the Bs out of the playoffs with consecutive 5-1 wins at the Garden. "No, I don't think we're going to be anywhere but Hotel Home."

Clark's words proved prophetic as the Penguins swept the last four games of the series to eliminate the Bruins in six.

Over the course of that season, Milbury had been talking to Sinden about being more involved in the front office. Sinden obliged his wishes that spring when he announced that Milbury would be promoted from the bench to assistant general manager. Rick Bowness, who succeeded Milbury in Maine, would follow his footsteps as coach of the Bruins. They remained a formidable team in the early 1990s but never got any farther than the second round of the playoffs after one last run to the conference finals in 1992.

That was a time, once again, when Milbury was the center of attention.

Following a 5-2 loss in Game 2 of that series—a rematch against the Penguins—the contentious assistant GM exploded in a postgame tirade directed at referee Denis Morel that was caught on camera, audio and all. Milbury met Morel as he left the ice in a narrow hallway at the Pittsburgh Civic Arena, also known as "The Igloo."

"I work my ass off all year to give this organization a chance to win and you stole it, you son of a bitch!" he screamed. "Just another fucking day at the office! Just take your fucking paycheck and go home, you phony piece of shit!"

While this was going on, a local television cameraman caught a red-faced collared priest standing in the background.

And so, the legend of Mad Mike continued to grow.

Two years later came another bizarre moment in his public life. Toward the end of the 1993–94 season, Milbury announced that he'd be leaving the Bruins to take over as head coach of the Boston College ice hockey team.

A graduate of Colgate University, where he played hockey and football, Milbury was always intrigued by college coaching. And he relished the idea of having absolute power and control over a program.

The news was met with surprise throughout the Bruins organization and the NHL. Over the past five years, it had been well known that Sinden was grooming Milbury to succeed him as the Bruins' general manager. Sinden was even talking plans of handing him the reins before the 1995–96 season. The Bruins that season were to open their new arena, then called the Shawmut Center, and introducing Milbury as GM would have been a perfect way to begin a new era for the franchise.

It's still a moment in Milbury's life that haunts him with thoughts of what might have been. But with his contract due to expire July 1, 1994, Milbury had his doubts that Sinden would ever totally step aside. And friends also say Milbury wasn't happy with Bruins owner Jeremy Jacobs's stinginess with the team payroll.

So for a while, Milbury had been secretly looking around the league for coaching or managing opportunities elsewhere. The Boston College opportunity intrigued him.

Publicly, Sinden wished Milbury all the best. But privately he was deeply and personally disappointed in his protégé.

On March 31, Milbury announced that he had agreed to a five-year, $750,000 contract that included a car and free tuition for his four kids. In doing so, he turned down the chance to negotiate a multiyear contract extension with the Bruins that would include a massive raise on his $300,000 salary, especially after he officially took over as GM.

"I left a million bucks on the table," he said at the time.

Leaving the Bruins—an organization with which he proudly held a two-decade relationship—hurt more than Milbury realized, and as he started to set up an office at Conte Arena on the BC campus, Milbury realized that the hockey program was more of a mess than he knew. And the more he learned of the problems there, the less he wanted to associate himself with it.

So in June he walked away. It was just two months after accepting the job and four months before his first season was to begin.

He declared "philosophical differences" with the school's athletic director, Chet Gladchuk, and claimed he never actually signed a contract. Milbury to this day refuses to give any further insight into the situation, but there are others who allude to NCAA violations and alarming illegal dealings within the program. Milbury wanted no part of it.

In an agreement he apparently made with the school, Milbury was released of any responsibility to the contract in exchange for a gag order regarding the hockey program and some of the discoveries he made.

Reports since then say the apparent crux of the matter was when Milbury found a discrepancy in the number of hockey scholarships promised and given out. Instead of going to Gladchuk, Milbury went right to Rev. Robert J. Monan, president of the college.

When Monan dismissed Milbury's concerns, Milbury saw impending doom.

"In that moment," one BC alumnus said in a *Boston Herald* column by Peter Gelzinis that ran November 10, 1996 in the midst of the school's football betting scandal, "Milbury knew that if the shit hit the fan, only one person would be wearing it."

Milbury kept his comments vague at the time of his departure from the school, but they did suggest underlying concerns about the condition of the program.

"Because of the premature announcement of my intention to go to Boston College, the process was sped up and unfortunately some very serious differences were overlooked," he said. "I guess to me there was a misunderstanding of the nature of the verbal agreements. Things were not there that I was led to believe were there. Whether it was intentional or not is irrelevant. I clearly didn't think it out well enough, or didn't have the specifics down well enough.

"It was," he concluded, "a mistake on my part."

He had no idea at the time how big it was.

Sinden wasn't about to take him back, and Milbury wasn't exactly looking to go crawling back to the Bruins. He had a burning desire to return to coaching, but not many teams had much of an interest. To his mild surprise, the Hartford Whalers, a New England rival of the Bruins, were looking for a coach but never pursued him with serious interest. A preliminary interview was all he was given.

When September arrived and training camps were opening around the league (despite the impending doom of an anticipated lockout), Milbury was without a team for the first time in his hockey career.

In need of a steady paycheck and a new challenge, he accepted a three-year offer from ESPN to work as an in-studio analyst for the NHL broadcasts. He made $225,000 that first season, which became the only one he would spend at the network.

Initially, though one might figure otherwise of the walking sound byte, Milbury was an early flop as a broadcaster. In preliminary mock telecasts to prepare for the 1994–95 season, Milbury was considered stiff and delivered one coaching cliché after another. But he watched his own tape and became a quick study. Once the cameras were rolling and the only event of the NHL that season—the three-month lockout—was the main topic, the well-read, well-spoken and unapologetically opinionated Milbury handled his new career with aplomb.

Of course, there was also the occasional controversy. Milbury's harsh criticism of the players during the lockout, especially with the knowledge that he had been an outspoken player representative during his career, made headlines.

Along the way that season, as coaches were on their respective hot seats, Milbury's name would be the first to pop up. With an out-clause in his ESPN contract in case a coaching job opened, Milbury often casually admitted an interest in getting back into the NHL. That only fueled speculation as NHL coaches hit the chopping block.

Then in March of that shortened season, the plummeting Los Angeles Kings, who had a disgruntled Gretzky, a dysfunctional management situation and the league's highest payroll ($25 million), called Milbury to offer him a dream opportunity: complete control of their franchise as general manager and coach.

But the beleaguered Kings organization, which crumbled in financial ruin under bankrupt former owner Bruce McNall, were not an ordinary situation. Milbury was well aware that the Kings were heading towards disaster with Chapter 11 and the uncertainty of an ownership transition on the horizon. So he turned it down.

In May, the Kings fired coach Barry Melrose, whom Milbury would have succeeded if he took the job in March, and Melrose joined Milbury in the ESPN studio for the playoffs. They made an entertaining duo that the network probably wished it could have kept together.

But for Milbury, opportunities continued to open up while the yearning to coach again continued to grow. And the Islanders, after a disappointing last-place finish in the Atlantic Division, had just fired their coach.

5

"The Right Man for the Job"

Maloney waited for the 1995 playoffs to end before he pursued the former NHL defenseman that he initially thought, and ultimately decided, would be the perfect fit to become the next coach of the Islanders.

It was assumed that he was waiting for Hall of Famer Larry Robinson, an assistant coach with the New Jersey Devils—the team that bored everyone, especially its opponents, to tears while neutral-zone trapping its way to the Stanley Cup title that spring.

But everyone knows what is said about people who assume.

No, Maloney was waiting only for Milbury.

After using his ESPN forum as a nightly pulpit to rip the defensive shutdown system that Robinson and the Devils employed and perfected, Milbury met with Maloney for the first time in late June at a hotel in Trumbull, Connecticut, a short distance from where ESPN's studios were located in nearby Bristol.

Maloney already had interviewed some other candidates as Henning's replacement, including impressive junior coach Craig Hartsburg, who went on to coach the Chicago Blackhawks and then the Mighty Ducks of Anaheim. There also was junior coach Don Hay, who later fronted the Phoenix Coyotes and the Calgary Flames. And former Calgary bench boss Dave King. Even one of Milbury's partners on ESPN's hockey highlights show, Barry Melrose, the former coach of the Los Angeles Kings, came in for a discussion.

Some of the Islanders' alumni also pushed for Maloney to hire Goring, the former star center who'd led the team's minor-league affiliate, the

Denver Grizzlies, to the first of two consecutive championships in the International Hockey League.

But Maloney already had been through one glory-days fiasco with Henning. As he put it, "I thought it was time for a fresh face and a fresh voice." Milbury's fresh mouth, of course, had been getting him into and out of trouble for years. Maloney had known him only casually until then, but he hadn't engaged in an at-length conversation with him until that June day in Connecticut.

"Of all the guys I talked to," Maloney said, "Mike easily was the most engaging and the most prepared."

Milbury whipped out media guides and rosters, asking Maloney as many questions about the Islanders as his interviewer had asked him about himself. He offered his opinions on Islanders players such as Marty McInnis and Darius Kasparaitis and Derek King. He didn't hold anything back, Maloney thought.

"Let's face it, Lornie was a nice guy, well liked by the players, but that's not always what's needed. I didn't think that's what was needed for us," Maloney said. "Larry Robinson, for everything he'd accomplished, was pretty much viewed in the same light. We had a lot of players we thought had underachieved. We needed someone with a proven track record of kicking them in the pants. Of getting the most out of them.

"We wanted fire, we wanted passion, we wanted a face, some personality. With Mike, everything about him seemed perfect for New York. And perfect for us."

Less than one week later, Milbury was introduced as the sixth coach in team history, given a five-year $3.5 million contract to right the wavering ship. At a July 5 news conference, despite Maloney's awareness that he also might've just hired his eventual successor as general manager, he proclaimed that Milbury simply was "the right man for the job."

There was so much work to do in the wake of the lockout-ravaged season. And Milbury was soon to find out what it's like to coach a team that didn't boast superstars such as Bourque and Neely.

The team he inherited was nowhere close to Stanley Cup contention. Under Henning, the Islanders had disintegrated during the 1994–95 lockout season, finishing in last place in the Atlantic Division with 35 points, ahead of only the Ottawa Senators in the entire NHL.

Henning, to be sure, is one of the nicest human beings anyone ever could meet. Still, that season he finished exactly where nice guys generally finish.

Henning was never more embarrassed than when his team flopped in a 5-1 matinee loss to the Buffalo Sabres on April 1, 1995. It made him look the fool on the day his friend and former linemate Bob Nystrom's No. 23 was officially raised to the Nassau Coliseum rafters.

In the end, Maloney thought Henning was simply too chummy with some of the veteran players on the team and that several of them didn't think they had to work hard any more in their first year removed from Arbour's stern father-figure presence.

One former player said members of the team were dumbfounded over some of Henning's personnel decisions, such as how he often played journeyman forward Troy Loney on Turgeon's first line while dynamic rookie Ziggy Palffy, who the next season would start a string of three straight 40-goal campaigns, was often in the press box or at the end of the bench.

Still, amid the chaos surrounding the late-season trade of Turgeon and the unhappiness of Muller, Henning also had to deal with emerging contract jealousies as well as season-ending injuries to defensemen such as Kasparaitis, Scott Lachance and Rich Pilon.

There were also far too many players performing below expectations to give Henning any chance to succeed while operating within the constraints of a condensed schedule. Thomas, for instance, had averaged 40 goals the previous two playoff seasons. But he scored 11 times in 47 games in 1994–95, while often talking about the burden of playing for a new contract that caused him to hold out the following training camp. He was traded before the start of the next season for forward Wendel Clark.

"I'm playing like I've never played the game before, and it's inexcusable," Thomas admitted to a few reporters after Henning had benched him and Turgeon for the entire third period of one defeat. "I'm really letting my teammates down. It's a joke. I've never been so low as I am right now and it's really frustrating. I'm expected to be a leader on this team and I've got my head up my ass. I'm mentally brain dead in my own end. Defensively, I'm the worst guy on the ice.

"Just watch the game, it's a joke. I'm trying to sign a new contract and I'm playing like a minor-leaguer."

Considering all of these factors—but mostly how Maloney's blockbuster trade, at least the Turgeon for Muller part of it, had blown up in his face—many Islanders thought Henning made for an easy scapegoat.

"My first reaction is disgust," captain Patrick Flatley said when Henning was canned on May 3. "I think it was wrong and I don't know how this can happen. Any successful organization has to have accountability.

"I don't think all parties involved in this decision," he said, clearly referring to Maloney, "are being completely honest or accountable."

To that end, Milbury easily could have remained in his cushy swivel chair in the ESPN studios, where he glibly picked apart coaches' errors and then retreated homeward to think up a few more one-liners. Although Maloney once joked, "Why the hell he'd want this job, I don't know," the challenge of restoring the Islanders to prominence drew Milbury back to coaching after a four-year absence.

"On a relative scale [TV] is less stressful, and when the game is over, it's over," Milbury had said. "When you've said what you've had to say, if it doesn't work out, nobody is going to remember it anyway, in all likelihood. It's just a blip on the screen.

"That can be a lot of fun. But so can coaching. This is a relentless job, and you have to love the wackiness of it."

From his first days as head coach, Milbury sought to expunge the apathy and complacency that had infiltrated the NHL's one-time model organization. But with his combustible personality, it was like throwing kerosene on a fire.

Wackiness, you say?

Tales about Milbury, and blustery quotes that have passed his always-moving lips, truly were the underlying constants throughout the remainder of the Gory Days for Long Island's hockey team.

On his first day of training camp in September of 1995, Milbury jumped in the face of rookie defenseman Wade Redden, the second overall selection in that summer's entry draft. Milbury nearly knocked the 18-year-old Redden off his skates with a two-finger poke to the chest, while screaming at him to pick up his intensity or hightail it back to the junior ranks. "It's one thing to be gifted, and another to be determined," Milbury told him.

"It shocked me," said Redden, who never played a game for the Islanders before he was traded to Ottawa. "I know he's been on me, but I needed a little kick in the butt. It was an eye-opener. He's definitely the boss out there."

Indeed, Milbury had written every player a letter that summer telling them that this would be the most grueling training camp of their careers. The 11-day camp was held in Maloney's hometown of Kitchener, Ontario, a sleepy community about an hour outside of Toronto. A few players soon dubbed it "Hell's Kitchener," a play on the seedy section of Manhattan known as "Hell's Kitchen" that produced former Islander Brian

Mullen and his brother Joey, himself a 500-goal scorer in the NHL.

Milbury was immediately annoyed that Thomas and affable defenseman Dennis Vaske didn't show up the first day because they had not signed new contracts. He singled out Vaske, saying he was "making a big mistake" because his reputation was that he needed every second of the conditioning time training camp allowed. "I heard he's a big fan of cheeseburgers," Milbury told reporters.

By the second day, Milbury had the team off the ice and at a nearby patch of grass to square off against each other in a friendly soccer match. It was not exactly the finest display of athletic prowess by professional athletes ever documented, although European goalies Tommy Salo and Tommy Soderstrom predictably dominated.

"I'm not even good, but they can't play. They're North Americans," Salo said.

The best of the non-Euro lot actually might've been Muller, who, no, still had not been granted his wish to be traded by Maloney when the summer ended.

The Islanders, their fans and the media all had seen the highlights of Milbury's shoe incident at Madison Square Garden by the time training camp arrived. And they had started to hear about the organist, the flea-bag hotel and the other wacky tales that trailed him from his 20-plus years in the Boston organization, all of which were concluded with trips to the Stanley Cup playoffs.

The Islanders' dysfunctional family certainly would get more than its share of headlines over the next several lost seasons from Milbury, who grudgingly became the only compelling reason for local papers—other than Long Island-based *Newsday*, which had no choice but to follow them—to even cover the team regularly.

Pick a quote, any quote.

If Milbury did it or said it, it probably made at least one person chuckle, one person cringe and one person start putting black paint on his or her face.

These are Milbury's greatest hits with the Islanders, from 1995-2002, presented as a public service and in no particular order:

•He once called Palffy's agent, Paul Kraus, a "moron" and later said Kraus was "depriving some small village of an idiot" during contract negotiations. "We hope that Ziggy will come to his senses," Milbury said in 1996. "We have no hope that Paul Kraus will."

•After trading away goalie prospect Roberto Luongo and making college goalie Rick DiPietro the No. 1 overall pick in the 2000 entry draft, he said, "As dangerous as this might be, we like to think Mad Mike maybe has something going for him. . . . This is it. This is my job. My job is squarely on the line. If we're not a better team immediately, if we're not a very good team over the long haul, then off with the head."

•He fired assistant GM Darcy Regier, who had remained in that position after Milbury had been named Don Maloney's replacement, two days after Christmas in 1996. Regier later was hired as general manager with the Buffalo Sabres.

•He chastised enforcer Mick Vukota in a Detroit hotel lobby after police were called because Vukota had trashed his room, thus getting the Islanders banned from that hotel. The two very nearly come to blows, with Vukota screaming back at him, "Yeah, like you're some role model!" The next day Milbury cleared the team bus, closed the door and gave Vukota his chance. But Vukota declined. Eventually, he was placed on waivers and has never been back in the NHL.

•After *New York Post* beat writer Marc Berman wrote an atypically glowing story about cheapskate owners Howard and Ed Milstein, Milbury teased Berman during a scrum with reporters: "You have something on your chin."

•His love-hate relationship with Palffy began in his first training camp when Palffy showed up out of shape. "Just look at him. The [team] more or less will be decided on the basis of merit, performance and conditioning. Ziggy is in none of those categories."

•He once made the entire team take off its practice jerseys on the ice, telling the players, "If you're not going to act like a team, you're not going to look like one."

•He once emerged for practice with a Webster's dictionary in hand and read definitions of 20 words such as "commitment," "sacrifice," "team" and "character," making the players skate up and down the ice after each one. He then turned and abruptly walked off the ice.

•He once spat from the bench in a game at Madison Square Garden in the vicinity of Rangers antagonist Ulf Samuelsson, long considered one of the league's dirtiest players, calling it "a derisive gesture of dismissal and disgust." After the game, Samuelsson fumed, "I'm teaching my two kids not to spit at home, and it's going to be tough to explain when they see that on TV." To which one Islander replied, "Right, because spearing and butt-ending is being a good role model."

•He literally made goalie Tommy Salo cry during a salary arbitration hearing. Another Islanders executive at the meeting blamed it less on Milbury being mean and more on Salo's agent, Rich Winter, not preparing his young client for the brutal honesty that is portrayed at arbitration hearings. "Mike didn't attack him with words," one person said. "He just answered questions [asked by the league-appointed arbitrator]."

•He once suggested 19-year-old defenseman Eric Brewer's inconsistent play made it appear as if "he's been sniffing glue."

•He once complained that if Palffy wanted "to be paid like a star, he better start [producing] like one." To which Ziggy, a Slovakian who learned much of his English by watching bad movies involving the late Chris Farley, replied, "What does he think? Every day's Christmas?"

•He once threatened to strip Patrick Flatley of the captaincy because Flatley stood up for a few young players who had arrived back at the team's hotel on the road past curfew. The next season, Flatley, the last remaining member of the team with a connection to the Glory Years, signed as a free agent with the Rangers.

•He called Anaheim center Travis Green, whom Milbury had traded one season earlier, "a gutless puke" for a hit from behind on Kenny Jonsson. "That's why Travis doesn't wear a fucking Islanders uniform anymore."

•He occasionally played first-year defenseman Bryan Berard, who would go on to win the Calder Trophy as the NHL's top rookie in 1996-97, at left wing to punish him for thinking too offensive-mindedly.

•He fired interim coach Bill Stewart, who had replaced him at midseason, following the 1998-99 season. Milbury was still riled up by Stewart's explanation for a 3-1 loss to the Rangers in March. "Have you seen our lineup?" Stewart had said. "Enough said." In 2000, Stewart was stripped of his position as general manager of the Ontario Hockey League's Barrie Colts, a junior club, for hiding 17-year-old Ukranian defenseman

Vladimir Chernenko in the luggage compartment of the team bus, smuggling him illegally over the border for games in the U.S.

•Milbury engaged in a verbal sparring war with Rangers counterpart Neil Smith during training camp in 1999 across Lake Champlain, with the Islanders practicing in Lake Placid, N.Y. and the Rangers working out in Burlington, Vermont. Smith charged the Isles leaked discussions that would've sent Palffy to their rivals in the worst possible salary dump of them all. Smith claimed the rumors upset Rangers forward Todd Harvey, who was part of the returning package. "I think Neil's trying to cover his butt," Milbury shot back. "He's not going to start throwing darts over here, saying that we're leaking stuff and then misleading his player when he doesn't have the nerve to tell him that he was in the trade discussions. We're talking about Zigmund Palffy here. That wouldn't be an insult to Todd Harvey, would it?"

•Smith also made an off-the-cuff statement that one of the Rangers' training camp squads had a higher collective salary than the entire Islanders roster. "I don't know if that's something to be proud of," Milbury said. "That's fiscal ridiculousness, for lack of a better term. . . . I took the corporate bicycle up and down Long Island in search of [minor-league free agent] Chris Ferraro. . . . Unlike my neighbors, the corporate jet wasn't available."

•When the Washington Capitals still played in Landover, Maryland, the Islanders often stayed at the Greenbelt Marriott, which generally was filled with autograph seekers whenever they visited. Late during Milbury's first season as coach (1995–96), there were no fans at the hotel upon the team's arrival. The driver of the Islanders' team bus whenever they stayed there, first name Joe, said to Milbury as he stepped off the bus: "Boy, you guys must really suck." Even Milbury had to laugh at the observation.

•During the 2000-01 season, he told the players that their dispassionate play would get coach Butch Goring fired, with Goring present in the room during a midseason closed-door meeting. When word of it leaked to the media, owner Charles Wang asked Milbury if Goring should be fired immediately. Milbury resisted and Wang told him to leave Goring alone for the remainder of the season. "I think in his own way, that was Charles's way of saying let him hang himself, which he proceeded to do," Milbury said. Goring was fired near the end of that regular season.

•Asked about the fans' reaction to him following his 2001 trades for stars Alexei Yashin and Michael Peca: "At least in addition to the 'You're an idiot' comments, there's an occasional 'Nice job' and 'I can't wait to get started' mixed in."

•Asked about the end of what had been a perpetual rebuilding program: "We needed men, guys that were developed players, and in some cases, character guys. We were all tired of wiping runny noses and changing diapers."

•Asked how he kept his job for so long, despite all of the losing, he said, "I never asked directly [to be fired], but there were times when I displayed enough of a screw-you attitude, when enough was enough, and I had taken enough abuse and tried to force their hand. It didn't work, so here I am."

•Milbury exchanged pleasantries with forward Craig Janney, who had played for him in Boston and was visiting Nassau Coliseum with the San Jose Sharks. Janney continued down the hallway and Milbury said, "No team ever will win with that guy in their lineup." Two years later, Milbury traded for Janney. "We needed offense," was his explanation.

•This one's not from Milbury, but it's too good to not include. *Newsday* reporter Jim Smith approached Russian center Alexander Semak to ascertain how well Russian rookie Grigori Panteleev spoke English. "Better than Bert," Semak deadpanned, alluding to the communication skills of then-rookie forward Todd Bertuzzi.

•While the St. Louis Blues, who'd just defeated the Isles 6-4 in a holiday matinee, headed for their bus in suits and ties, Milbury ordered his team back onto the ice in full uniform for a 60-minute practice.

•While an ESPN analyst, he referred to New Jersey's trapping defensive style as "glorified soccer on ice" and railed for the NHL to install legislation against it. Midway through his first season as coach of the Islanders, they employed a 1-2-2 trap. "Fuck you," he told reporters with an ever-sarcastic smile.

If you want to hear the most telling quotes from Milbury, if you want to glean the most grounded insight into his personality, ask him about his kids. He has four practically grown children from his first marriage, which ended in divorce, and two small sons with his second wife, Ginger, a former team employee.

"Like Charles [Wang] says, if this doesn't work out, it's only hockey. I do have a life," Milbury said in an interview with the *Daily News'* Botte in the summer of 2001, when the tide finally appeared ready to turn in his favor. "My older kids are all giddy now because they know what I've gone through. But the little guys, it's just really easy to go home and get a smile out of them. And it's really easy for them to get one out of me."

Milbury's first wife, Debbie, actually was a right wing on the first team he ever coached. He volunteered to teach the women's club team while he was a student athlete studying urban sociology at Colgate University. They remained married for more than 20 years and had four children together. Milbury couldn't be prouder of any of them, despite the financial strain he accepted to afford each of them exceptional educational opportunities.

As of 2001, his oldest son, Owen, was attending graduate school in London. His second son, Luke, was taking courses at Berklee School of Music in Boston ("Interesting child," Milbury says). His oldest daughter Alison attended Brown and also studied abroad. His daughter Caitlin was close to finishing up at Tabor Academy, a prestigious New England prep school.

"I've already started to put some money away for the little people, but it's going to come to about a million bucks for the older four," Milbury said of his youngest sons, Jack and Jake. "The ironic thing would be for the Islanders to let me go in the year I finally finish my kids' last tuition payments. That would be poetic justice for my tenure here, wouldn't it?"

Milbury claims these financial obligations precluded him from ever resigning his post, although he admitted he often hoped to get fired by the Islanders, especially during the lean Milstein years.

Milbury, whose $850,000 annual contract was extended for an undisclosed number of years prior to the 2002-03 season, fittingly has a Japanese proverb that translates to "Before success, there must be chaos," hanging on a wall in his office at Nassau Coliseum.

But his personal life regained a sense of normalcy when he fell in love and married his second wife, Ginger, with whom he'd worked closely while she served as the team's media relations director during his early years in the organization.

"It was a true love story," Milbury told a couple of reporters in a relaxed moment during training camp in Lake Placid in September of 2001.

Ginger, as well as Milbury's older children, simply longed for the day when he would feel that love from a fan base that chanted for him to go away as often as they chanted derogatory things about the hated Rangers.

"Words can't describe how much I want to see him win," his son Luke said in a 2001 interview with *Newsday*. "I've been to a couple of games and I've heard the 'Mike Must Go' chant. My heart kind of sinks."

"To me," Ginger said in the same story, "when I hear it, it's the only thing I hear."

At least, Ginger joked, she got something out of the years of losing. Milbury, she said, developed a therapeutic ritual following loss after agonizing loss. He would stay up all night scrubbing their four-bedroom Colonial home in Garden City, Long Island, obsessing over all that needed to be done to resuscitate the flatlining franchise. If the team lost a game that evening, Ginger knew what to expect.

"I know he's going to come home," she said, "and we're going to have a clean kitchen in the morning."

The 1995–96 Islanders could've driven even the most sane of men batty. Imagine what it must've been like for Milbury, who already was halfway there before he'd even coached them in one game.

His Islanders debut, on October 7, 1995, fittingly came in Boston's antiseptic new arena, the Fleet Center, which had replaced historic Boston Gah-den. It was a 4-4 tie with Muller netting one of the goals.

Ten days later, however, the Isles had opened the Milbury regime with a record of 0-4-1, culminated by a horrible 5-1 loss to the Rangers in Long Island, with the first Blueshirt goal coming from free-agent defector Ray Ferraro. "To be candid with you," Milbury said, "it looks like this is the worst-coached team in hockey."

The five-year commitment management had made to Milbury allowed him to make such statements without fear of repudiation. Maloney, in the final year of his contract and with the Muller fiasco destined to forever mark his resume like a scarlet letter, wasn't so lucky.

The losses kept coming, one more bizarre than the last. Three days after Milbury's Isles were smoked, 9-2, by Wayne Gretzky's Kings in Los Angeles, Palffy failed to jump onto the ice for a line change in Anaheim with less than one minute remaining in overtime. By the time the Isles realized they'd been playing shorthanded for several seconds, the Mighty Ducks had scored with three-tenths of a second remaining for a 2-1 victory.

Of Palffy, who'd also been benched in the Los Angeles game, Milbury said, "Ziggy went from being a world-class player one night to something entirely different. He's the epitome of what our team is right now."

After Milbury had lit into the team following another hard-to-swallow defeat, winger Derek King said to members of the media, "Don't go in there, it's not a pretty sight. His spit's all over the walls."

It was only a matter of time before the fans' spewing wishes—that "Don Must Go"—would become reality.

"I don't know who's less popular on Long Island," Maloney quipped, "me or Joey Buttafuoco."

He was referring to a Long Island auto mechanic whose claim to infamy was having sexual relations with a teenaged girl named Amy Fisher, nicknamed the Long Island Lolita, who shot Buttafuoco's wife in the head in the early 1990s.

Unfortunately for Maloney, his assessment was only slightly off the mark.

With Muller banished from the team and Maloney unable to accommodate his desire for a trade, the Isles were 5-15-3 under Milbury when Pickett's management group announced Maloney's firing on December 2, 1995. One of the back-page headlines read, "Done Maloney."

"Unfortunately, Donnie is probably better qualified to be a general manager in this league now than he was four years ago," said Ralph Palleschi, the Isles' chief operating officer.

"I think maybe the Islanders are paying for my inexperience," Maloney said the night of his firing. "My heart was in the right place. But I knew I was playing with fire, quite frankly. I felt like Manuel Noriega, with all those ['Don Must Go'] chants going on."

Within a few seasons, those chants were revised to include Milbury's first name.

Regier initially was named Maloney's replacement on an interim basis, but CEO Bob Rosenthal announced that Arbour, the VP of hockey operations, would conduct a "thorough and expeditious" search for the full-time general manager.

Prevailing thought was that if Milbury adamantly wanted the job, it was his. It couldn't get more expeditious than that.

After initially waffling, Milbury accepted the opportunity to join Mike Keenan, then with the St. Louis Blues after a power struggle with Rangers GM Neil Smith, as the only men at the time to serve in the dual role of GM/coach in the NHL.

Milbury was named the third GM in team history on December 12, ten days after Maloney had been sent packing. He immediately denied accepting Maloney's offer of a five-year, $3.5-million deal knowing he'd be next in line to usurp the GM's job at the first sign of duress.

"I'm not that big of an asshole," Milbury said. "Don's the guy that gave me a great opportunity at a time when I was looking for one. I owe him a huge debt of gratitude. Frankly, I feel rotten about the whole situation. I feel I let him down; I hope the team feels the same way."

For his part, Maloney, who eventually resurfaced as the assistant GM with the Rangers, didn't blame Milbury for his demise.

"I never felt a sense of undermining by Mike. Never," Maloney said in April of 2002. "If somebody decided in the bigger picture that Mike should have both jobs, so be it."

Six weeks after his promotion, Milbury finally accomplished what Maloney had not for the previous nine months. On January 23, Muller was traded, along with the rights to Redden, in a three-team deal. The Isles netted 18-year-old defenseman Bryan Berard, who was selected one pick ahead of Redden as the first overall selection in the 1995 entry draft, and forwards Martin Straka and Ken Belanger.

Muller was finally gone, but the losing wasn't. And the two jobs only gave Milbury double the opportunity to affect a franchise that, improbably as it may have seemed at the time, still had a long way to fall.

6

And Get This . . .
With No Money Down

By the fall of 1996, finding even one person associated with the Islanders—including Pickett himself—who wanted Pickett and his minions to remain in charge of the flailing franchise was as improbable as finding someone wearing the fisherman jersey around Long Island with even the slightest hint of pride.

The Islanders, their dwindling fan base, the NHL, and even the media were desperate for a new voice and, most important, a new bank account behind the team. That desperation, however, only resulted in one of the most bizarre, disturbing and ultimately laughable chapters in the history of the franchise and sports in general.

First of all, everyone initially believed in John Spano. *Everyone.* Anyone who says differently is lying. That includes Islanders alumni such as Potvin, NHL commissioner Gary Bettman, Milbury, and the fans who deliriously chanted "Save Us Spano" at the team's home opener a few days after the news surfaced in the October 10, 1996 edition of the *New York Post* about his $165 million purchase of the team and its cable deal from Pickett. And why wouldn't they believe? The 32-year-old Dallas businessman was precisely what the Islanders needed at the time. Well, give or take a few hundred million dollars.

He promised a rebirth and people believed him. He demanded the best of everything and nobody questioned him. He would've been perfect, if only he hadn't been a mirage. He would've spent money, if only he had some. The best thing you can say about him—other than that he left the Islanders no worse than he found them—is that he temporarily injected hope (even if it was false hope) into Pickett's long-dormant and listing operation. He showed that making a go of the Islanders was possible. He simply wasn't the right man for the job.

In like a lion and out like a sham, the crimes Spano perpetrated against Pickett, the Islanders, several banks and a veritable Who's Who of wealthy investors eventually landed him in federal prison for up to 61 months for bank and wire fraud.

Still, the most overlooked aspect of the sordid Spano debacle, conveniently forgotten in the ensuing malaise that resurfaced around the team for another three or four seasons after his departure, is that he very nearly got away with it.

Very nearly.

But how?

For anyone who ever received a late notice from their mortgage lender or their credit card bank when their payments arrived a day or two past due, Spano's tale of deception and decimal shifts were something straight out of a late-night television infomercial. Something along the lines of "You, too, can own a professional sports franchise. And get this, with no money down."

As Milbury remembered screaming at Spano in a telephone conversation when the house of cards eventually collapsed like a bad episode of *The Brady Bunch*, "What you did wasn't right! There are a lot of people here who put their lives toward getting this thing right and you made it a mockery. It was all a game, a sham. It was all about you and your greed!"

"I was hard on him and I had a right to be," Milbury said. "What he did was worse than criminal."

Less than one week after Spano's purchase agreement with Pickett became public, the new white-knight owner (pending NHL approval) took the five beat writers covering the team at the time—Peter Botte of the *New York Post*, Jason Diamos of the *New York Times*, Colin Stephenson of the *New York Daily News*, John Valenti of *Newsday* and Lou Friedman of the Associated Press—to an informal get-to-know-me luncheon at an upscale local Italian restaurant.

Spano had Isles VP of communications Pat Calabria and media relations director Ginger Killian arrange for a limousine to pick up Spano and the media contingent at Nassau Coliseum following the team's morning skate in preparation for a game that night against the Hartford Whalers.

Later that night, the writers reflected how the limo ride was the most entertaining part of their day. It didn't dawn on them until months later how prophetic parts of their first face-to-face conversation with Spano would become.

Spano started by acknowledging Botte's exclusive story with colleague Larry Brooks about the sale, with one notable correction that should've served as the ultimate red flag, but didn't. While he claimed to be "flattered" by what really was a throwaway line in the story, Spano wanted it known that *The Post*'s categorization of him as a "Texas billionaire" was inaccurate. "I suppose there are worse things to be called," Spano said, "but I'm not there just yet."

The all-encompassing conversation that followed simply wasn't something sportswriters were accustomed to with old-guard ownership types in New York, such as Pickett or baseball owners George Steinbrenner of the New York Yankees or Nelson Doubleday of the New York Mets.

Spano immediately seemed to be just another frat boy at the party—asking the writers about their personal lives, about their favorite movies (his was *Caddyshack*), about the best and worst things about being a sportswriter. The quote of the day came from Valenti, who befuddled Spano and everyone else in the car with his contention that "the worst part about sportswriting is having to go to the games." Valenti, a sitcom character if ever there was one, still works for *Newsday* but no longer covers sports.

Spano also asked the writers if they knew whom he needed to contact to purchase tickets for an upcoming concert at Nassau Coliseum. "Mr. Spano, you're the owner of the Islanders now. I don't think it will be a problem," one of them replied. Longtime Islanders television announcer Stan Fischler later admitted to having a similar conversation with Spano about obtaining tickets for a New York Rangers game at Madison Square Garden.

Soon after, the limousine conversation among the writers switched to the weekly lottery in New York State, which was slated to total more than $20 million that Saturday. "Really? How does that pay out?" Spano asked as he leaned forward in his seat. "Can you get all of that money up front?"

Who'd have known?

Even the writers were desperate for the shell game Spano apparently was selling. Not that he was the most engaging personality nor the most colorful quote they'd ever come across, but they wanted to believe him. He made their jobs more interesting. They imagined covering the impoverished Islanders when they actually had some financial backing and a daring frontman committed to using it, as opposed to the final days of the penurious Pickett regime.

Through the course of the regular season, Spano would call reporters—unsolicited—to ask them what local politicians were telling them about the possibility of securing a new arena to replace Nassau Coliseum. He'd call to ask them about rumors he'd heard about the personal lives of Milbury or some of the players on the team. He'd call to ask them about trade rumors they'd heard around the league. He'd ask them about the NHL's complicated rules regarding free agency, always with an eye on improving the team in the future.

When informed only older NHL players generally switched teams, due to the severe restrictions placed on those players under the age of 31, Spano privately told reporters of a plan he had devised to circumvent that rule. Joe Sakic and Peter Forsberg, the two marquee 20-something centers with the Colorado Avalanche, were slated to become restricted free agents in the summer of 1997.

"Restricted," in NHL parlance, means if the Avalanche declined their right to match any offer either player received from another club, the signing team would be obligated to compensate Colorado with up to five future first-round draft picks, depending on the value of the contract. Spano's plan was to attempt to sign both players to lucrative above-market deals that summer, forcing the cash-strapped Avalanche to decide which player they'd retain by matching the Islanders' offer.

Of course, Spano and the Islanders never made it to the NHL's free-agency period. By that summer, there were more pressing loopholes to try to get around.

Bettman, who fought years of media criticism about not wanting three teams in the New York market, immediately trumpeted Spano as "the perfect man to rescue a team like the Islanders." Pickett told *Newsday*'s Valenti shortly after his sale agreement became public that the 32-year-old Spano was "the type of owner that the Islanders need. He's got youth, he's got money. He's a hockey fan, an Islanders fan. He's got it all."

Pickett left out an active imagination, an amazing proclivity for stretching the truth and a quietly strange charm that caused people in positions of power and prestige to fully believe Spano was the jet-setting, elbow-rubbing, filthy rich entrepreneur he claimed to be.

There are still those who are convinced that Spano would be in control of the team in the new millennium had he not repeatedly missed a scheduled $16.8 million installment payment to Pickett upon closing the deal in April of 1997.

He had been hand-picked and rubber-stamped by Bettman, who steered Spano in Pickett's direction despite Spano's previous failure to close similar attempts to purchase two other National Hockey League franchises, the Dallas Stars and the Florida Panthers.

He had New York roots, boasting a Manhattan upbringing, and maintained a vacation residence in Long Island's exclusive section of The Hamptons. He claimed friendships with the likes of Potvin, whom he met during his courtship of the Panthers, and Pittsburgh Penguins star Mario Lemieux, as well as soap opera actress Susan Lucci and famed horse trainer Nick Zito.

According to the biography Spano provided to the Islanders when the sale agreement was announced, the Dallas-based equipment leasing company he owned, The Bison Group, headed a conglomerate of 10 subsidiary companies with more than 6,000 employees worldwide.

According to a 1997 *Sports Illustrated* story, he claimed to own a Lear Jet and a Gulfstream and "every great car that was ever made."

According to childhood friends, college buddies and various former acquaintances and business associates, he often spoke about a lucrative trust fund set up by a nebulous deceased relative that supposedly was the basis of the fortune he parlayed into a nine-figure net worth less than 10 years after he had graduated with a bachelor's degree in business administration from Duquesne University in 1986.

"People in the office were doing cartwheels," one former Islanders employee remembered. "Everyone was kidding how it was too good to be true, but no one ever really means it when they say that."

Who possibly could've known?

At least until nearly nine months later, when an exhaustive series of investigative stories by *Newsday* revealed Spano's ponzi scheme for the scam that it was.

The private planes, it turned out, were leased or chartered, usually on the Islanders' tab. There was no home in The Hamptons registered to anyone named Spano. The Bison Group, as defense lawyer Nicholas J. Gravante eventually claimed at Spano's arraignment, held no "appreciable" assets. The trust fund, which Spano later attempted to link to a notorious deceased mobster as a way of explaining his difficulty accessing the money, could never be proven.

And Spano's financial rise and fall left the Islanders and numerous other business partners in the wake of what assistant U.S. attorney Joseph Conway described as "a tangled web of lies and broken promises"—eventually landing Spano, who has refused repeated requests through Gravante to be interviewed, holed up in a minimum-security federal prison in West Virginia.

Sinden, the longtime general manager of the Boston Bruins and Milbury's mentor in the game, remembered Spano approaching him to introduce himself in the bar of Manhattan's exclusive St. Regis Hotel, in June of 1997. Sinden had been waiting for Torrey, who also was in town as the Panthers' representative for an upcoming meeting of the NHL's board of governors, to arrive so that they could go out to dinner.

"This guy came over and introduced himself: 'I'm John Spano, the owner of the Islanders,'" Sinden recalled. "We're at the bar, there are well-dressed people all around, it's happy hour. And here's Spano, in short sleeves and no tie. He comes over and starts talking about hockey.

"He says, 'What do you think about Mike Milbury?' Now, that's a terrible question to ask *me*. Then he starts asking me about players, and they had a few reputable ones at the time. And I started telling him a few things.

"All of a sudden, he pulls out his cell phone and says, 'Mike, Harry just told me something about one of our guys that you told me the opposite.'

"My God, he called him from the bar, right in front of me," Sinden continued. "Then he hands the phone to me, and says [to Milbury], 'Here, talk to Harry.'

"I was taken aback by it. I was going to confront him about it the next day. But the next day, he doesn't show up at the [board of governors'] meeting. That was the meeting they found out about him."

Former New York Rangers president and general manager Neil Smith indicated eyebrows and red flags went up all around the NHL when Pickett's longtime lieutenants, Skehan and alternate governor Jack Krumpe, arrived at that meeting with no explanation of Spano's whereabouts.

In the next three weeks, Spano's tapestry of deception was exposed— much of it in an award-winning series by *Newsday*, which fanned out reporters all over the country to uncover the truth behind Spano's life story.

All the while, Spano and Pickett engaged in a public war of words in the local papers that finally gave the irrelevant Islanders what they had been seeking for years—loads of publicity in the summertime. It just wasn't what they, nor anyone else involved, had in mind.

Spano had been unanimously approved by the NHL's board of governors as the new owner of the Islanders on January 24, 1997. He celebrated, according to people who were there, with one of his infamously wild parties at Long Island's posh Garden City Hotel, which often included prostitutes and other debaucheries.

On April 7, the closing date of the $165 million deal, Spano handed Pickett $80 million for the team, secured by a loan from Boston's Fleet Bank, an aggressive lender in the professional sports field. Spano also was scheduled to forward Pickett another $16.8 million upon closing, the first of five agreed-upon annual installments of the $85 million balance of the deal for the team's lucrative cable television rights. Spano gave Pickett his word that the proverbial check was in the mail, convincing him not to postpone the closing.

And one of the wildest financial goose chases in sports history was on.

In a seething memo that Pickett fired off to Bettman more than two months later, asking him to intervene, Pickett's lawyers outlined dozens of excuses Spano gave them for purportedly failing to deliver the payment, including problems with "ravenous South Africans and the Irish Republican Army," as well as an alleged bomb threat in the London Underground.

According to the memo, Spano also told Pickett to expect a wire transfer of $5 million on June 5. When it arrived, it was for $5,000. After also bouncing a $17 million check dated June 5, Spano left Pickett another message on June 17, giving him the reference number for another $17 million transfer he purportedly had authorized. When that check arrived, it was worth $1,700.

"Remember that line from *Jerry Maguire*? 'Show me the money!' Someone probably needed to say that to John, at some point," one member of Pickett's management team said. "How could anyone have known? Some pretty reputable people vouched for this guy."

Or so everyone thought.

From Bettman's standpoint, Spano's tale forever altered the NHL's process for approving prospective owners. The league hired an investigator, former FBI agent Ben C. Nix, to look into Spano's background. According to *Newsday,* he was paid only between $500 and $750 for his information.

At Pickett's insistence, Bettman eventually agreed to step in, ordering Spano in early July to desist from any involvement with the Islanders, pending league mediation. On July 11, Spano ceded operating control of the franchise back to Pickett, who eventually negotiated with Fleet Bank a repayment of the $80 million loan, which Spano had secured with the Islanders' assets as collateral.

When federal authorities formally charged Spano with bank and wire fraud on July 17, they cited, among other things, a letter from Lloyd's Bank of London signed by a senior vice president named Clive Jones in the trust department, confirming the existence of a $107 million trust in Spano's name. The only problem was that Lloyd's claimed it didn't employ anyone by that name, nor did it even have a trust department.

Fleet Bank also reportedly relied on documents signed by two big-time Dallas professionals—Joseph Lynch, a senior vice president at Detroit-based Comerica Bank, and high-powered attorney T. McCullogh Strother—attesting to Spano's net worth of up to $230 million. Both men later testified to federal investigators that they never personally verified Spano's status.

According to the government's complaint, Spano also twice forged documents to buy himself time with his creditors. One of them was a letter to Pickett on Comerica Bank stationery claiming Spano had sufficient funds to cover the $17 million. Prosecutors called the document "an obvious forgery," explaining that the fax machine markings atop the first page were "virtually identical" to those of a fax machine at Bison Group's Dallas office.

One of Spano's former lawyers also admitted he once had an attorney wait at Heathrow Airport in London for a courier Spano vowed would be coming with a certified check from Lloyd's for delivery to New York. Spano later claimed the couriers got lost en route to the airport, and the check never arrived.

Newsday also discovered that not only did Spano carry a $1.95 million mortgage on the nearly $3 million home he and his wife, Shelby, owned in the exclusive Dallas-area enclave of University Park, but he also owed more than $85,000 in back taxes and penalties on the home.

In addition, he allegedly bilked Lemieux, former Penguins owner Howard Baldwin and high-ranking officials of a company owned by former Dallas Cowboys quarterback Roger Staubach out of several million dollars in various shady investments. And the Islanders charged that he stiffed them for more than $200,000 for chartered planes, limousines, hotel stays and other expenses in his nine months in the owner's seat.

On July 21, authorities appeared at Spano's home and at his office in Dallas with a warrant for his arrest. He was not to be found in Texas.

Instead, he was staying at a $390-per-night room in the Cayman Islands, where he'd told the Islanders he was going to withdraw money from one of his numerous offshore accounts.

"How in the world did you get this number?" Spano demanded when reached by *Newsday*'s Valenti at his vacation hideout. "You call me again, and I'm going to take matters into my own hands."

Two days later, the 33-year-old Spano turned himself in to Long Island authorities.

So how did this quiet man of modest means talk his way into the world of the business and social elite in such a relatively short time?

School records viewed by *Newsday* showed John A. Spano Jr. was born in New York on May 31, 1964 to John and Anne Spano. He was baptized in Yonkers, N.Y., and attended schools in Pennsylvania, California, Florida and central New York, where his parents grew up.

His Islanders biography stated that he attended "St. John's Academy," when there was no such place. Instead, he graduated in 1982 from St. John's H.S. in Ashtabula, Ohio—a neighboring town to Madison, Ohio, where his father had settled the family in 1977 following a job transfer while working for a company called CE Cast Products.

Years later, Spano testified in a civil deposition that the inheritance he supposedly parlayed into his fortune came from a paternal grandfather named Angelo Spano. But *Newsday* discovered that probate records indicated Spano's grandfathers were named Antonio Spano and Charles D'Ambra. One was a grocer and the other a barber, and neither left estates totaling more than $250,000.

Spano later attempted to put out word that his family benefactor was none other than Anthony Salerno, a former organized crime boss who died in prison in 1992. Efforts to prove any remote connection, though, were fruitless.

Wherever he had convinced himself his future fortune was coming from, however, Spano stuck to the story of pending inheritance beginning with his high school days, according to childhood friends interviewed by *Newsday*. That charade continued during his time at Duquesne, said former fraternity brothers of Zeta Beta Tau. After college, though, Spano took a job with a fledgling automobile leasing company in Pittsburgh called Intellease. His salary was $20,000 per year. From there, he moved on to Dallas, where he was hired as a credit manager at a branch office for a California-based automobile leasing company called Reseda Finance.

The two years he spent working there might've taught Spano more than he learned in his four years at Duquesne, at least in regard to banker's lingo and the ability to raise money from banks based on misrepresented information.

After that company went belly-up, Spano, according to his biography, returned to New York and incorporated his own company, Bison Group.

In truth, he took a job with an Ohio-based company, named Bison Leasing Co. Inc., which leased automobile and airline equipment. One of the co-owners of the business was named Benjamin Mann, who reportedly had pleaded guilty in 1986 to two misdemeanors in Buffalo, N.Y. for defrauding the Small Business Administration.

That company also defaulted on nearly $2 million in loans and was dissolved in 1993. Still, Thomas Raglow, an equipment lease salesman there, believed the education Spano received working there taught him enough about the machinations of the business to cause him to think much loftier goals were attainable.

"It involved wire transfers, financial statements, and if they did all these real deals, they would know how to do a phony deal," Raglow told *Newsday*. "You can create a statement saying you're worth any dollar amount. If enough people verify the information, then you're worth that amount, until someone can verify you're not."

By 1993, Spano had migrated to Dallas and incorporated Bison Group as his own company. He immediately portrayed himself as a multimillionaire—including being seen about town in a red Ferrari with Ohio plates. No one questioned his financial clout.

During a six-month period in 1995, he attempted to purchase half of the Dallas Stars from then-owner Norman Green, but he always came up with one excuse or another to not close the deal.

"He was like a kid who steals a chocolate bar, gets away with it and then moves on to other stuff," Green told *Newsday*. "He got away with a little and then a little more, and it all worked."

Following his flirtation with the Stars, Spano made a similar bid for the Florida Panthers in May of 1996. Panthers owner Wayne Huizenga decided not to sell the team when South Florida pledged a sweetheart deal on a new arena for the team to play in, but Spano clearly had established himself as a gold-plated future investor in the eyes of the NHL.

He also had befriended Potvin, the captain of the Islanders' four Stanley Cup champions in the 1980s who went on to work for the Panthers as a television analyst. Shortly thereafter, Potvin phoned Pickett and arranged a meeting for lunch at Pickett's winter home in Palm Beach, Fla.

"The thing that struck me was here's a kid, 32 years old, and I was trying to figure out whether he'd be a good owner," Pickett told *Newsday*. "I didn't know what to make of him. You know, at any time, he could say the most charming, logical thing in the world. I don't care what you talk to him about.

"We talked about hockey and everything he said about hockey made sense—from rebuilding the team to getting a new building to promoting the team to selling tickets. . . . I guess I was sold. I thought he was the savior."

Of all the people duped by Spano's scheme, one victim stood alone as perhaps the most affected and the most sympathetic. The others—the Picketts, the Potvins, the Bettmans, the banks and the rest of the millionaires involved—eventually could look back and laugh at Spano's crimes from the sanctity of their limousines. For Tom Croke, then a 45-year-old fan of the Islanders, Spano's reign represented nothing more than a cruel jab at his livelihood.

Croke, a single computer consultant from Huntington, L.I., was one of the cofounders of the activist fan group Save The Islanders Coalition (STIC) that had given Pickett's regime so many headaches since its inception in 1995. In November of 1996, soon after agreeing to purchase the team, Spano met with Croke and a few other officers of STIC at the Islanders' offices at Nassau Coliseum. By Christmas, Spano had invited Croke to occasionally sit with him in his luxury suite at games, asking for his advice on the team's outdated computer systems. The discussions ultimately led to a job offer on Feb. 8 from Spano, Croke detailed in a July 1997 interview with *The Post*'s Phil Mushnick, as a special adviser with a salary of about $135,000. Spano told Croke to report to work at the Coliseum on March 17.

"I told him that would give me time to jettison clients and break off talks with an outfit I was negotiating with," Croke told Mushnick. "I left on a cloud. My favorite hobby, the Islanders, would become my profession. My family even threw me a party."

Croke added that he had "zero suspicions" about Spano at the time. "Why would I be suspicious?" Croke said. "He was the new NHL-approved owner of the Islanders."

When Croke showed up for his first day of work, however, he was met by disbelieving office workers claiming no knowledge of his hiring. "They had no idea why I was there," Croke said. "They must've thought I was some nut. It was humiliating."

Croke called Spano in Dallas and was promised that all would be straightened out. Soon after, though, Spano stopped taking Croke's calls. "That's when I knew he had a screw loose," Croke said.

Croke eventually recovered much of his computer business, but an attempt to retrieve money he believed owed to him over several months of lost wages never materialized.

"In a way, it's my fault. I should've gotten everything in writing from the start, should've taped the phone conversations," Croke said. "But if the NHL considered him credible, why wouldn't I? The whole thing was so humiliating. But I don't hate him. He's a troubled man. He's the Wizard of Oz. He was the man behind the curtain."

Talk to any of the central characters of the Spano saga, and every one of them can recall one or two examples of something he once said or did that should've been the tipoff that he was not all that he represented himself to be.

The night before the Isles were to play in his adopted hometown for a late-season game against the Dallas Stars on April 2, 1997, Spano invited the entire team and its traveling party to his Dallas-area mansion. As Islanders defenseman Dennis Vaske remarked the next day, though, "[Spano] has a great house, but I was expecting something out of *Dynasty* for all the money he supposedly has. I mean, Kaspar [former Isles defenseman Darius Kasparaitis] has a nicer place."

Former Southern Methodist University basketball star Max Williams, who struck it rich years later in the oil business, shared office space with Spano during his early Dallas years. Williams entered some failed business dealings with Spano in the early 1990s, recalling in a *Newsday* story, "It was always like trying to sweep smoke." He also recounted a tale about Spano's then-fiancé, Shelby, trying to sell him diet pills on the verge of her marriage to a supposed multimillionaire.

Bob Gutkowski, the former president of Madison Square Garden, sued Spano for $20,000 owed his company, Marquee Group, for consulting work it did for the Islanders. "He'd always talk a good game," Gutkowski told *Sports Illustrated*. "You'd ask him, 'John, are you sure you have the money to do this?' And he'd become indignant and say something like, 'I have a private plane. Of course I have the money. Why would I be having this conversation if I didn't?'"

Even Potvin, whom Spano purportedly had promised to make president of the Islanders, said, "If he had that stature, why didn't he have staff working with him? He was always very much alone."

Of course, he did have some help. When Spano hired the prestigious accounting firm Deloitte and Touche to do the Islanders' money-crunching, the employee there put in charge of the Islanders' account was his old friend, Benjamin Mann, who'd had a history of criminal fraud even before he and Spano went into business together in the early 1990s. Soon after the Spano mystery unraveled, Mann was fired from Deloitte and Touche.

Jim Lites, the president of the Dallas Stars during Spano's negotiations with Green to purchase half the club in 1995, also remembered Spano once telling him that he couldn't close the deal until his partners from South Africa arrived to view the operation and meet everyone. "One guy showed up and 'cheerioed' us for a whole day," Lites told *Sports Illustrated*. "I can laugh now even if it didn't make any sense. . . . The excuses were always laughable."

The man who 'cheerioed' the Stars' staff was a South African businessman named Douglas de Jager. A few years later, even de Jager's company, Lenco Holdings Ltd., filed a lawsuit against Spano after he'd failed to pay for a $1.9 million shipment of pots and pans he claimed to have sold on their behalf to Nordstrom, the Seattle-based department store giant. Nordstrom officials claimed to never have heard of Spano.

"In the end," Milbury said, "we all were left wondering what was true and what wasn't true."

7

The Last Islander

Perhaps there's a line in the first chapter of this book—in which Milbury refers to a former Islander as "a fucking asshole"—that begs for a little background.

Never mind who he was talking about; it doesn't matter. The line was less about that person and more about the long shadow that has covered the franchise and Milbury for so many years. Sometimes the greatness of the past can become a burden on the present and future. Especially when the present and future always seem so bleak.

But what stands out is Milbury's choice of words. His antagonistic candor. And, of course, his target—the legacy. Islanders fans have a hard time dealing with anyone blaspheming anything from their storied past. Even Jiggs McDonald, television announcer during the Stanley Cup era, is a hallowed name on Long Island.

But at the heart of the matter, Milbury doesn't hate the tradition of this franchise as much as he simply can't attach himself to it. As a former Bruin, a former opponent of those dynasty teams, how could he? For Milbury, his Islanders history involves heartaches, headaches and blood-boiling bullshit. Not Stanley Cup parades and lifelong hero status.

Milbury has never been showered in confetti along the Hempstead Turnpike parade route. Beer bottles and trash, perhaps, but never confetti.

The first day Milbury officially stormed into the lives of Long Islanders, the day he was hired as head coach in the summer of '95, he candidly described his desire to have his Islanders make a break from their storied past while promising a new age of similar glory during his tenure.

"I've heard enough talk about people wanting to put the past behind them that it must be an issue for some people. It just doesn't happen to be an issue for me," Milbury declared that day. "That was somebody else's past, not mine. In a way, that's maybe why I'm here, and not somebody else. I'm part of a fresh approach to this thing. As much as I respect what was won then, I don't live that day to day. And neither should these guys. And they won't."

A few moments earlier, Milbury made the famous proclamation: "Screw the Devils, screw the Rangers. I'm an Islander now."

Several years later, he would defiantly claim to be "the last Islander" of them all.

In between, Milbury always made for an easy target for the team's proud alumni. It was a running cacophony of anonymous jabs, behind-the-scenes whispers, and, at best, backhanded compliments that drove an indelible wedge between the people who made the organization the masterpiece it once was and the man determined to repaint it with his own brush.

Milbury often had attempted to defend himself by citing how many jobs his administration actually had provided members of those famed Cup teams, despite his stated intention to create his own legacy of success.

Anders Kallur, an unsung forward who scored as many as 36 goals in one Islander season during the championship run, was the team's director of European scouting. Bob Nystrom was the team's director of corporate relations, Kenny Morrow the director of pro scouting. Lorne Henning and Butch Goring had been members of the coaching staff. Clark Gillies temporarily was brought in to work with young power forward Todd Bertuzzi. Billy Smith came back in 2001 as the goalie consultant. Bryan Trottier, more than once, was offered a minor-league coaching position before he accepted a job as an assistant coach with the Colorado Avalanche. Ed Westfall, the first captain in team history, and Wayne Merrick, a former center from the dynasty years, worked for the team as broadcasting analysts (Milbury and Westfall, despite sharing a link with the Boston Bruins, are hardly considered to be chummy).

Yet all of this apparently wasn't enough to appease other former greats, such as one of his greatest nemeses, Denis Potvin. As if everybody working for the New York Yankees once wore pinstripes, as if Mikko Makela should've been hired to usher people to their seats, as if Mike Hordy had sent in a resume to become the team's new mascot.

After Goring was fired as head coach near the end of the 2000-01 season, Potvin, in town as a television analyst with the Florida Panthers, discussed with a couple of New York reporters the continuing mess that was the Islanders.

"It's been a bad situation here for a long time," a visibly disgusted Potvin said. "We're all very close and, of course, we supported Butch pulling through and having a tenure here. Nobody's had that here.

"Well," Potvin then said, "except for Mike Milbury."

He then brought up the team's new owners, Wang and Kumar, who said before Goring's ouster that Milbury was their guy and that he was not going to be fired.

"I don't think any of us have a response," Potvin said. "I sure don't. For me, I'm in Florida now, and for me, the Islanders are long forgotten."

This was quite a concession from Potvin, who'd tried for years to return to the Islanders in one front-office capacity or another. Milbury, it just so happened, was always what got in his way.

John Spano never got the chance to throw his Monopoly money at any free agents, never got to do much of anything, really, to affect the Islanders' hockey personnel before he turned left and right for the camera and was fitted for a penitentiary jumpsuit.

That is, with one highly notable exception.

Barely one month before his jig was up, Spano released a statement through the Islanders' public-relations staff. "SPANO: HANDS OFF MY GM!" read the headline in *The New York Post*.

Midway through his first and only season in the owner's box, Spano had convinced Milbury to give up his coaching hat to concentrate solely on managerial duties, with associate coach Rick Bowness taking over behind the bench. During the playoffs—and during the six-week span in which he'd tried to dupe John Pickett into believing his $16.8 million installment check was in the mail—Spano also announced that any NHL teams hoping to lure Milbury away from the Islanders were sadly mistaken.

"Mike and I had a discussion regarding his role with the Islanders and reports that he may be a candidate for jobs with other NHL teams . . . He is not going anywhere," Spano said. "In short, Mike has put together a tremendous nucleus of young talent. With my complete support, I am certain he is the person to lead the Islanders back into Stanley Cup contention.

"Mike Milbury and nobody else will be in charge of the hockey operations for the Islanders. Therefore, I will refuse any requests from NHL teams to talk to Mike regarding employment. Mike is entirely in agreement and will remain our general manager."

In the previous days, Milbury had dropped hints with Boston reporters that while he did not expect to leave the Islanders, he declined to rule out the possibility, especially if he was offered the job as Sinden's replacement.

The fact was, Sinden had indicated his existing assistant GM, Mike O'Connell, eventually would inherit the post. Sinden also told reporters he had no intention of asking the Islanders for permission to speak with Milbury.

Milbury called speculation about his departure "idle gossip," although several team insiders knew his covert courting of the Boston media—and notions that he also was a candidate for a GM's position with the Washington Capitals—simply were born from a veiled effort to block Spano from hiring Potvin as team president, and thus, as Milbury's new boss.

"In December or January, John told me that he was thinking about bringing in Potvin to work on the business end of the franchise, whereupon I told him that was crazy, that I did not want to work with Denis Potvin and that there were going to be problems," Milbury told the *Post*'s Larry Brooks the day Spano's ouster officially was announced by the NHL. "Then, in mid-May, there was a lot of talk going around about Boston being interested in bringing me up there. At the same time, I'm hearing more concerning Potvin.

"So while we're at a meeting of our scouts, in fact, John asked me, in a bantering way, to dispel those [Boston] rumors. And I told him I thought we had something we needed to discuss.

"I told him again that if Potvin were coming, I could not envision reporting to him or working with him. I mean, I don't want to say anything about Denis Potvin, but haven't others called him 'a shameless self-promoter?' [Spano] gave me his word that Potvin was not going to be hired, and so it was then that I told him that he should issue the press release.

"And despite all that's happened since, involving the ownership, I have no second thoughts. This is where I want to be."

Still, Milbury had a clause expressly written into his contract allowing him to leave should an opening develop for a general manager with another organization. When asked how he would react to someone coming in above him on the hockey side, Milbury replied, "I think if anybody came in, in the capacity of the hockey operations department, who was impacting my job, I'd have to review it. I would think I would have to reexamine my position."

Potvin had tossed his hat into the ring to be the team's general manager when Don Maloney was fired, but Milbury eventually got that job. Shortly after introducing Spano to then-owner John Pickett, Potvin also angled to become the team's president, not that he had the requisite decision-making and business experience to merit such a lofty position.

Potvin, of course, was the franchise's first star player, the first overall selection in the 1973 amateur draft. He spent 15 seasons with the Islanders, winning three Norris Trophies as the NHL's best defenseman. He played 1,060 regular-season games, scoring 310 goals and adding 742 assists for 1,052 points. In 185 playoff games, he was 56-108-164. He was enshrined in the Hockey Hall of Fame, with Bossy, in 1991.

He rightfully still receives a hero's welcome whenever he returns to Long Island as the Panthers' television analyst or for various ceremonies in which banners are raised to the rafters honoring franchise greats like Arbour, Torrey, Gillies, Nystrom or Trottier. "Some of my favorite memories are from here," Potvin once said. "I'm almost exhausted by the bad news. I travel around the league, I always hear the same comments, 'Denny, we're sorry to hear what's going on in Long Island.' The alumni is not happy, I can tell you that. We all feel that way. There is too much history here."

Potvin's alliance with Spano immediately spawned rumblings that he soon would return to work for the Islanders in the front office. But those dreams were dashed for good when Spano's true identity was revealed.

"It's very simple. Spano basically told me he couldn't pay me what we had discussed. And that put an end to that," Potvin told the New York *Post*'s Botte on July 5, 1997. "What he told me was—and this was the last conversation we had, back in April—he told me he was running out of money. I took that, at that point, as giving me a pretty clear message that he couldn't deliver what he had promised . . . The presidency is what we had talked about all along."

Milbury's take? "I just think that's his excuse for not having gotten the job."

In the end, Potvin at least regretted his role in Spano's involvement with the Islanders. "John and I had a relationship for almost two years," he said. "It's been a mess [in Long Island] for three or four years, but to tell you very openly, this just tears my heart apart to see what has happened to the organization. If I had the money, I would've bought the team.

"The intent was to bring somebody in because Mr. Pickett, I know, didn't want to be involved in hockey any more. And I was introducing him to someone who by all accounts—by the NHL, by Pickett himself, by the banks and everybody else—always checked out pretty well.

"Who was I to question if he could do it or not do it?"

Potvin was talking solely about Spano at the time, yet Milbury rarely was afforded the same benefit of the doubt from Potvin or many of his former teammates.

In a story published January 25, 2001, the *Post*'s Barry Baum reported that several former Islanders from the Stanley Cup dynasty years had either met or held telephone conversations with Mike Picker—the top envoy to the club's new owners—to call for Milbury's immediate firing.

"[Owners Charles Wang and Sanjay Kumar] know how we feel," one anonymous player was quoted as saying. "The team has gone in a totally wrong direction. It's ridiculous. The franchise was torn apart."

One of the players who met with Picker reportedly was Jean Potvin, a spare defenseman on the team's first two championship teams in 1980 and '81 and Denis Potvin's older brother. Several former Islanders claimed to have felt "put off" by Milbury, whom they considered an outsider as a former Bruins player and coach. They also resented what they perceived as his aloof attitude and felt he never was more than the black sheep of the Islanders' family.

"I don't want to hear there's a five-year plan again. I'm tired of hearing it. It's a tough situation to go through year after year," Clark Gillies said in the story. "I don't think these players want to play here. There's a total lack of effort. Until they want to take pride in that jersey, it'll be the same thing over and over."

Others trashed Milbury for what was widely perceived to be a series of poorly executed trades and draft choices during his tenure, regardless of whether some of them were financially motivated and/or mandated by ownership. "He hasn't made any sterling decisions as far as I could tell," one former Islander said.

Even when Gillies tried to be nice to Milbury on the day the Islanders clinched their first playoff berth in eight years in April of 2002 (mostly due to Milbury-engineered trades for stars Alexei Yashin and Michael Peca and the acquisition of goalie Chris Osgood in the waiver draft), many in the team's front office viewed Gillies's words as little more than a forced, backhanded compliment.

"I must say, I've liked the way Mike's handled things this year a lot better and how he's shown more patience than in past years. I have to give him credit," Gillies told the New York *Daily News*. "If [owners] Charles [Wang] and Sanjay [Kumar] allow him to add a free agent or two this summer, with the mix they already have here, I think they have a pretty good hockey team.

"I know Charles said he sent Mike to charm school," Gillies added, bringing up a joke the owners liked to use when talking about Milbury. "While he might need a few more lessons, Mike has really stayed out of it and let [coach Peter Laviolette] handle the team. I like that he hasn't been as outspoken as he has in past years. He's also had some real money to work with and I really think he's done a much better job."

Initially, Milbury publicly attempted to maintain a diplomatic facade about the years of criticism he garnered from the people whose legacy his teams could not avoid or draw upon.

"Look, these guys were great Islanders. They want it to be right and I could understand that. But I didn't comment on how they sell insurance or run their stock brokerage business," Milbury said. "I've been beaten up pretty good, and I didn't particularly care for it. I didn't think it was appropriate. I think this organization has been overly generous to its alumni...We have nothing to apologize for as an organization for the way these guys have been treated."

Eventually, by the spring of 2001, he'd had enough.

"They can take this—they'll have to, because I'm gonna say it anyway," Milbury said in an interview with *Newsday*'s Hahn. "Rain has been pouring, literally and figuratively, on this building and leaking for a long time. There's been no rush of support from anyone from anywhere.

"I told my wife, 'I'm the last Islander.'

"I'm the last one. Everyone else has gone. They've left the Island. There's only us people in this organization. The other guys only used to be Islanders."

8

Milstones, Meet the Milstones

The only optimistic approach that could have been taken following the Spano fiasco was that things couldn't possibly get worse for the Islanders.

We'll pause here for laughter.

The Pickett family regained control of the franchise for a short time and immediately began the search for another owner. Obviously the next person to come in would be under intense scrutiny from Bettman all the way down to the beat reporters who covered the team.

It didn't take long for Bettman to steer another group toward the faltering franchise, this one led by Howard Milstein, head sibling of a powerful and rich New York real estate empire, and Steven Gluckstern, a co-owner of the Phoenix Coyotes who, with Richard Burke, moved that franchise to the desert from Winnipeg (and with little foresight into an arena not built for hockey, but that would become Wayne Gretzky's problem years later).

Milstein and Gluckstern seemed a far more stable partnership. Milstein had billionaire bucks and visions of developing a new arena while Gluckstern had experience as an NHL owner. The two created New York Sports Ventures, purchased the franchise from Pickett for $195 million and took over operations on February 25, 1998.

Of course it wasn't a totally smooth transaction. SMG, the company that managed Nassau Coliseum, wasn't happy with the Milstein-

Gluckstern group after meetings with them regarding the plans for a new Coliseum. It took a four-hour meeting at Bettman's office in Manhattan to finally convince SMG to approve the sale and close the deal. SMG was never comfortable with Milstein, who made it abundantly clear that his interest in the team was based on a greater interest in development rights for the 70-plus-acre Coliseum property. SMG was in direct control of such matters, and Milstein wasn't one to want to take orders or follow someone else's rules.

It was the beginning of a contentious relationship. And if the Spano situation left the franchise in a mess, the Milstein-SMG battle turned the mess into a ruin.

Indeed, it could get worse for the Islanders. And it did.

Still, it was hard for anyone around the team not to feel a sense of relief that the Spano situation, at least, was behind them. The new owners spoke about reconnecting with their fans and with the tradition of the franchise and even dared to discuss plans to have a new arena in place by 2001.

The night of the sale's approval saw the Islanders drop a 4-1 decision to the Dallas Stars at the Coliseum in the first game back from the Olympic break. They lost 5-4 to the Bruins in their next game, but newly named team president David Seldin (remember this name, it will come up a lot) tagged the following Tuesday night game against the Flyers as "a night Islanders fans don't want to miss."

The team, which had rid itself of the fisherman logo but was still wearing the wavy, aqua blue and bright orange-colored jerseys from that era, donned their classic uniforms that night. The new owners put on a pregame show that included trotting out a host of alumni from the glory years—highlighted by Mike Bossy and Bryan Trottier. They also officially named Trevor Linden (who was acquired just before the Olympic break in what Milbury later admitted was his most regret-laden trade, sending future stars Todd Bertuzzi and Bryan McCabe to Vancouver) the team's seventh captain, with Denis Potvin there to hand Linden his new jersey with the "C" sewn on the shoulder and everything.

Bossy and Trottier even put on skates, took sticks and went the length of the ice toward an empty net for a 2-on-0 that Bossy fittingly completed with a goal.

Cheesy, but an altogether happy moment for Islanders fans after years of sadness and grief. The sound system blared Bruce Springsteen's song "Glory Days" to cap the event.

Optimism abounded that night. Before a somewhat disappointing crowd of 12,085, the Islanders carried the emotion of the pregame festivities toward a 3-1 victory over the Flyers to keep themselves within six points of the final playoff spot in the East. They won their next game over the Buffalo Sabres, keeping pace.

But then, as has happened many times during the team's forgettable years, the bottom dropped out at the worst time. The team went into a six-game winless streak (0-4-2), which sank all hopes of making the playoffs. It also saw the end of Bowness's tenure as coach. Milbury, who earlier in the season put Bowness "on alert" for the team's poor performance, replaced the coach with—who else?—himself on March 11. The team responded by going 0-3-1 in Milbury's first four games back behind the bench. The team missed the playoffs for a franchise-record fourth straight season.

In fashion similar to Henning's ouster in 1995, the players reacted with disappointment and pointed blame on themselves for the likeable Bowness's firing. Some were also a bit upset with the timing of the decision, especially in the midst of a playoff push.

"We'll see what happens," Ziggy Palffy said. "There's 19 games left. We're fighting for a playoff spot. In a couple of weeks, there's been a lot of changes. I don't know if the coaching change is going to help . . . but what can you do? It's part of hockey. One time you're up, one time you're down."

For Palffy and the Islanders, there were too many times that they were down. Perhaps the lone memorable moment in that season came on April 4 at the Coliseum, when the Islanders and Rangers—both eliminated from the playoffs—were involved in an ugly blood feud that is hardly a highlight moment in the history of the rivalry. In fact, only 14,640 fans showed up—a rare occurrence that an Islanders–Rangers game, although a sellout on paper, did not produce a packed house at the Coliseum.

The trouble started when Milbury called a timeout midway through the third period, just after the Islanders scored to take a 3-0 lead. Rangers coach John Muckler was incensed.

"Bush move," Muckler growled. "Milbury doesn't have to call a timeout and embarrass all our players. He wanted to stand up and take bows."

So Muckler sent out his goons to retaliate, and the final minutes of the game turned into a bloodbath of nastiness and thuggery.

Milbury was seen mouthing the word "sorry" to Muckler after the timeout.

"Those who know me know I take my timeouts at unorthodox times," he said. "It was . . . an effort to make a point to my team." The

Islanders had blown a 4-0 lead a few weeks earlier and Milbury wanted to remind them of it.

The Rangers simply wanted to pound the shit out of the Islanders, who were without heavyweight Gino Odjick after Odjick had been ejected in the first period for not having his jersey tied down in a brawl with Darren Langdon.

So Bill Berg fought Linden, Langdon took on 6'9", 250-pound rookie Zdeno Chara, and Jeff Beukeboom picked on J. J. Daigneault while Bruce Driver tussled with Palffy.

But it got nasty when a punchy youngster named P. J. Stock jumped the passive Mariusz Czkerawski and put a beating on him. Islanders goalie Tommy Salo saw Czerkawski's predicament and raced over to help him. That gave Rangers rookie goalie Dan Cloutier the green light to race the length of the ice and jump Salo. What ensued was a beating that had everyone in the building wincing. Cloutier pounded Salo with about 20 unanswered punches.

One hundred and fifty-four minutes of penalties were assessed at the end of the altercation. Six players were ejected.

And Daigneault opined this of the Rangers, who were about to miss the playoffs for the first time since 1993 and had the league's highest payroll at $44 million:

"I think they had to justify their payroll somehow."

The 1998-99 season would be the first full year with the Milstein–Gluckstern ownership in place, and there was much anticipation. The group did a lot of talking about arena plans, winning and bringing back the classic jersey full-time.

They kept just one of those promises: the jersey was restored to its old form, with a few minor enhancements—a deeper blue and a sharper orange and four stripes added to the shoulder to represent the four Stanley Cups. But the most important aspect was that all remnants of the fisherman jersey were completely gone.

But concerns about the stability of the franchise were not. The new ownership group did everything with a reinventing-the-wheel sort of arrogance. It had many insiders concerned.

Late in the previous season, just after the new ownership took control, Seldin told Milbury that he wanted to experiment with an expanded coaching staff, like in football (Seldin's background was getting the NFL Jacksonville Jaguars off the ground as an expansion franchise). Many figured the control freak in Milbury wouldn't agree with such a scheme, but he surprisingly endorsed the idea. Of course there was a catch revealed later.

"Mike didn't argue because they were negotiating with him a five-year contract extension," one person involved in those meetings said. "So of course he said, 'That's a great idea.'"

The person then laughed and said, "It was obviously a disaster."

It began with Milbury as head coach and GM. He had five assistant coaches—Henning, Wayne Fleming, Bill Stewart, Stefan Luner and Greg Cronin—and two other organizational coaches—Steve Stirling and Gilles Gilbert. Each coach had his own specialty that he was in charge of, like offensive and defensive coordinators in football. Seldin even considered a fighting coach and had a team manager named Mike Santos meet this candidate before a game late in the 1997-98 season. Santos brought him to the team's locker room to observe the players he would be "coaching," and then-assistant equipment manager Eric Miklich was asked to outfit the man, described as Middle Eastern-looking and about 5'5". He was supposedly a martial arts expert and had never seen a hockey game in his life.

Miklich put the man in full gear—pads, glove, skates, jersey and helmet—as requested. Then the man, covered head to toe, said, "I need to know where the vulnerable spots are."

So Miklich playfully popped him in the nose.

"Right there," he said.

The man was never seen again.

There is also the story of Darren Anderson, described by one Islanders executive as "one of David Seldin's only friends." Anderson worked with Seldin for the Jacksonville Jaguars, and Seldin wanted to give his buddy a cushy job with the Islanders. So he created one that paid a six-figure salary. He dubbed Anderson—who had no previous experience in hockey—vice president of hockey operations. It was immediate cause for alarm, considering that the legendary Al Arbour held that position before Anderson arrived. Arbour had retired.

But it didn't matter. What operations of hockey Anderson was responsible for is still to this day a mystery to many who remain with the franchise. Milbury and his staff made sure not to allow him much of a say in matters, nor did they include him in decisions, so he was rarely seen or heard. And when he did show up for work, he did very little more than sit at his desk.

"He was [*Seinfeld* character] George Costanza come to life," the executive said.

Anderson did sit in on meetings, though he was once angrily sent home by Milbury when he spoke up concerning matters he knew nothing about. In the end, it was decided he was simply a spy, albeit a well-paid spy, for Milstein and Seldin.

But that kind of meddling—Anderson was fired the minute Wang and Kumar took over and the football-style coaching staff didn't last the 1998–99 season—wasn't the greatest annoyance brought almost daily by Seldin. It was his penchant for creating catastrophe just when things were on the verge of being under control.

One example was when he met with the radio station that had broadcast Islanders games—WLIR, a strong FM signal—to renew the team's contract. When WLIR voiced some concerns about poor ratings, Seldin flippantly replied, "If you guys aren't happy, let's agree to walk away."

Seldin apparently figured either that WLIR wouldn't dare give up exclusive rights to the Islanders or that he could cut a better deal elsewhere. He didn't figure that the Islanders were not at all a sought commodity in the New York broadcasting market.

So when WLIR's representatives decided to call Seldin's bluff—two Islanders executives with him at the meeting gasped when they did in fact agree to walk away—the Islanders were left without a radio station to broadcast their games. That is, until they signed on with a new all-sports station, One-on-One Sports, which used an AM signal located in Newark, New Jersey. The station could barely be heard at the Coliseum, let alone in the deeper reaches of Long Island.

Not that anyone was listening anyway.

But Seldin's worst miscalculation came that fall in a meeting with Nassau County officials and SMG regarding the Coliseum.

All summer long, Seldin and Milstein had negotiated with SMG and Nassau about the development of a new arena. Milstein, a real estate mogul with an eye on developing property, wanted the land himself and even went as far as having a scale model created to show his plan. It included a cluster of office buildings, a convention center and an arena, with a parking garage and a corridor of shops and restaurants. Politicians didn't like it because it was too urbanized, too many skyscrapers. Even a second, more scaled-down model wasn't received well.

So with fear he would turn Uniondale into a small city, they refused to work with Milstein to oust SMG and allow him to take over the development of the property. Milstein didn't want to share anything. For him, it was all or nothing.

SMG wielded great power over Milstein. Not only because it had the county as an ally, but because of the long-term lease it held as the manager of the building. The lease, signed by John Pickett in 1985, bound the Islanders to the Coliseum until 2015. In accordance with the lease, the Islanders could not play home games anywhere other than the Coliseum. The lease also called for the team to yield as much as two-thirds of revenue, such as ticket sales and advertising and all of parking, to SMG and the county. Financially, it was an immensely debilitating agreement from the perspective of the franchise, but at the time Pickett mistakenly overvalued the worth of luxury boxes, which, as part of the agreement in the lease, he built with his own money and from which he took all revenue. By the mid-1990s, it was obvious that the Coliseum didn't have nearly enough luxury suites to make enough of a profit. And there was little room to add more.

So the lease grew to become a leech for the franchise. Spano, in his short term, even grumbled about it, but at least he came up with a few workable plans that the local politicians to this day still applaud. When Milstein arrived, he figured his financial and political might as a real estate giant would bully SMG out of the picture. But SMG wasn't going anywhere and made sure that point was understood.

When Milstein made a paltry offer of $7 million to buy out the remaining 17 years of the lease, SMG scoffed. So Milstein had his lawyers pick apart the lease to find a loophole. Late that summer, they thought they had found one when an engineer installing a new center ice scoreboard purchased by the team (another fiasco, because it turned out to be a basketball scoreboard with no place for penalties or shots on goal) noticed a crack in one of the hoists in the ceiling of the Coliseum that held up the scoreboard. It needed to be replaced.

The Milstein group made it out to be a life-threatening discovery. With his attorneys filing a lawsuit against Nassau County and SMG, Milstein ordered the Islanders out of the Coliseum and into temporary offices in Manhattan. The team cited publicly that it was "structurally evicted" because of the cracked hoist and named a host of other problems with the building.

The media quickly labeled the latest controversy "Hoistgate." Seldin created a website called "Coliseum-coverup.com" to list the infractions that gave the Islanders the right to move out of the arena. All an effort to publicly embarrass the county and SMG.

Meanwhile, the team was in Lake Placid for a training camp that was supposed to last a week, but it wound up stranded there almost a month.

Nassau politicians were livid. Engineers were brought in to inspect the building and it was deemed safe, though problems were detected and reported.

The three sides came back to the negotiating table again to finally put the embarrassingly public feud to an end. Seldin was representing the Milstein–Gluckstern ownership, and, after a few hours, the three sides thought they finally had an agreement in principle. The county executive, Thomas Gulotta, even went as far as ordering his public affairs department to begin writing a press release.

Then Seldin spoke up, and all hell once again broke loose.

With all sides in agreement, Seldin figured he had the county in a vulnerable position. So just as they were discussing the deal, Seldin announced that the Islanders were no longer happy with the plan. They reconsidered and decided they still wanted SMG—most especially the lease—out of the picture. The team, mainly Howard Milstein, also wanted more control of the development of the Coliseum property. If not, no deal.

Gulotta exploded. He left the meeting and in an impromptu press conference ripped the Islanders owners, calling them "pigs at the trough" and saying the lawsuit was "nothing more than a ruse" to get rid of the lease and SMG so the team could get a bigger cut of the revenues. In confidence, two Milstein insiders said that much was true. But only because with the lease as it was, the team could not survive financially. The team claimed losses of $20 million in 1998-99.

A Supreme Court ruling finally forced the Islanders back into the building in time for the '98-99 regular season to begin. But the bad blood was already spilled, and Islanders fans were already back to feeling woe for their woebegone team.

9

A Coliseum in Ruins

Since the day it was born from a sincere idea spawned by foresight and post-World War II optimism, Nassau Coliseum has lived the tortured life of a bastard child under the neglectful watch of the historically greedy, wholly unfit parent that is the Nassau County/Long Island political machine.

It stands today as a depressing reminder of an idea that never reached its intended fullest potential, mostly because of outside factors constantly dragging it down. Even when it was first constructed and lauded for its innovative design to allow excellent sight lines for sporting events, the place was still somewhat of a disappointment. Construction was never officially completed, just half-assed at the end enough to cut costs, allow events to start up and get the money rolling in for the many hands that stuck out in the receiving line.

Much like its main tenant, the Islanders, Nassau Coliseum enjoyed a brief yet booming heyday during the team's Stanley Cup era from 1980-83, when the building, affectionately dubbed "Fort Neverlose," was sold out for virtually every home game during the regular season and was standing room only for the playoffs.

But that's also when the arena started showing its warts—and the drawbacks of poor design. While the interior portion was considered, by design, one of the best in the NHL for viewing a game, it was terribly inept in functionality and comfort. The seating area includes two levels—an upper bowl and a lower bowl—that are both accessible only by a narrow street-level concourse that wraps the building. The arena's single concourse also includes concession stands and rest rooms, and when crowds reach 14,000 and up to the 16,000-plus sellout capacity, the Coliseum concourse is a frustrated sea of weaving humanity. Many observers consider those times when the concourse is filled a dangerous fire hazard.

And for Islanders–Rangers games, it is a chaotic, volatile mosh pit that just begs for trouble.

But, incredibly, there hasn't been a newsworthy situation to bring such concerns to light. Tragic events are usually the catalyst for reform or destruction, for either of which the Coliseum, completed in 1972 and since then never once renovated, remains in desperate need.

To understand the Islanders' plight at the Coliseum and the incredible mother-eating-her-young relationship the building has had with the franchise, one must start from the very beginning.

This all started well before the Islanders were even an idea.

It was early winter in 1960 when the rapidly growing Long Island landscape was still taking shape. The region had blossomed after the landmark development of Levittown, which had been an icon for American postwar prosperity and expansionism to the suburbs.

And not far from Levittown, in fact less than ten miles due west, the United States Air Force had housed a 1,122-acre military base called Mitchel Field. It was there in 1927 that one of the most significant moments in aviation history took place when Charles Lindberg and his plane, *The Spirit of St. Louis,* set off for Paris from that airstrip to become the first man to make a nonstop transatlantic flight.

In 1961, the air force announced that it would be closing the base. Immediately, interest arose regarding what would become of the vast portion of valuable land that was hugged between the Meadowbrook Parkway, a road that served as a cross-island interchange between the Northern and Southern State Parkways, and Hempstead Turnpike, which was a conduit to bustling Jamaica Avenue in Queens. Agencies such as the U.S. Army Signal Corps, the Internal Revenue Service, and the filthy rich and ever-expanding Roman Catholic Diocese of Rockville Centre all made inquiries.

The most prevalent idea for the land was to construct a civic center for Nassau County, which was growing into one of the most affluent in the nation. The idea was opposed by a lesser argument to turn it into a civilian airfield, but in 1961 the county executive, A. Holly Patterson, formed a panel to make plans for a county center. Those advocates of the airport idea, with the backing of the Federal Aviation Administration, threatened to block any development of the land unless the county agreed to house an airfield at the site.

By 1963, however, the county had acquired slightly less than half of the property, with 154 acres going to Hofstra University, a neighbor to the immediate west, and 220 acres given to Nassau County Community College, which sprouted up among the vacant airplane hangers and deserted barracks on the northern portion of the property. The federal government kept about 130 acres, with the rest doled out among New York state and other agencies. There is a large area that, to this day, remains a protected site to preserve the Hempstead Plains and the Meadowbrook Stream.

It then took until 1968 for plans to construct the Coliseum to be drawn and approved by the County board. Original outlines called for a 14,000-seat arena—at the time referred to as Mitchel Field Coliseum—with a budget that started at $21.5 million. County executive Eugene Nickerson proposed the Coliseum project as part of a complex of seven buildings, including a 750,000-volume library, to be known as the John F. Kennedy Educational, Civic and Cultural Center.

But, as of 1968, only the Coliseum was approved.

Nickerson's plan, ironically, was sort of in line with what the county has been talking about since the mid-1990s—a project now called "The Nassau Hub," which would turn the mostly unused 70-acre Coliseum property into a sports and entertainment complex with a new arena, convention center and open-air mall of restaurants, bars, a multiplex, an arcade and even an idea for luxury condominiums.

Like the current plan, Nickerson's vision in the 1960s was to create a smaller, cleaner and less congested version of the bustling cosmopolitan scene in Manhattan, which is a 40-minute drive to the west. Nickerson also wanted to add low- and middle-income housing, as well as luxury apartments, to the site. The proposal called for 1,000 units of housing to be built for returning Vietnam veterans.

Nickerson also called for a Coliseum, a hotel and five office buildings, along with a research and light industry complex, all situated on 576 acres.

"It will be something beautiful and inspiring," Nickerson said in the mid-60s when discussing his dreams for Mitchel Field. "And it will not be afflicted with the desperate ugliness of New York City."

But Nickerson would never come close to seeing his vision come to life. The lame-duck Democrat did, however, watch in frustration as his Republican replacement, Ralph Caso, took command of the project and the credit of finally putting it in motion with his own ideas and doing it with the help of his own political cronies.

The Coliseum has always been a lightning rod of dirty politics. Even under Nickerson there were charges and reports of poor management of the project, conflicts of interest among those in charge of planning and, naturally, political favoritism. For most of the decade, the Coliseum plans were strangled by red tape—something that would become the bane of the arena's entire existence even before a shovel hit the dirt.

Caso, who would later cut the ribbon at the completed Coliseum in 1972, cut through the red tape, wielding a saber of political might. As supervisor of the Town of Hempstead, in which the Coliseum resides, and minority leader of the county board, Caso was involved in the Coliseum planning. When he took over as county executive in 1970, he snatched the project out of the hands of the development agencies set up by Nickerson and named a political ally to a cabinet position with direct responsibility over Mitchel Field.

Caso then scrapped all plans for housing on the site, saying bluntly, "They will never be considered. Housing is completely out." This with many low-income families waiting on deck in hotel rooms set up for them by Nickerson's regime.

And so went a famous and longtime war between Democrats and Republicans in the county. And the property, along with the Coliseum, has always remained in the middle.

To Caso's credit, he put an end to the rhetoric involving the Mitchel Field site, and in a relatively short time, construction finally began on the project, though it involved only the arena portion, with a county-funded cost that had by 1970 ballooned to $28 million. It was scheduled to open by autumn 1971.

The arena was ballyhooed all over Long Island. It would have the capacity for 14,000 spectators—much more than the Island's only two other prominent venues at the time. Commack Arena, home of minor-league hockey's Long Island Ducks, sat only 4,500 fans and was located further east on the Island in rural Suffolk County. Island Garden, which shoehorned in about 3,500 people and was the home of the ABA New York Nets, was situated in an unappealing industrial park in neighboring West Hempstead.

The new Coliseum would not only be much larger, it would also offer far more comfortable seating, with upholstered theatre-style chairs that had completely unobstructed views at every seat.

The Nets, who moved to Long Island from Teaneck, New Jersey, were the obvious first potential tenants for the building, though local politicians considered offers from NBA teams. The Ducks, an entertaining, pugnacious gang from the iron-fisted Eastern League, with an icon in player/coach John Brophy (who was the inspiration for the 1970s cult-hockey movie *Slapshot*), were not at all under consideration.

Caso hired Bill Shea—he of Shea Stadium fame and the family that helped bring National League baseball back to New York in 1962 with the expansion arrival of the Mets—to advise him on how to properly run a major sports venue. Shea said 'yea' to the profitable Nets, but 'nay' to the loveable Ducks.

"Why fool around with something that's not major league?" Shea said in a April, 1971 interview with *Newsday*.

Caso concurred, saying, "We're big-time all the way."

And so marked the beginning of the end of the Ducks, a team of great legend and little else in the Long Island sports annals.

What Shea's influence and Caso's thirst for the big leagues did was—intentionally or not—start the process that brought the National Hockey League to Long Island. It also laid the groundwork that would lead to the creation of the New York Islanders hockey franchise.

First, the Coliseum had to be completed. In the spring of 1971, with the arena's grand opening now pushed up to April 1, 1972, Shea was already down on the building. "I wish it were larger," he lamented to a reporter while touring the construction site. "Madison Square Garden will have 2,000 more seats."

But, Shea added, "the thing that may make this building right is its better viewability than the Garden."

Still, as a *Newsday* story documented, some of the luxuries planned for the arena ended up being sacrificed by no-frills cost cutting. The arena restaurant, located at the event level 24 feet below street level, "isn't much bigger than a neighborhood tavern," *Newsday's* Joe Donnelly wrote. "It is the dream of some housewives; more kitchen than dining room."

And all around the massive white-concrete oval of 32 poured-concrete columns and glass-enclosed concourse was nothing but empty, undeveloped land. Plenty of parking. Not much else to do.

"Lions and Christians, no charge," read a crude cardboard sign stuck in a window of the Coliseum box office, which was still under construction.

The workmen were having fun with the Coliseum. Fans would have to wait for their fun a little longer.

Meanwhile, Caso and Shea continued to entertain ideas for their arena. The Nets, with a determined and otherwise desperate owner in Roy Boe, were a lock as the first main tenant. And talk of a potential future merger with the NBA had Nassau officials excited about the prospects of big-time professional basketball as a main event. But most major markets housed two teams in their arenas—basketball and hockey—not unlike the New York Knicks and Rangers at Madison Square Garden. The more teams, the more games and the less nights the building would be "dark," or unused.

So Caso and Shea, with visions of nightly sellouts throughout lucrative winter months, invited National Hockey League president Clarence Campbell to visit the nearly completed Coliseum in June of 1971. Campbell came away impressed.

"It's much bigger than I was led to believe," he said. "It's a long way from completion, but I'm certain it will be an excellent building."

Then Campbell echoed the sentiments of just about everyone who first laid eyes on the innovative inner structure of the arena.

"Basically, the thing I was most enthusiastic about is that it has excellent sight lines," he said.

Caso said that afternoon that he intended to make a strong pitch for an NHL franchise. Campbell said the league, which had just undergone rapid expansion from its original six teams to 12 in 1967-68 and then to a total of 14 in 1970-71, agreed not to expand again until 1974 at the earliest. "However," Campbell said, "that agreement could be modified with the unanimous consent of the owners."

Accompanying Campbell with Caso and Shea was a man who would have significant influence over any chance of the NHL expanding to Long Island. That was, ironically, Rangers owner Bill Jennings.

"I feel it's inevitable," Jennings admitted in a *Newsday* interview, adding that before such a decision could be acceptable a new team would "have to make a deal with us."

The territorial fee was figured somewhere around $5 million, on top of a $6 million expansion fee paid to the NHL, with interest that ballooned it to almost $10 million, over the next 10 years.

That wasn't enough to deter the unflappable Boe, who, along with a band of 19 partners, stepped up to create the Islanders after the NHL awarded an expansion franchise to Long Island on November 8, 1971. The team would join Boe's Nets as the Coliseum headliners and be ready for action, along with a fellow NHL newcomer, the Atlanta Flames, for the 1972-73 season.

The Coliseum, meanwhile, was finally—though unofficially—opened for business on February 11, 1972 for an exhibition game between the Nets and the Pittsburgh Condors. The Nets won the game, 129-121, with their star player, Rick Barry, scoring 45 points.

More notable than the game, however, was the condition of the spanking-new arena, which still had yet to receive several finishing touches. Not all of the anticipated 15,500 seats for basketball had been installed. A crowd of 7,892 fans showed up despite an advertisement that said that only 7,000 seats would be ready for the game.

One woman who had four tickets for herself and three children discovered her seats—Section 317, Row M, Seats 12-16—had yet to be installed. Exhausted vendors complained about making constant treks up and down the steep 57-step upper bowl, while ushers, who were just learning the lay of the land themselves, did their best to help people find their seats. Most of the sections were marked in chalk and ushers could only hope fans wouldn't erase them.

Even the scoreboard had yet to be installed. One that the Nets used at Island Garden was hung in place for the game. And, believe it or not, that small, simple scoreboard remained in relative obscurity high in the rafters of the Coliseum for over 20 years. No one bothered to take it down until a new JumboTron scoreboard was installed in the late 1990s.

And on that unofficial first night, in what would eventually become a chronic problem throughout the arena over many years, a minor water leak developed in the locker room hallway.

Still, for the Nets it was a significant upgrade from the cramped, factory-like confines of Island Garden. Nets guard Bill Melchionni said it was "like going from an outhouse to a bathroom with plumbing."

Back then, at least you were confident the plumbing worked.

The arena quickly became the jewel of a burgeoning Nassau County, despite an otherwise barren landscape that surrounded it. Despite the hapless team the Islanders iced in their inaugural season, the Coliseum still drew an ambitious average of 12,908 fans in 39 home dates.

The very first hockey game played at the Coliseum was on September 27, 1972, when the Islanders and Rangers faced off in an exhibition game. The Rangers won, 6-4, but the score gave some Long Island fans reason to think their new team might not be so bad. The Rangers, after all, had reached the Stanley Cup finals the year before.

But such optimism would be quickly dashed, though at least a following was being established. A crowd of 12,221—shy of the 14,000 capacity for hockey—witnessed the very first Islanders regular-season game on October 7, 1972. The Islanders lost a 3-2 decision to the Flames. Ed Westfall scored the Islanders' first goal in their new home at 17:29 of the second period. Five days later, on October 12, the team would earn its first win at the Coliseum, a 3-2 victory that included the first penalty shot in team and Coliseum history, which was taken and scored by rookie Billy Harris.

That season was wildly entertaining, but mostly for the wrong reasons. The Islanders managed just 12 wins out of 78 games, but 10 of those wins, at least, came at the Coliseum. The team suffered through some embarrassing moments, such as the firing of coach Phil Goyette, who was replaced in an interim basis by Earl Ingarfield and Aut Erickson. Goyette, after being fired, wished his replacements luck. "They're going to need it," he added.

Up to that time, the season had been an abysmal experience to some players. But for defenseman Arnie Brown, it was a nightmare. Brown, a respectable, experienced player who was acquired from the Detroit Red Wings just before the start of the season, was miserable as an Islander. This was in part because he spent most of his career (1964-71) with the Rangers and he wasn't thrilled to be a member of an expansion team. And Rangers fans who took in hockey games at the Coliseum knew it and chastised him accordingly.

"I don't want to be here," Brown told his teammates early that season. "I'm doing anything I can to get out of here."

So after one game, with fans riding him hard, he got fed up and climbed the glass to get after them. He even made an attempt at them when he reached the runway that leads to the locker rooms. By February, he was finally traded.

The Arnie Brown story might be one of the earliest pieces of evidence that the Coliseum would be a different sort of building. Most hardcore arenas—from old Chicago Stadium to Boston Garden to the Philadelphia Spectrum—had an unforgettable and, at times, intimidating atmosphere. But those were historic, venerable buildings filled with legend and lore.

At the Coliseum, the stories ranged from the sublime to the ridiculous.

There are many bizarre stories that exist involving the Coliseum. Few can be completely factual, but some have enough witness accounts—and certainly an abundance of entertainment value—to permit their re-telling.

Perhaps the most outrageous story ever to unfold at the Coliseum took place during a game late in the 1999-2000 season. The Islanders were getting pummeled by their opponent—we're leaving out the name of the team and the date of the game to protect the persons involved—and a backup goaltender for the visiting team was sitting bored in the runway that leads to the visiting team locker room (at the Coliseum, most visiting goalies sit there because the bench is too cramped).

Throughout the game, an overzealous female fan, who is well-known throughout the league and goes by the suggestive nickname "Trish the Dish," was flirting with the goalie, whom she apparently knew from previous visits. As the story is told, she was wearing a short skirt and no panties and, from her seat near the runway, made sure the backup goalie was aware of that fact.

Security guards by the runway were also made aware.

After the visiting team took to the ice for the start of the third period, the goalie signaled for her. When she arrived at the runway, the goalie told the security, "It's okay, I just want to show her the locker room."

A few minutes into the period, a star player from the visiting team headed off for an equipment adjustment. And when he reached the dressing room, he walked in on the goalie as he was receiving oral sex from the more-than-willing Trish. The star player exploded in anger and called for security, who, naturally, acted as if they had no idea how she got to the room. They escorted her out of the locker room and back to her seat.

"The most incredible thing was," one witness said, "she didn't even get kicked out of the building."

The season before that, one Islanders player was involved in an equally bizarre situation. It happened during play on the ice, when the player—who is no longer with the team—noticed a disturbance in the crowd and realized it was his wife and, well, girlfriend in a fight. As the puck was sent to the other end of the rink for an icing, the player wheeled around and skated to the corner of the rink containing the door that leads to the home team's locker room. Next to that runway is a section of stands where mostly players' wives, girlfriends and family sit. He started slamming his stick against the glass, screaming at them to break it up.

The player recently had the girlfriend join him during a long road trip. Now, with respect to the pure image most professional athletes reflect, sometimes a married player has a steady girlfriend or two on the road. Occasionally, he'll meet up with her, and some of his teammates might even know about it. But rarely does that player allow the girlfriend exposure with him. It is done, of course, out of respect to himself, the girlfriend, his wife and family and his teammates.

But this particular player made it no secret that the girl was with him during this trip. She was often seen around the team in four consecutive cities, and they were often seen together around town. Finally, then-coach Rick Bowness decided it was time to have a talk with the player to tell him to keep the girl out of sight. The girl, it was later learned, was the babysitter for his children.

Apparently, by the time the team returned home to the Coliseum, the wife had heard about the little trip the girl took with her husband and wasn't pleased. The player was well aware of it when he saw the two converging on each other in the stands.

"He was two-handing the glass," a witness said. "And screaming at them."

Security divided the two and the player regained his composure and set himself for the ensuing faceoff. As he waited, with his stick resting across his knees, stooped over, the player could be heard among the sparse crowd, screaming at the ice beneath him.

"Fuck!" he barked. "Fuck! Fuck! Fuck!"

On October 26, 1995, Pittsburgh Penguins superstar Mario Lemieux scored a hat trick in a 7-5 win over the Islanders. The goals were the 498th, 499th and 500th of his career. But the Coliseum scoreboard never once acknowledged the historic feat, nor did it acknowledge Lemieux, who was playing in his first game in Long Island after missing the entire 1994-95 lockout season with back problems.

The Islanders admitted they were unprepared because two of the goals came in the final minutes of the game, and it's not like anyone ever expects Lemieux to score a hat trick, right?

The Penguins were livid. Lemieux just shrugged.

"I was waiting for it," he said after the game. "I was surprised they didn't announce it."

During an Islanders–Rangers game in 1996-97, Wayne Gretzky's first as a Ranger, the Coliseum scoreboard kept replaying clips from Billy Smith's memorable battle with Gretzky in the 1983 Cup Finals. Smith slashed Gretzky in one of those games and Gretzky fell to the ice as if he were shot. The scene was played over and over to the delight of Islanders fans.

Neil Smith, who was general manager of the Rangers that season and had signed Gretzky as a free agent, charged after Islanders VP of communications Pat Calabria, demanding the Coliseum stop showing the clips.

Still, most of the time, the team doesn't need to do much to encourage the Coliseum fans, who clearly are a breed all their own. There was once a promotion by the fast-food chain Wendy's that offered free chili to ticket holders if the Islanders scored six goals in a game. On one particular night, the Islanders had 11 goals and the crowd urged the team for a 12th goal with the chant: "Dou-ble-chi-li!"

On another night, they offered an optimistic cheer as the team was winding up a strong finish to the 1991-92 season despite the fact that it ended without a playoff berth: "Next year!" they shouted. "Next year!"

And on that Saturday night in April, 2002, when the Islanders clinched their first postseason berth since 1994, the Coliseum faithful waved white T-shirts and chanted a word that had, at least in recent years, become unspoken taboo on Long Island:

"Play-offs! Play-offs!"

During the emotional first-round playoff series with the Toronto Maple Leafs, the Coliseum rocked with the fervor of a desperately needed release. The cramped, squat building was suddenly praised for its throwback feel and the energy it produced because of the low ceiling and tightness of the seating in respect to the playing surface. Islanders players were giddy about the boisterous crowds and the decibels they were able to produce.

During the run to the playoffs, fans picked up many cult heroes, but none as surprising as Oleg Kvasha. The frustrating enigma, who was acquired in the curious June 2000 trade with Florida that saw goalie Roberto Luongo shipped off Long Island, was the target of boos from Coliseum fans earlier in the season because of his lackluster (and lackadaisical) play. But after a flurry of clutch goals late in the season, the fans started warming up to the aloof young Russian.

"Ohhhhh-leg, O-leg, O-leg, O-leg, Ohhhhh-leg, Ohhhh-leg!" they sang, sounding like a raucous soccer crowd.

When it started, Kvasha—who admitted to hearing the boos and also admitted it upset him—didn't realize they were singing for him. A teammate patted him on the bench and said, "That's for you, Olie!" Kvasha crinkled his brow and listened closer. When he heard it, too, he had to lower his head into his shoulder pads to hide his smile.

"I'm going to do everything I can do make sure it stays that way," he said, when asked about it afterward.

The fans had their favorites, but none greater than the love affair with an unsung everyman named Steve Webb, a soft-spoken battering-ram fourth-line forward built like a fire hydrant and one of those rare players that fans can directly identify with on many levels. Just the previous season, he was still clinging to a spot in the NHL with the Islanders. By the end of the 2001–02 season, the entire Coliseum was chanting his name after every crunching hit he laid on a Maple Leafs player:

"Steve Webb!" "Steve Webb!"

Perhaps more telling of Webb's arrival as a factor was when the series shifted to Toronto, and Maple Leafs fans responded with chants of "Steve Webb Sucks!"

Until the 1993–94 season ended with the Stanley Cup in the hands of the Rangers, the most-heard chant at Islanders games—whether the team was playing the Rangers or not—was the "19-40!" chant, which reminded the Rangers of the year they'd won their previous Cup and re-minded everyone else there was only and will be only one despised rival of the Islanders. Islanders fans have an incredible complex regarding the Rangers. Rangers fans have more of a contempt for the Islanders, but it's nothing near the outright hatred felt by the Islanders fans toward the Blueshirts.

Patrons of Madison Square Garden chanted "We Want Fish Sticks!" in reference to the Islanders' once and never-again fisherman logo. Also, to this day, not even one game passes without a whistling tune that ends with them yelling "Potvin Sucks!" That chant is in reference to the Denis Potvin hit that broke the ankle of Rangers star Ulf Nilsson in the 1978-79 season.

During goalie Felix Potvin's brief time with the Islanders in 1999, it provided a funny connection. The Rangers fans would yell "Potvin Sucks!" and some Islanders fans would reply, "We Know!"

After the Rangers claimed the championship in '94, the "19-40" chant had to be scrapped. But the crowd still enjoyed regular repeats of "The Chicken Dance," to which the crowd in unison would sing "The Ran-gers Suck!" when the chicken clucks at the end of each verse. There is also a less popular, but just as hilarious version of the "Clap Your Hands" song, which has to be heard to be enjoyed at its fullest extent. Here are the lyrics:

If you know the Rangers suck then clap your hands
(clap, clap)
If you know the Rangers suck then clap your hands
(clap, clap)
If you know the Rangers suck, and they'll never win the Cup,
If you know the Rangers suck then clap your hands
(clap, clap)

And, much like the "1940" chant, the Rangers don't have to be present for either this or the Chicken Dance song to be sung, at least twice and sometimes more, during Islanders home games.

There have been many villains to come and go at the Coliseum (Dale Hunter might be the greatest of them all, though Darcy Tucker has recently challenged that title), but perhaps none have felt as much wrath as Theoren Fleury. The volatile and troubled mighty-mite speedster, who was a disappointing symbol of Ranger overspending and mismanagement in the late 1990s, involved himself in a host of shenanigans on the Coliseum ice that only encouraged abuse from the fans. During a pregame skate before a preseason game in September 2001, fans were giving it to Fleury, who often stands along the boards and returns the trash-talking. But this night, some fans were getting personal and Fleury wanted to get the last laugh. So he picked up a puck at the end of warmups and flung it into the crowd, where it just missed a fan's head.

Then, in the first regular-season game against the Rangers at the Coliseum, Fleury flapped his arms in response to the Chicken Dance song and in the direction of Islanders tough guy Eric Cairns. Cairns had jumped Rangers forward Steve McKenna following a Rangers goal, which happened just seconds after Cairns had refused to fight Rangers tough guy Sandy McCarthy. (Cairns, however, had a hand injury and could not fight. Later in the season, at Madison Square Garden, Cairns went toe to toe with McCarthy and took him down).

As a fuming Cairns sat in the penalty box screaming across the ice at the Rangers bench, McCarthy pointed to his biceps while Fleury stood in front of the bench flapping his arms wildly. Islanders fans were in an uproar. Rangers fans howled with delight.

After the game, Fleury said with a sly grin, "I was just dancing along with the song."

When Fleury passed the Islanders' locker room on his way to the team bus, he paused to offer a sinister smirk to one Islanders player talking to reporters by the doorway. When he saw Fleury, the Islanders player stopped in mid-sentence and barked, "Cocksucker!"

For the next Islanders–Rangers game, the Islanders fans came ready to exact revenge on Fleury. And they hit him below the belt. They showered him with chants of "Crackhead Theo!" in direct, disrespectful reference to Fleury's substance abuse problem that caused him to take a leave of absence during the 2000-01 season. Fleury responded by offering the old "up yours" salute to the fans as he left the ice at the end of the game. He was fined $1,000 by the NHL for the obscene gesture. Fleury's problems during the 2001-02 season, which stemmed from a family situation, seemed to have many lowlights at the Coliseum.

Webb, in the regular-season series finale against the Rangers at the Coliseum, finally exacted the revenge Islanders fans were thirsty for ever since the "Chicken Dance" episode. He sent Fleury skates-over-helmet with an open-ice hit that brought the house down and left Fleury flat on his back.

Fleury usually had something to say about the fans after each Islanders-Rangers game at the Coliseum. But he was adamant about the "Crackhead Theo" chant being an issue. At first he claimed it was all part of the entertainment, but as it grew he felt the need to at least correct his detractors.

"I don't mind the booing and all that stuff," he said. "But when you get personal, you're crossing the line. Especially when you call me a crackhead. I have never, ever, ever used crack in my life."

But details never were a concern for Islanders fans, who have been likened to a rowdy college crowd, perhaps the original hockey version of what developed at Duke University in the late 1980s, the college basketball "Cameron Crazies." Typical of a hearty, blue-collar New York crowd— a rare breed in expensive sports arenas these days—they can spontaneously produce a chant or song that catches on throughout the arena. During the Stanley Cup era, the fans were rowdy, arrogant and unforgiving— even against the home team. Once during a disappointing loss in January 1983, fans starting chanting "Let's Go Jets!" in anticipation for the AFC championship game that season.

But for a good portion of the late 1990s, fans seemingly had to entertain themselves on many nights. Deep into losing seasons, when cantankerous crowds were sparse but terse, one could hear chants of "We Suck!" and "Last Place!" descending from the upper bowl.

One player had enough and lashed back on January 2, 2001, a night that Montreal goalie Jose Theodore added yet another indignity with a game-sealing, empty-net goal in a 3-0 Canadiens win. For those who thought things couldn't get worse, there was this misguided gem in the postgame interview session from forward Mark Parrish when asked about the unhappiness of the paltry crowd of 7,916 with both the team and GM Mike Milbury, again the subject of vociferous beheading chants. As much as we love the fans and want them to come out here and watch us, if they're going to boo us like that, we'd appreciate it if they'd just stay home, to be honest with you, Parrish said. That's not going to help us out all too much. Real smart. Although Parrish, a true stand-up guy, apologized one day later and often made self-deprecating references to the incident for much of the next two seasons.

When the fisherman logo arrived, much to the dismay of the majority of fans, furious chants of "No More Fish Sticks!" practically shook the Coliseum's foundation. There were also calls of "Save Us Spano!" at the arrival of the infamous Texas businessman, who would be proven to be full of shit and empty of cash.

And when all else failed, which the team did quite often, the embattled Mike Milbury was chased to his car with echoes of "Mike Must Go!" in his pounding head.

A memorable night for frustrated Islanders fans came February 12, 2000, when a small but boisterous collection gathered in Section 332 to protest the state of the decaying franchise and Coliseum. Holding signs that condemned everyone from NHL commissioner Gary Bettman to county executive Tom Gulotta and the Coliseum managing company, SMG, the fans showed their deep knowledge of the Islanders' debilitating lease situation with chants of "SMG, Set Us Free!" Over 11,000 fans showed up for the game on a rare night that saw attendance hit five figures in a season that averaged a franchise-worst 9,748 per game.

The Islanders gave them even more to cheer about by slamming the Jaromir Jagr-led Pittsburgh Penguins in another rarity: a blowout win.

The team, which had no responsibility in organizing the fan uprising, did acknowledge the fans' effort by showing a telling clip from the Joe Pesci movie, *The Super,* on the scoreboard JumboTron. It was a scene that blatantly acknowledged the crumbling state of the Coliseum and exactly who was to blame.

The team's game-night operations staff also played songs such as Twisted Sister's "We're Not Gonna Take It" and Sting's "If You Love Somebody, Set Them Free" during timeouts.

And, in another moment that has remained in the lore of the Coliseum, there was an incident in the hallways between the locker rooms during that game that begs to be retold. Cairns and Penguins bad boy Matthew Barnaby had fought on the ice with under a minute left in the second period. Each was sent to his respective dressing room and the period played out.

But Barnaby, a noted yapper, made his way down the hall toward the towering Cairns, who shouted back. A television camera from Fox Sports New York followed Barnaby down the hall and caught the two heavyweights as they met at a curtain that divides the hall. A gate is supposed to be up whenever two players are sent off for fighting, but the security guard was, for some unexplained reason, not at his post in the middle of the hall.

But the camera was.

So seen live on television was Barnaby taking a shot at Cairns through the curtain. Cairns then delivered a crushing blow that buckled Barnaby, but by this time the teams had already headed off the ice and security had caught up to the scuffle.

As Barnaby walked back to the locker room, he screamed at the cameraman, "Get out of my way, you Mexican bitch!"

Penguins defenseman Darius Kasparaitis, a former Islander who still has many friends at the Coliseum, giggled at Barnaby.

"You dummy," he said. "He's Italian!"

The Coliseum was a building that had been praised and panned throughout its existence. Shining moments came during the Stanley Cup era, when the building was sold out on a nightly basis and rocked with the fervor of a region that, after less than a decade of exposure to the sport, had become a passionate center of the hockey universe.

The league was so enthralled by its success on Long Island that it rewarded the Coliseum with hosting duties for the 1983 NHL All-Star Game. Wayne Gretzky stole the show—and, with his popular mullet-cut flowing down his shoulders, took home, yes, a Camaro Z-28 (there's a self-deprecating inside joke there that only true Long Islanders would get)—by scoring four third-period goals for the Campbell Conference in a 9-3 win.

Years later, however, with the memories of those glory years fading and the Coliseum yellowing into a dank, moribund relic, it became a target of widespread criticism and the butt of jokes throughout the league.

They called it the Nassau Mausoleum.

San Jose Sharks captain Owen Nolan called it something else one night during the 1999-2000 season, after the Sharks easily beat the Islanders, 4-1, before an announced crowd of 6,690 lonely souls.

"It's a depressing place to play," Nolan said.

That season, *Newsday*'s Alan Hahn did a three-page investigative piece on the condition of the Coliseum. Hahn got his hands on a copy of the lease—known by those involved with the Islanders and the county as "The Bible"—between the Islanders, Nassau County and SMG. The story outlined many unreported problems with the arena that went overlooked during the aforementioned "Hoistgate" situation. Some of the most alarming information concerned fire safety codes. The building, *Newsday* reported, had only recently been equipped with an updated fire system that included smoke detectors, heat sensors, sprinklers and pull-down alarms in strategic areas on the concourse. Before that time, the Coliseum—though it had been passed by fire inspectors each year—only had sprinklers around the building and few pull-down alarms.

The story also pointed out that the luxury suites—built by Pickett in the late 1970s and added to in the early 1990s—were not wheelchair accessible and could also be considered a fire hazard considering the number of people each suite holds and the narrow hall that connects them to the exits.

But the greatest revelation were the details of the decaying condition of the neglected Coliseum. A leaky roof—Hahn obtained documents that proved the team had several times requested it be replaced—was so bad that fans sitting in Section 205—prime season ticket holder seating—usually had to be moved to another area because of a steady flow of water on rainy nights. Visiting media also got a front-row view of the indoor rain—and patrons holding open umbrellas over their heads—because the leak was directly in front of the press box.

Weather also affected the concourse, which would flood around the poorly sealed doorways during a heavy rain. As far back as the Stanley Cup era, the locker room hallway would sometimes become a shower of beer seeping through the ceiling from the concession stands above.

And do you remember the woman who bought four tickets to that unofficial opening game in 1971 only to discover that her seats had not yet been installed? Well, one night during the 1999-2000 season, a woman literally carried her broken seat to an usher and deadpanned, "I need a new seat."

The Coliseum seats in the upper bowl, a mosaic of drab green and faded royal blue, are the most unpredictable. Cushions are worn practically to the aluminum base. Torn material is replaced with whatever union workers at the Coliseum can get their hands on. In 1999, an order for new seat material was put in, but the material never came. And that's just a small example of how work was done there.

The union workers at the Coliseum, much like the county that runs the building, have a stronghold over the team. For the most part, they are willing to do work that is required. But they can't without the authority of the financially strapped county, which rarely approved major capital improvements.

During his tenure in the late 1980s, Islanders coach Terry Simpson got into trouble when he finally tired of waiting for a request to be met. Simpson had asked for the satellite dish on the roof of the Coliseum to be adjusted, so that he could get more games from around the league to do some scouting on his own. After waiting for it to be done, Simpson, an electrician in his earlier years, eventually climbed a stairwell to the roof and did the work himself. When union workers discovered it, they filed a complaint against Simpson and the Islanders.

One person with knowledge of the labor and maintenance workings at the Coliseum said that foremen are told to keep journals of work that needs to be done. The person said the journals are usually filled with suggestions, but rarely are they carried out. Any job that does get done has just one requirement: "They are told to do it at minimal cost," the person said.

Records obtained by the county revealed this to be true to the letter. Or to the penny, as it were. A statement of operations listed expenditures between 1989 and 1996 at an average of $50,000 a year on maintenance and repair for the Coliseum. During a five-year period in the 1990s, the average dropped to merely $22,000 per season. (In that same time frame, the county claimed earnings of $1.7 million in total revenue.)

For perspective, the New Jersey Sports and Exposition Authority claimed expenditures of $800,000 to $1 million annually on maintenance and repair on Continental Airlines Arena at the Meadowlands Sports Complex in East Rutherford, New Jersey. The Devils and NBA Nets—they being the same Nets that began at the Coliseum in the early 1970s—both call the arena home.

One executive for the New Jersey Sports and Exposition Authority was contacted by *Newsday* about the story, and when the Coliseum expenditures were revealed to him, the executive was shocked.

"That's hard to believe," he said. "I can't believe they can continue to operate."

Bob Gutkowski, the former Madison Square Garden president who in recent years has worked in the entertainment industry, said major musical acts and other big-time shows were less inclined to play the dreary, obsolete Coliseum. Incredibly, on a night when just about every major venue in the country hosted some kind of celebration event with headline acts, the Coliseum was locked and dark on New Year's Eve 1999.

What's more amazing is that, despite the declining reputation, the building continued to operate at a surplus for the county and for SMG, which reportedly earns between $2 million and $2.5 million a year on the Coliseum, mostly because of the lucrative lease that awards it all parking and concession revenue and one-third of ticket and advertising revenue. The Coliseum, many reports have said, is SMG's biggest money maker out of a host of buildings it runs throughout the country.

But with money coming in, both the county—a victim of its own poor financial management and blatant arrogance—and SMG have refused to invest in the building. Going by letter of the lease, neither says they had to.

In fact, there is an irony to the decay of the Coliseum. With just average TLC, it might be, at the very least, acceptable. But just when Nassau politicians began to acknowledge the neglect that the Coliseum endured, they had a new excuse to spin. Because there had been so much talk of replacing the Coliseum with the Nassau Hub plan, as Gulotta told *Newsday*, it didn't make sense to put any more money into the Coliseum.

"In view of the potential for a new sports complex," he said, "there is a reluctance to devote tax dollars to a building that is going to be replaced."

This he said in February of 2000, well after cost-cutting measures allowed the building to fall into its decrepit state to begin with. Meanwhile, a new arena for Long Island remains strictly a conversation piece two years later, with little hope of a new structure in the foreseeable future.

And, until Wang and Kumar arrived and started pumping their own money into the place in 2001—something the previous owners refused to do—the Coliseum remained a literal ruin. A decaying landmark of a vision from over 30 years earlier that never lived up to its promise.

"The taxpayers own this building," said one furious Democrat, who had been for years fighting the Republicans about the handling of the Coliseum, "and it's gone totally to hell."

10

Cheap Skates

In the summer of 1998, money had once again become a bigger issue than replacing the Coliseum or even fixing it—this despite Milstein's Millions. He had already reneged on what he promised when he bought the team by refusing to put enough of his own money into the team to get the players needed to win. Instead, with little promise of a new arena in sight, Milstein ordered that the franchise would operate on a strict budget. Winning became secondary. Perhaps even tertiary.

Still, Milbury got himself a new contract. But Palffy, the all-star sniper, entered the '98–99 season without one and held out until December while his agent, Paul Kraus, and Milbury again publicly lambasted each other through the media. Milbury had a number of one-line gems regarding Kraus, but the most memorable was his assertion that it was a shame Kraus lived in the city "because he is depriving some small village of a pretty good idiot."

Kraus and Palffy finally relented on the holdout when they accepted a five-year, $26 million deal. No one knew at the time that Palffy would never get to the second year of that contract in an Islanders uniform.

At the time the Islanders were already spiraling into oblivion, and Milstein—with his eyes now off acquiring the Coliseum property and on ridding himself of the Islanders and purchasing the NFL's Washington Redskins—started cutting back drastically. The team no longer stayed at

the usual luxury hotels and many amenities were taken away. Occasionally, they flew commercial instead of using a charter for their flights.

During one trip to Greensboro, North Carolina to play the Carolina Hurricanes, Palffy was told the team would be staying at the Holiday
Inn. Palffy stormed onto the team bus.

"The fucking Holiday Inn?" the usually jovial Palffy yelled. "Cheap
fucking Islanders, we're staying at the Holiday Inn."

But Palffy would wind up one of the lucky ones, as he was spared of
the enduring misery when he and his big contract were traded at the end
of the season. In the meanwhile, with Milstein's bid to buy the Redskins
for a reported $800 million a public matter, fans and the NHL started to
realize that the Islanders were once again stuck with an owner who didn't
want them and certainly didn't want to spend to make them better.

So with all of that incredibly positive influence, it's a wonder the
team continued to lose.

The Milstein regime, meanwhile, continued to prove it was terribly
out of touch with running a sports franchise. Take for instance an awful
idea to run an ad campaign mocking the Rangers. It listed characteristics
of an Islanders fan and made reference to "ignorant Ranger fans" and how
Islanders fans have to endure "very rude comments from ignorant Ranger
fans in the kind of language that should not be used in front of children."

And then one night the PA announcer was instructed to read an
announcement that an upcoming game against the Rangers had been re-
scheduled to a 2 P.M. start time. He was also instructed to read it like a
wise-ass in a cheap appeal to the crowd.

So he added that "for Rangers fans, that's when the big hand is on
the twelve and the little hand is on the two."

Among it all, however, nothing was quite as bizarre as Milbury's
behavior. Years later he would half-jokingly refer to this time in his Islanders tenure as when he tried to get himself fired. At the time, it certainly
seemed he was doing a pretty good job of it.

Milbury, as much as he wanted to, couldn't quit. His contract extension was guaranteed over five years and paid him $750,000 per year. If
he was fired, the team would still have to pay him the rest of the contract.
If he quit, the team was not responsible for the rest of the contract.

Milbury had kids in private school and college. And he was starting
a new family with his second wife, Ginger. So no doubt he needed the
money. But he, too, wanted nothing to do with the Islanders.

By 1999, hardly anyone else did, either.

Still, he continued to work and continued to shuffle the roster like a bored rotisserie player. Down on Salo practically since the day he met him, Milbury made a confounding trade in January of '99 when he sent Bryan Berard—a confident and talented young defenseman who won the Calder in 1997 but whose development, especially in his own end, had since slowed almost to a halt—to the Toronto Maple Leafs for struggling goalie Felix Potvin. Salo's days were obviously numbered, but it was wondered why Milbury didn't make sure to have a deal in place to move Salo before Potvin came to town.

In fact, the deal was made while the team was in Montreal for a game. Milbury called Salo at the team hotel hours before the game and told him it might be best for him to stay at the hotel instead of going to the arena.

Earlier Milbury had signed first-round pick Roberto Luongo to a three-year contract, but Luongo, 19 at the time and playing junior hockey, wouldn't be available to the Islanders until the following season.

Still, in acquiring Potvin, Milbury took indirect shots at Salo, who was 27 at the time and still boiling from the arbitration hearing of the previous summer and being the afterthought to more promising youngsters such as Eric Fichaud and Luongo.

"We think the goaltending future of the Islanders for—I don't know how many years—is in great shape," Milbury said after acquiring Potvin and signing Luongo.

Rookie Marcel Cousineau got the start that night in Montreal, and the team, predictably, lost the game, 3-2. Salo, however, was not moved that day and a day later was in Washington D.C. doing the same, sitting in a hotel room waiting.

"Something is going on if your No. 1 goalie is sitting in the hotel watching the game on TV," Salo said. "Hopefully, he can move me as fast as he can. I can't see any other way. I don't want to be here and do nothing. But I don't see my job here any more—not when I am left to sit in my room."

Goaltending coach Stefan Lunner, who was hired by the Islanders because he had worked successfully with Salo in the past for the Swedish National team, was puzzled by Milbury's decision.

"If you asked me if I'm confused, the answer to that is, 'Yes, I'm confused,'" Lunner told *The Post*'s Marc Berman. "I didn't see the goaltending as the problem for this team."

The following day, with his quote prominent in Berman's story, Lunner walked into the Islanders' coaching office, where the coaching staff was discussing Lunner's comment.

Lorne Henning, ever the deadpanning wise-cracker, didn't even look up from the paper when he greeted the unsuspecting Lunner.

"Nice working with you," he said, well aware that Milbury, too, reads the papers.

But Lunner stuck around until the end of the season, while Salo remained for another two months after his replacement, Potvin, was acquired. The fact that Salo wasn't moved right away might have been a bigger slap in the face of the young Swede. It was also what galvanized a deep and personal contempt that Salo to this day still feels for Milbury. It started when the two met and Milbury had little patience for Salo's soft and sensitive personality. In other words, Salo doesn't take well to criticism. And Milbury oftentimes can't stop being critical.

Salo and young defenseman Kenny Jonsson, both Swedes with a history as teammates on the Olympic gold medal-winning national team in 1994, were good friends. But Milbury didn't like seeing them so close and yet noticeably distant from the rest of their teammates. So he pulled Jonsson aside and told him to stop spending so much time with Salo. Jonsson, ever the obedient solider, followed orders and inexplicably started to avoid Salo. And Salo took it very personally.

Then the clincher came during an arbitration hearing during the previous off season, the infamous meeting in which Milbury was said to have been so critical of Salo to the arbitrator that Salo broke down and cried right at the negotiating table. The hearing, which took place at the Marriot Eaton Centre in Toronto, lasted from 9 A.M. until 11 P.M. that evening, mostly because Salo was so emotional that his representatives, including agent Rich Winter, had to take a break from the hearing to help Salo regain his composure.

"That's pretty good, huh?" an angry Salo said of Milbury months after the hearing. "That's really good of him, huh?"

But there are some truths about that meeting that have never been revealed. One was that Winter and his group apparently failed to prepare their client for the typical circumstances of an arbitration hearing. Two sides argue a case for compensation. From a team perspective, you naturally highlight the negatives in order to keep the cost down.

"Mike didn't attack him with words," said a person who was involved in that hearing, "he just answered questions."

Of course Milbury's answers were harshly critical, perhaps more than necessary.

Still, there were fair complaints to be made, and in one case, one of Salo's representatives walked into one. It involved a discussion about conditioning. Milbury said that Salo finished dead last in a team fitness evaluation the previous season. One of Salo's representatives then mentioned a recent off-season conditioning camp the Islanders held and asked how he measured up then. Milbury said he couldn't give him an accurate comparison because not every goalie was present. One didn't show up.

"Which goalie?" the agent asked.

"Salo," Milbury replied.

After the trade, however, Salo held his tongue and just took pleasure from leaving the down-spiraling Islanders and joining the playoff-bound Edmonton Oilers.

"It feels good when you're in a situation where that can happen," Salo said. "It feels different when you have a GM and coaches who believe in you when you play. I never got that from Mike. Never. From the first moment I came there, [he didn't like me.] I don't know why. Here, I think I'll get the opportunity. Maybe I'll show him he was wrong about me."

Potvin, meanwhile, who had been involved in a holdout with Toronto, lost the first four games he started as an Islander.

Milbury, wanting to further distance himself from the losing—to concentrate on his GM duties, he claimed, but with no budget and an unstable ownership, he was kidding no one—removed himself as the team's coach and instead of selecting the obvious choice to take over, in the experienced Henning, he tapped the youthful Bill Stewart.

Stewart then put Salo back in goal and sat Potvin. Salo responded with two wins and a tie. But that trend didn't last, either. The Islanders were a terrible mess.

"What direction the team is going in is a difficult question," Trevor Linden said. "I don't think [Milbury] can answer that, I don't think the players can answer that. I don't even think ownership can answer that."

Milstein wasn't looking to answer anything. The beat reporters were in Washington for a game against the Capitals and heard the elusive Islanders owner was there on his new business venture: an attempt to purchase the Redskins. One reporter called Milstein's personal PR office to find out where the Islanders owner would be and was told that Milstein had canceled his meeting and wouldn't be in Washington.

But Berman found out about a news conference Milstein was having in D.C. with Washington reporters and raced over to it. He wasn't allowed to ask any questions.

That night at the Islanders–Capitals game, the beat writers chatted with Washington reporters, giving them the real scoop about Milstein as a professional sports owner. Suddenly in the nation's capital, Milstein was viewed in a far more negative light as the potential new owner of the Redskins.

Eventually, Milstein's bid was voted down by the NFL owners.

Throughout the developing chaos, Stewart had the Islanders playing harder and started earning some mild praise, though the losing continued. Even Milbury dared to suggest the young coach might remain behind the bench past the current season.

But Stewart's undoing began in a costly moment of frustration. Following a loss to the Rangers at Madison Square Garden that capped a 13-game span with just one win and two ties with 10 defeats, Stewart ripped the cheapskate organization for putting forth a meager product.

"Have you looked at our lineup?" he said in a postgame tirade. "Enough said. We've got people trying their butts off right down to the last man. Obviously at this time we don't have the resources. You can't take one ounce of blame toward the people inside the locker room. Certainly, if we had the resources to acquire National Hockey League talent, would it be a different story? You answer the question. I think it's quite clear."

An Islanders media relations staffer quickly phoned Milbury to tell him of Stewart's rant and forewarn him about what would be in the papers the next morning. After the game, the team was en route to Fort Lauderdale for a game against the Florida Panthers the following night. The team arrived in Fort Lauderdale via charter around 3 A.M., and one assistant with the team got a call on his cell phone.

It was Milbury.

"Tell Bill to call me right fucking now!"

The following morning, Stewart was sitting poolside at the Sheraton Suites desperately apologizing to Milbury over the phone. He then summoned the beat writers and begged them to help him clean up the mess he had made the night before.

"I want to smooth things over with Mike," he pleaded. "I'm not against the ownership . . . I want to be a part of this."

But Stewart had already made a mess. A high-strung man with a short fuse and unshakable confidence, Stewart took over the team and immediately took shots at the former coach, Milbury, by suggesting his team needed to be taught how to play hard and compete.

He also had some memorable rants, which made him another side-show to what was already another lost and forgettable season.

Stewart, an otherwise intelligent coach, took himself more seriously than anyone else did. So for the players, his postgame tirades were more entertaining than inspiring. One player he couldn't stand was Eric Brewer, then an immature 19-year-old defenseman, who occasionally got into uncontrollable giggle fits.

"If that fucking Brewer laughs at me again," Stewart once told his coaches, "I'll fucking kill him."

After a loss in Detroit, Stewart was again tearing into his team when Brewer caught the eyes of a few of his impish teammates and caught the giggles again. Stewart immediately grabbed an oar used to mix the Gatorade jug and flung it across the room. The oar missed Brewer's head by inches.

Veteran defenseman Rich Pilon immediately got up and chastised his coach, who stormed out of the room.

After another game, this one at the Coliseum, Stewart was lacing into his team when he took his arm and cleared an entire table of blended nutrition shakes. The stuff was a thick, pink substance, and most of it sprayed in the faces of veteran forwards Craig Janney, Ted Donato and Sergei Nemchinov.

Once Stewart left the room, Janney and Donato laughed it off. But Nemchinov, who is widely respected as a kind, soft-spoken man and revered for his roles as a Russian star and, as a Ranger, one of the first Russians to have his name engraved on the Stanley Cup, sat motionless. Pink liquid dripped from his nose as he stared blankly while players milled about around him.

Nemchinov finally grabbed a towel and wiped his face. He then got up to go to the bathroom.

"Fucking Stewie!" the affable Russian growled in rare anger. "I play for Red Army and nothing ever like this! I kill this man!"

Nemchinov was soon sent to the Devils for a draft pick, as Milbury made a few deals before the trade deadline that he called "a little tree pruning." Actually, it was $6.4 million of pruning in payroll.

First, Robert Reichel, a talented offensive center who seemed to fit well with Palffy, was dealt to the Phoenix Coyotes for Brad Isbister. That would prove to be a great pickup by Milbury, considering Reichel went to Europe the following year and did not re-sign with the Coyotes.

But while that might have been a winner, the trade that goes down as one of the worst deals in hockey history was when Milbury finally ex-Isled Salo to Edmonton in exchange for Mats Lindgren, a down-to-earth friendly person, but otherwise a mediocre two-way center who is, at best, a third-line player on even a bad team.

"He's scored on every level but this one," Milbury said of Lindgren, perhaps in hindsight using the wrong choice of words for the low-scoring, low-impact Swede.

After the trade, Berman spoke to Palffy's agent, Paul Kraus, who begged for his client to be the next to go.

"I just hope to hell Ziggy's out of there," Kraus said. "He's there by himself. There's not a guy on that team that can play with him. Trevor Linden is not an elite player any more."

Then Kraus, who took a verbal beating from Milbury in the media during their contentious negotiations involving Palffy's contracts, got in a shot of his own.

"How does Mike wake up in the morning and look at himself in the mirror?" he said. "He's been told to dump salary and look like an idiot."

The season mercifully ended with a mere 24 wins, the team's worst production since Milbury's first season as coach produced just 22 victories in 1995-96. Stewart, despite his groveling, was dismissed, though he never told his assistants.

"All we have to do is work out a contract," he told them after his season-ending meeting with Milbury, in which Milbury had apparently told him he'd not be returning.

They never saw him again.

In fact, the next time anyone heard from Stewart, it was in the news. After his time with the Islanders, Stewart became a junior coach and was arrested during the 1999-2000 season for attempting to smuggle a Russian player across the Canadian–U.S. border. He had the 17-year-old player hide in the luggage compartment underneath the bus.

A season later, while coaching in Germany, legend has it that Stewart faked a heart attack to get a timeout during a game.

With his own wake of controversy and failure, Seldin gave up his title as team president and went to work privately for Milstein, who in turn completely distanced himself from the franchise and gave his younger brother, Edward, decision-making control.

An affable, less contentious man named John Sanders replaced Seldin. And Eddie Milstein, too, was far more cordial and warm than Howard Milstein. Eddie was well-meaning and also a huge fan, which oftentimes made him come off as goofy. But he had good intentions and many good qualities. Just not enough money to buy out his brother, which is what he secretly wanted to do.

With the controversy of an ongoing salary purge hanging over them like a black cloud, the team then announced in an obvious PR move that Butch Goring, a key member of the Stanley Cup dynasty teams, would finally become the Islanders' next head coach. This after they had passed him over many times before. Goring, who spent over a decade as a successful coach in the minors, at his introductory press conference said he "bleeds Islander blue."

For the next two seasons, the bleeding seemed to never stop.

The placement of a friendlier Milstein, a kinder Sanders and the lovable Goring were earmarks of apparent wagon-circling by the owners. Inside, however, an out-and-out downsizing of the franchise to minute proportions was well under way.

Milbury was told the payroll, which had already dropped to $20 million, had to be pared further—by any means necessary. Criticism be damned.

After losing in excess of $20 million, Howard Milstein had enough of this sinking franchise, especially now that his sole purpose for buying it in the first place—to develop the property around Nassau Coliseum and build a new arena—was just about a dead issue.

So budgets between $10 million and $15 million were discussed— a ridiculous $5 million payroll was even suggested—and Milbury considered every possible way to pull it off while keeping the team relatively competitive. It would be nearly impossible. Milbury told them a $15 million budget would have to be the lowest they would go. It would still be the lowest of the 28 teams in the NHL that season.

The summer carnage began with Linden, who was shipped off to Montreal for the 10th overall pick in the 1999 draft. Everyone knew, of course, that the real prize available to rich NHL teams was Ziggy Palffy, who, ironically had just closed on his new house on Long Island when he was told he was going to be traded. Palffy, a fan favorite who loved living on the Island and enjoyed being an Islander, was dismayed at what had become of the franchise.

Plus, he said, he really liked the house he bought.

By mid-June, only one team had contacted Milbury regarding Palffy. That would be the Rangers.

Years as bitter rivals and a silly slanderous ad campaign meant little with Palffy on the block. Milbury and former Rangers GM Neil Smith worked out what would have been a terrific deal for both sides. Palffy and veteran defenseman Rich Pilon would go to Manhattan in exchange for impressive youngsters Niklas Sundstrom, Todd Harvey, the Rangers' first-round pick and college prospect Pat Leahy. The deal also included the Rangers padding the Islanders' pockets with an extra $2.5 million in cash. Once NHL commissioner Gary Bettman got wind of that sort of financing, however, he immediately stepped in and ordered it to be no more than $1 million.

Then the word got out—neither side will admit which was the first to leak it to the press—and New York was in a tizzy: the Islanders are going to send their best player to the Rangers?

Fans went crazy. The media went crazy. And PR directors from both teams began discussing how they would handle the strange circumstance about to happen.

With a need for a competitive bid to keep the Rangers from controlling the market, the league stepped in again to help the Islanders search for another party with an interest in Palffy. The Los Angeles Kings then decided to make an offer that included Palffy and veteran forward Bryan Smolinski, who was headed for restricted free agency, thus necessitating that the Islanders dump him as well. The Islanders wanted hot prospects Scott Barney and Justin Papineau in return for those two players. Milbury and Kings counterpart Dave Taylor were quickly able to come to an agreement.

That's when Milstein met former MSG president Dave Checketts at a Knicks playoff game and said he wanted the Rangers to sweeten the pot. Since Bettman cut $1.5 million from the cash exchange, Milstein wanted the Garden's parent company, Cablevision, to rework the team's cable deal so that the team could get more money up front. Or perhaps issue the Islanders a loan, borrowing off the value of the cable contract.

Cablevision said no. The Rangers, sensing Milstein's infamous greed sprouting again, then walked away from the deal.

The Islanders ended up with Olli Jokinen instead of Barney, whom Milbury coveted far more than Jokinen. It was discovered that Barney, an intriguing power forward prospect who was a rising star as a junior player, suffered a severe back injury and therefore was untradeable. In fact, Barney wound up sitting out the entire 1999-2000 season and underwent back surgery in May of 2000. He has yet to return to professional hockey.

When the league found out about Barney's injury, it ordered the Kings to make available to the Islanders other prospects. The league felt Jokinen, the third overall pick in 1997, would make the trade look more reasonable. But Milbury and his staff had little interest in Jokinen. In fact, with two top 10 picks in the 1997 draft, they had no plans to select Jokinen, a skilled and big but relatively lazy, slow-developing Finnish center. On their charts, he wasn't even top 10. Milbury and Clark took Luongo at No. 4 and Brewer at No. 5.

The deal, however, was completed, with Jokinen suddenly talked up as the centerpiece and the interesting perspective that the Islanders now had each of the players who became picks three through five from the 1997 draft. Along with Jokinen in the deal came fellow youngsters Mathieu Biron and Josh Green and the Kings' first-round pick for that draft year.

It hardly compared to the offer of NHL-quality players the Rangers made, but for Islanders fans, there was some relief that they at least didn't have to see Palffy wearing a Rangers uniform next season. It was difficult enough seeing the likes of Pat LaFontaine do so.

Milbury and his staff used the plethora of picks (fourteen total, four first-rounders and three in the top 10) that June to stockpile their prospect coffers. But while the distant future had some hope, the near future was as bleak as ever.

11

Deserted Isle

Before training camp even opened for the 1999-2000 season, the franchise already appeared to be headed toward more transition. Bob Gutkowski, the former president of Madison Square Garden and a Long Island native, had spent the past year trying to gather investors to back him in an attempt to buy the Islanders from Milstein. In August, he thought he was close when Charles Koppelman, a recording industry mogul, agreed to be his main money man, with a few others.

In August 1999, Gutkowski signed a letter of intent to purchase the team. When the story appeared in the papers, fans were already giddy about yet another possible white knight. And Gutkowski, a smooth, media-savvy front man with little money but lots of ideas, played the role up and played it well. He responded to fan e-mails about as quickly as he responded to reporters' calls. He even dared to mention in an interview with *Newsday* that should his group follow through with the purchase, Milbury would be gone. That, of course, had fans roaring with approval.

Gutkowski became a popular man among Islanders fans. But there was one problem: Koppelman wasn't all that interested in hockey. He wanted the building and rights to developing a new one. His vision was of a state-of-the-art arena that would house the Islanders, yes, but also dominate the New York area for major concerts and shows. Once again, the arena was more important than the team. There was also some talk of creating bonds in the name of the team, similar to the "Bowie Bonds" of the 1980s.

But with SMG around and Nassau County in a woeful financial state, Koppelman quickly learned what Milstein had already experienced a year earlier. This was a pursuit of failure.

While Koppelman kept himself out of publicity, Gutkowski encouraged talk of his group's interest in the team to percolate. Each week he would tell reporters the sale was "a few weeks away." In truth, his group never got past the stage of working out a deal with SMG. In one discussion, they made an offer of about $7 million to SMG to buy out the rest of the lease. At about $2 million per year in profit and 16 years left, that was well short of reality. Once the group saw SMG as a hurdle, it started to back off. Gutkowski did so grudgingly.

The truth is, no one in the know ever took them seriously. Eddie Milstein even went as far as saying that he didn't want to sell the team. He, in fact, was hoping to put together a few investors to back him in buying out his brother Howard and Steven Gluckstern, who both wanted out. Eddie Milstein would throw darts at Gutkowski, saying, in essence, "show me the money" after every newspaper claim that a purchase was imminent. One offer the group made was for about $150 million, Milstein said. That was $45 million shy of what Milstein had paid for the team two years prior.

No one, not even Bettman, knew what to believe any more. All he did know was that growing rumors that the Islanders would eventually be moved to another city were untrue.

"That franchise isn't going anywhere," he said almost defiantly.

But he couldn't avoid acknowledging the reality of what the team was becoming, slowly but surely, right before his eyes. And this was a man who, when he first arrived on the scene, considered the Islanders an excess in a New York market that would be better off if it had only the Devils and Rangers to share it.

"I wouldn't characterize it as embarrassing," Bettman said of the Islanders' pitiful situation. "It's unfortunate and it's frustrating."

And by midseason, it started to take on the pathetically adorable look of a cut-rate minor-league franchise. The sophomoric Ranger bashing continued with a scoreboard video that played a clip from the movie *Godzilla 2000* that showed a fighter jet pilot circling Manhattan. A voice from the command station would then announce, to the delight of the Coliseum crowd: "I want you to blow up Madison Square Garden!" As the missiles destroyed the movie-made Garden, Islanders fans would roar with approval.

It was one of the few times anyone cheered at all at the Coliseum. With a league-low average player age of around 25 years, the team predictably started out poorly under Goring and were well out of playoff contention before Christmas. It was then when the final stages of salary dumping took place. Longtime defenseman Rich Pilon was taken by the Rangers off waivers and goalie Felix Potvin was traded to the Vancouver Canucks for three young players who would figure in the team's immediate future: center Dave Scatchard, goalie Kevin Weekes and forward Bill Muckalt. The team had already called up Luongo, who was dynamic in his first few starts.

Weekes and Muckalt would later prove to be tradeable assets for the franchise. But Scatchard, a gritty, character center who struggled under Marc Crawford with Vancouver, flourished both on and off the ice as an Islander.

He experienced a touching emotional moment in early January that season when the Islanders were in Boston to play the Bruins. Scatchard is the type of professional athlete who lives two lives: one as a happy-go-lucky playboy and the other as a caring and concerned mentor for sick children. Often, Scatchard on his own will befriend a sick child and grow very close to the child, usually showing up at the family's house to play video games or just hang out. What makes Scatchard special is that he never, ever, wants media attention for it. That, to him, would cheapen his intentions. On this night in Boston, Scatchard scored a pair of goals in a 5-2 win that snapped a five-game losing streak for the Islanders. You might say the win and rare offensive outburst were motivation enough, but Scatchard had a greater cause for his energy. He revealed this during a televised interview during the second intermission, just before he broke down in tears.

One of his young friends, a 12-year-old boy named Nicholas Beresford whom Scatchard met when playing for the Canucks, had succumbed to leukemia. Scatchard dedicated the game to Nicholas and promised the family he'd score a hat trick. After the second goal, Scatchard pumped his fist to the ceiling at the Fleet Center.

"I think he was up in heaven helping me out," he said afterward, still fighting tears. "I would have liked to get the hat trick for him."

From January on, things started to change on the Islanders' ice. They were indeed bad, but not awful. Their greatest weakness was inexperience. Veteran teams complimented them often, either out of respect or just pity. Goring had the group playing hard. Leaders were emerging in Scatchard and Isbister, a strong-skating, hard-hitting winger. Tim Connolly slowly but steadily started coming into his own. Mariusz Czerkawski was named to the All-Star team and was on his way toward a career-best 35-goal season. Together they managed an 11-15-3 record in the final two months of the season. And considering all that was going on around them, that was fairly impressive.

But there were many lowlights that reminded everyone that these were still the Islanders. For one, the financial purge carried over to the travel budget. The team no longer flew charters to every game. It flew commercial.

No, it's not the worst situation. At least the Islanders traveled by plane and not bus or train. But consider this image that actually took place on March 26, 2000:

The Islanders played the Hurricanes that Sunday afternoon in Raleigh, North Carolina and lost, 4-1. They then packed up and bused to the airport for a flight to Nashville, where they were to play the Predators on Tuesday night.

And what discount airline flies from Raleigh to Nashville? Why, that annoyingly over-friendly Southwest Airlines, the Wal-Mart of air travel, with their open-seating boarding system and bare-minimum service.

So picture, if you will, 22 hockey players straight from a game, three exhausted assistant coaches and a frustrated Goring, two overworked equipment staffers who had to come early and make sure all of the equipment was checked in by well-tipped skycaps, and two trainers looking for some semblance of healthy food (in, of all places, an airport) to feed the players, while a frazzled media relations director is handing out those numbered boarding cards and telling the entire party it has to stand in number order.

Some players actually tried to trade their little boarding cards with passengers in the 1-through-30 line for autographs just so they could get choice seating.

Goring, who was always ornery after a defeat no matter how lost the season already was, approached a gate agent with the hope of some much-needed red carpet treatment. After all, he was a four-time Stanley Cup champion, a Conn Smythe Trophy winner and the coach of an NHL team. Damn it all, he was Butch-fucking-Goring!

"Do you have first-class seats?" he asked one of Southwest's perpetually cheerful agents, who didn't even blink.

"All of our seats are first class, sir!" she sang back to him.

Goring's sour look as he turned away from her was priceless. He then boarded, curled himself up in one of the first rows and stared out the window without saying a word to anyone.

As the rest of the team slowly filed onto the plane, resident goofball defenseman Jamie Rivers started making cattle sounds and cracking jokes. Many of the players did their best to make light of the situation. It's a good thing most of the team was young.

Hell, they were so young the dressing room stereo was regularly heard playing a Backstreet Boys CD. At times it sounded like a teeny-bopper slumber party. Twenty-one-year-old Josh Green, a rugged young power forward on the team, was once seen walking out of the showers to his stall signing to himself along with the song "Larger Than Life." Rivers, a music buff and musician, burned his own mixes for the road and was one of the main culprits who promoted the cheesy bubble-gum pop.

One thing was for sure: during his brief time with that year's team, veteran headbanger Rich Pilon didn't like the stuff one bit.

The antagonistically jovial Rivers, however, had a noticeable hold on the locker room and was usually the ringleader for the fun during the countless hours of downtime. He would pick up courtesy phones at airports to leave phony pages for members of the team or staff or for made-up names with lewd connotations. He and Scatchard, in the San Jose airport during a long delay, entertained themselves and the rest of the team—along with other waiting passengers—by attaching a five-dollar bill to a string and then laying it out in the middle of the walkway. As someone stopped to pick up the bill, they would quickly yank it away.

That is, until one man stepped on it with his foot before stooping to pick it up. When Scatchard pulled the string, it snapped off of the bill. The man then picked up the bill and shoved it into his pocket while the entire gate of waiting passengers roared with laughter.

The hockey, however, wasn't a laughing matter. Connolly began to show an apathetic disregard toward losing, which made it easy for him as an 18-year-old to endure the season with flashes of talent mixed in with mistakes, save for some annoyances by veteran enforcer Gino Odjick, who would constantly hound Connolly to pass him the puck.

But for 19-year-old Eric Brewer, who the season before showed promise despite the oar incident with Stewart, each night was a nightmare. He was twice sent to the minors by the frustrated coaching staff and a fed-up Milbury, who sucker-punched his talented young defenseman by saying he "has every skill imaginable, but sometimes it looks like he's sniffing glue."

A flustered Brewer said he couldn't understand why he was playing so poorly and called his play "inconsistency at its finest."

"Mistakes for me are really bad," he added. "I just eat myself up on the bench instead of letting it go."

It didn't help that the Islanders were already thin at the blue line after the veteran Pilon was claimed by the Rangers, the eggshell-fragile Jonsson suffered another concussion because of a hit from behind by San Jose Sharks forward Todd Harvey, neophytes Zdeno Chara and Mathieu Biron were still quite raw and the threadbare patchwork of cheap journeymen—Dallas Eakins, Jamie Heward and Rivers—just wasn't going to get it done.

Going into the season, Brewer put pressure on himself to be a big-ticket defenseman and cowered into his own self-pity as he failed miserably with no one possessing the ability to step forward to help him out of it.

But management already was concerned with his attitude from the start of the season. Many outsiders viewed Trevor Linden the season before as a good mentor for Brewer, but insiders noticed the youngster's personality changing rapidly. He, like Linden, spent more time on his cell phone and more time playing up a big-time self-image. He appeared to walk the walk of a superstar before he actually became one.

So, many Islanders insiders said, he arrived in 1999-2000 with his head screwed on wrong and never was able to correct it. He might have had the most talent and potential of anyone in the Islanders' dressing room that season, but he wound up one of the worst defensemen on the organization's minor-league team. And that might prove to be the greatest failure in Milbury's tenure.

Perhaps even greater than the mishandling of another young blue-chipper that season: goalie Roberto Luongo.

Right smack in the middle of Connolly's apathetic calm and Brewer's unstoppable meltdown was the regal air that surrounded Luongo—the prodigal franchise goalie of the future who made his NHL debut in December with a 43-save victory over the Boston Bruins and then proceeded to carry himself on a level well above the rest of the team.

And everyone noticed.

Clark Gillies and the Islanders hold the Stanley Cup aloft after winning the championship in 1983.

© Bruce Bennett/BBS

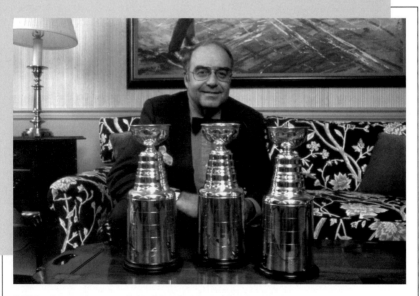

Bill Torrey, architect of the Islanders' rise from expansion team to NHL dynasty, sits with three of the team's Stanley Cups.

© Bruce Bennett/BBS

Pierre Turgeon—
known to Islander
fans as "Sneaky
Pete" for his quiet
demeanor and
quick-strike ability
on the ice—led the
Islanders to a 1993
playoff run.

© Scott Levy/BBS

Former Islanders owner John Pickett (left) with legendary coach
Al Arbour.

© Bruce Bennett/BBS

"Mad Mike" Milbury knew he had his work cut out for him when he signed on to be the Islanders' sixth head coach.

© **Bruce Bennett/BBS**

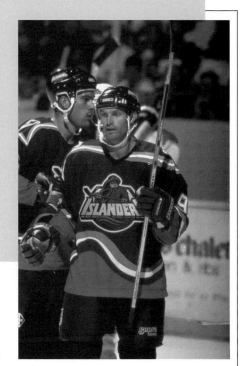

Kirk Muller, wearing the onerous jersey: "Obviously, I'm not a fan favorite here."

© **C. Andersen/BBS**

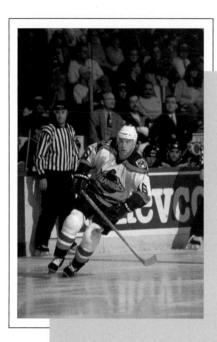

The hat trick Ziggy Palffy scored in his last game with the Islanders summed up his career with the team. For five seasons, "Ziggy Stardust" wowed Islanders fans with his awesome dekes, moves and shots.

Stranger than fiction: John Spano (right) conned Milbury and the rest of the Islanders organization.

Bryan Trottier, the greatest two-way center in hockey history, began his career as the heart and soul of the Islanders by scoring a hat trick in his first home game.

Denis Potvin (right) demonstrates his stingy style of defense which opposing teams hated.

Butch Goring, considered the final piece of the puzzle in the Islanders' dynasty, couldn't help turn the team around from behind the bench.

© Jim McIsaac/BBS

New Islanders owners Charles Wang and Sanjay Kumar set to work on returning the team to its former glory.

© John Giamundo/BBS

Alexei Yashin dominates the Rangers in their January 30, 2002 game, scoring a hat trick in the first period.

Michael Peca is sent flying by Maple Leafs right winger Darcy Tucker in Game 5 of the first round of the 2002 playoffs.

Shawn Bates celebrates after converting a penalty shot for the first time in the Islanders' playoff history.

© Jason Pulver/BBS

Emotions reach a boiling point in Game 6 of the first round of the 2002 playoffs as Eric Cairns (right) is separated from the Maple Leafs' Shayne Corson.

© Scott Horodyski/BBS

Luongo was just 20, but since training camp he'd talked about wanting to play in the NHL. His performances left little doubt he could, but with the veteran Potvin and a veteran backup in Wade Flaherty, the Islanders were careful not to rush their prized prospect.

Then a Goring bumble in training camp sparked what has since become a quiet fury Luongo still holds against the franchise.

It started innocently enough, when Goring was asked about the status of Flaherty, a well-liked backup who seemed the odd man out because of Luongo's emergence during exhibition games. It seemed logical that the Islanders would keep Luongo with the big club to be tutored by fellow Francophone goalie Potvin. Luongo beamed each time a reporter raved about his performance or asked him if he felt he was ready for the NHL.

"I'm not afraid," he said, sitting at ease in the stands of the Igloo in Pittsburgh before his first start of the preseason in September. "For me, the first year in the NHL is going to be a learning year. Whether it's this year or next year or three years, I might as well get it over with now."

Early in camp, Goring suggested Luongo might be ready. "Certainly he has made a very strong case for being here," he said. Back at the Islanders' offices, Milbury winced.

Then later in camp, Goring was talking about the goaltending situation and made it a point to say that Flaherty, a personal favorite of his, wasn't going anywhere. Suddenly a quietly boring off day turned into a feeding frenzy for the pack of media around Goring, who then said, "I think that our feelings are Felix or Luongo will be here. One of the two."

The team's radio announcer, Chris King, quickly attempted to correct Goring, who was apt to mix up words and names and metaphors without missing a beat.

"Flats and Roberto, you mean," King said.

But Goring wasn't mistaken.

"Flats," he said again, "will be here."

Reporters exchanged quizzical glances. That meant to them that either Luongo was being sent to the minors or Potvin, who was acquired the previous winter for Bryan Berard and then signed to a one-year, $2.7-million contract that was high for Islanders' standards, was on the trading block.

But Goring swore there was no controversy. The reporters at the time figured otherwise and went to track down Milbury. The team's masterful PR spin doctor Chris Botta quickly worked behind the scenes to douse the flames that Goring seemed to be fanning with each comment.

Later that day, Botta called each reporter with an explanation and a comment from Milbury.

Goring was then forced to name Potvin as "the No. 1 goaltender" and admit that even though Luongo would be headed to the minors, he was trying to keep the young goalie competing in camp. So the obvious was only confirmed: Luongo would be headed to the club's AHL affiliate in Lowell, Mass. for his first professional season.

"He'll be disappointed," Goring said, "but he'll be fine."

Milbury, through Botta, said "that was the plan from the beginning."

But that plan was caught in a glitch because Goring's original slip had a doozy of a follow-up. The next day, Goring thought the problem was behind him and of the impending demotion announced that Luongo was "fine with it."

What Goring failed to say was that he never personally spoke with Luongo about it.

Hahn then wandered into the locker room and gave Luongo a tap on the shoulder.

"Sorry, man," he said, opening his notebook for reaction.

A somewhat confused Luongo shrugged.

"When are you leaving?" Hahn asked.

"Huh?"

Luongo had no idea.

His eyes stared at the locker room floor as he sat in his stall and was told what Goring had just said in the hallway outside. He stopped unbuckling his equipment and took a breath as the other reporters gathered around his stall.

Potvin, sitting next to him, shook his head.

"It's obviously disappointing," the visibly upset Luongo started.

"You guys have been talking to him," he then said. "I haven't talked to him. I don't know what's going on."

Luongo wasn't sent to Lowell for another week, but when he got there he fared well. And it wasn't long until he returned to Long Island; his call-up came in late November, when it was revealed that Flaherty had a shoulder injury and when trade rumors involving Potvin reached feverish levels.

He made his first start on Nov. 29, with a 2-1 win over the Bruins in Boston in which he made 43 saves. He was stellar in a 2-1 loss to the defending champion Dallas Stars at the Coliseum. Potvin then made the next two starts in Islanders losses and Milbury finally made it clear that Luongo was staying for good. "He's got to play," Milbury said of Luongo, "he's got to play a lot. That's my objective for him."

But not even Luongo was safe from criticism. Following a January loss to the Bruins in which Luongo gave up seven goals, Milbury ripped the youngster for apartment hunting the afternoon of the game. Luongo had been living in the Marriott hotel next door to the Coliseum since his call-up in November. The Islanders pay for a player's room and board at the hotel for the duration of his call-up or for up to a month. Luongo was told he had to find a place soon or start paying his own bill.

So he got in touch with a real estate broker and the morning of the Bruins game was called to check out a place that was available. Luongo met the broker right after the morning skate, around noon, and was back to the hotel by 1 P.M. for lunch. That night he was shellacked by the Bruins, who were determined not to let the young goalie beat them again.

After the game Luongo admitted he felt "very shaky." A few days later, Milbury suggested why during a meeting with beat reporters.

And then Luongo responded with his usual expressionless shrug during a televised interview with Fox Sports New York's Stan Fischler.

"I don't want to say Mike is lying," the 20-year-old said plainly, "but . . . it wasn't a matter of the whole day like he said."

Luongo's rookie season ended without gaudy numbers or Calder Trophy hype (he was 7-14-1 with a 3.25 goals-against and .904 save percentage), but it was clear he had established himself as an NHL-caliber goaltender and certainly the Islanders' goalie of the future.

Yet he wasn't treated as such. It was revealed after the season that Luongo was the victim of another cheapskate move when he was curiously sent down to Lowell in March and not called back up until Weekes suffered an injury in the final week of the season. Luongo started the regular-season finale and earned a win. It was his 24th appearance of the season, one shy of a total that would have kicked in a lucrative bonus in his contract.

The Islanders claimed that the numbers were just coincidental. They insisted Luongo was sent down because Weekes had emerged as a No. 1 and the organization wanted Luongo to get consistent starts. Therefore, he was sent to Lowell. ECHL refugee Steve Valiquette was called up as the backup and actually played well in six appearances.

Luongo's agent, former Montreal Canadiens goon Gilles Lupien, helped the Islanders defuse the situation when he said that he and Milbury both agreed that Luongo should have played the entire season in the minors because neither wanted the youngster rushed into the NHL. "So playing 24 games was a bonus in itself for Roberto," the typically affable and up-front Lupien concluded.

But despite the controversy and confusion, with Luongo and Weekes, who was 10-20-4 with a 3.41 goals-against and .902 save percentage, the Islanders appeared to at least have a solid and coveted foundation set in goal.

Eddie Milstein eventually gave up his dream of buying out his brother, but he didn't stop being actively involved in the season. He also didn't apologize for the stingy travel budget and the low payroll. Whenever any of the controversial topics were mentioned, he would change the subject to discuss the promising youth of the team and the future it had.

And on the afternoon of the trade deadline, he made an executive decision that would reverberate throughout the franchise for seasons to come.

Milbury had had his eye on Florida Panthers prospect Oleg Kvasha for years. There was a ton of potential in the tall, fast Russian, who was loaded with skill. They called him Baby Bure in the Panthers organization, because he seemed to have the same offensive prowess as Florida's All-Star sniper Pavel Bure.

The Panthers were closing in on a playoff berth and were looking to bolster their lineup. Florida GM Bryan Murray had an affinity for Kenny Jonsson, and Milbury had maintained concerns about his durability and toughness. So Milbury and Murray talked over a deal that would have included Kvasha going to the Islanders in a package for Jonsson.

Leading up to the deadline, Milbury and Murray thought they had a deal. There was even some discussion that would have made the deal bigger by sending Mariusz Czerkawski to Florida for Mark Parrish and perhaps another young Russian sniper named Ivan Novoseltsev. It seemed a given that a headline trade would happen that day. Reporters from both cities called each other to exchange notes.

Jonsson, who continually said he wanted to remain with the Islanders, left his cell phone off that day.

Milstein, however, didn't. And when he was called in for a meeting to approve the trade, he hedged. He then called Murray and canceled the deal.

Milbury, clearly frustrated, did his best to suck up the power play by his meddling boss.

"It wasn't meant to be," he said.

Neither was Gutkowski's attempt to buy the team, as confidence in his group's sincere interest faded farther into oblivion with each passing week. Meanwhile, former New York State senator Alfonse D'Amato, the man hired to represent SMG in grandstanding public hearings held by Nassau County's Democratic-majority legislature regarding the Coliseum, was working his friend and business partner, Charles Wang, behind the scenes.

The ultra-private but sports-crazed Wang had been approached by Gutkowski to join his group with Koppelman, but Wang declined. He was a basketball fan at heart and did once consider partnering with Robert Wood Johnson in the latter's purchase of the New York Jets football team. Another friend, Cablevision chairman Charles Dolan, owned Madison Square Garden and the Knicks and Rangers. So for Wang, sports ownership was intriguing.

But the truth was he didn't have a great deal of interest in hockey. He had attended only a few hockey games in his life, and those were at Madison Square Garden as a guest of Dolan.

Still, D'Amato knew what buttons to push with Wang. He mentioned the Coliseum property, which included the potential of a lucrative convention center, and, of course, the Islanders' desperate situation and desperate need for a hero. That appealed to Wang, who is a staunch Long Island patriot.

Rumor had it that the Milsteins were ready to dump the team to the first bidder. Software billionaire Paul Allen, a noted hockey fan who has always been on Bettman's short list of potential owners, became a name whispered throughout the league as an interested suitor.

For years the possibility of an Islanders move from Long Island was widely discussed. Bettman continually shot it down publicly, but during those tumultuous years in the 1990s he had to wonder to himself if pulling the plug was the only option left.

And sometime during the 1999-2000 season, it is believed that Long Island was indeed on the verge of losing its only pro sports franchise and a once-proud symbol.

It had literally reached the 11th hour.

12

A Wang and a Prayer

Charles Wang's dream is to rival Dolan one day in the sports world. He imagines owning an empire that includes a state-of-the-art arena and teams from both the NBA and NHL. He envisions a modern complex with a convention center, a parking garage, a restaurant, and perhaps even a nightclub along Hempstead Turnpike—all things that would fulfill the dreams of Patterson, Nickerson, Naso and, yes, even Spano.

D'Amato, ever the slick promoter during his reign as a popular senator in New York, had Wang hooked. By early March they quickly dispersed Gutkowski and his feeble campaign to buy the Islanders. Within a month's time they'd completed a $190 million purchase of the franchise.

Milstein got back every penny he paid for the team and disappeared as quickly as Wang arrived on the scene.

For Wang, whose controversial 1999 compensation of $650 million placed him at the top of *Forbes*'s annual pay survey and subsequently thrust him into the billionaire category, it was the first small step toward his grand plan. Ever so shrewd and calculating, Wang also made sure to learn from the mistakes of those who came before him. He was not a hockey fan, he readily admitted, but he is a fan of Long Island. He knew what the people wanted to hear.

Long Island was not about to lose its only pro sports franchise.

But more than just saving a team that was already at death's door, the purchase of the Islanders was a challenge for the ultra-competitive

Wang, who built his company, Computer Associates, from a fledgling retail distributor into a computer industry superpower.

"We love it when people say, 'This is impossible,'" Wang said on April 26, 2000, the day the sale was officially announced. "We thrive on it. Watch us."

He and partner Sanjay Kumar were a comedy routine from the get-go. They never once tried to downplay nor apologize for their collective lack of knowledge of the sport. Wang, who was born in Shanghai, and Kumar, who was born in Sri Lanka, walked into the jam-packed news conference at the Garden City Hotel carrying a copy of *Hockey for Dummies,* written by John Davidson, and cracked self-deprecating joke after joke.

"Where we were raised," Wang said as the slap-happiness continued during a casual sit-down luncheon in a suite at the hotel later that afternoon, "an ice cube was not only a luxury, it was a miracle."

"It was a very unconventional thing to have a blade on your feet and walk around on a sheet of ice," Kumar added. "They'd think you were some kind of nut."

Some said at the time that they were nuts for getting themselves into this mess. And then even more so a month later when Wang and Kumar announced that Milbury would be retained. It was during a 90-minute meeting in mid-May that Milbury, as usual, proved himself to be the devoted company man that Maloney, Spano and Milstein each saw him to be. The ability to say all the right things—or exactly what your boss wants to hear—is a Milbury trait. Along with making an immediate allegiance to whomever is in power.

"This guy is talking about building a team," an astonished Kumar reported to Wang after the interview.

"That's the last thing I expected from him," Kumar said. "I expected him to say, 'I've been down and beaten. We had to sell off all of our good assets. Give me some money. We're ready to rock and roll.' I fully expected that. But instead, I walked out of the meeting scratching my head. He wants to build a team."

Milbury also played up the self-pity angle by suggesting that the new owners make a change if they saw fit.

"I care so much about this franchise that I won't get in the way," he said.

While violins moaned a sorrowful song, Wang and Kumar were all ears. And for the next three years, their running joke was that all Milbury needed was a few sessions of charm school. He became the centerpiece to their franchise-wide reclamation project. Not only would they turn the

Islanders into winners again, but they would salvage the career of a man who long ago had reached the end of his rope. He'd already proven that there wasn't enough left to hang himself.

The newfound optimism and rekindled passion in the Islanders organization brought some immediate results. Good karma came in the form of a longshot victory in the NHL draft lottery. The mediocre finish to the season managed to move the Islanders out of the basement in the league standings and seemingly out of contention for the No. 1 overall pick, which prompted Goring to once crack after a huge overtime win in Dallas, "I'm really fucking up their plan to get that first pick, aren't I?"

But on June 1, despite being ranked fifth out of the five teams in contention for the No. 1 pick and just an eight-percent chance of success, the Islanders' number came up. And on the same day the Rangers introduced Glen Sather as their new GM and the Devils were set to open the Stanley Cup Finals against the Dallas Stars, the Islanders elbowed their way into the New York sports pages with some rare good news.

"It feels like the worm is beginning to turn here a little bit," Milbury said.

Milbury already knew what he wanted to do with the pick. Trade it. He immediately began making and taking calls from interested teams that might have had an impact player to deal in return.

One target pushed by a few members of the scouting brain trust was Ottawa Senators center Alexei Yashin, who had just completed a controversial year-long holdout while demanding his current contract, which was set to expire June 30, be rewritten.

But Wang and Kumar, sensing negative reaction to such an acquisition, had cold feet. The Senators already had said they wouldn't deal Yashin until after an arbitrator ruled whether he was indeed a restricted free agent or that his holdout meant he still owed the team the final year of service.

In the weeks leading up to the draft, Milbury was dying to do something big, something to gain some positive attention and perhaps announce that the Islanders were no longer a laughingstock. He also wanted to show his new bosses that he could get the job done in a big spot.

While he tried to keep Wang and Kumar open-minded about Yashin, there were other quality players such as Sandis Ozolinsh and Roman Hamrlik who were up for grabs via trade, and Milbury considered those options, as well. He also debated with his scouts about what to do with the pick. There were two forwards (Wisconsin University freshman Dany Heatley and Slovakian Marian Gaborik), a defenseman (Czech Rostislav

Klesla) and a goalie (Boston University frosh Rick DiPietro) widely hailed as the top four prospects available. Of the group, Heatley and Gaborik seemed the most NHL-ready, but neither figured to be an immediate impact player. Neither carried much luster, nor showed any gumption.

And Milbury likes gumption.

Still, the hockey staff met and interviewed each of them, which might not have been newsworthy had the list not included DiPietro, who met with Milbury at the Islanders' offices a week before the draft. DiPietro had luster. He certainly had gumption. And he had that Boston pop to his personality that makes Milbury swoon. If ever there was a person who used unfettered spunk as a credible asset, it was DiPietro, who treats just about everyone near his age as if they are a frat brother and elders as if they are uncles.

Milbury then considered the situation. In Luongo, he had a young-ster with dynamic skill and an ice-cold confidence, yet an aloof, sort of haughty demeanor that at the end of the season alienated him from his teammates. He also proved to be a high-maintenance type of player who needed coddling.

In DiPietro, he saw a youngster with perhaps less talent (though considered an unprecedented stick handler), but with a fiery competitive-ness along with an entertainingly excitable and warm personality that elec-trifies a room. DiPietro was the kind of kid whom you could tell he played like shit, yet two minutes later would ask you where you wanted to go to dinner.

Mind you, Milbury never once saw DiPietro play a single game. He watched a few tapes, but nothing more. There was one attempt to catch him in Providence, but DiPietro didn't play that night. So Milbury had little of his own hockey knowledge to consider. Instead, this was a decision he made—a major one, at that—based on pure emotion.

In effect, from the minute DiPietro met Milbury, he had him at hello.

And so on the eve of the draft, which was hosted by Calgary, an inevitable buzz surfaced just before the midnight sun set behind the Alberta city. Milbury had his plan in the works.

Luongo would be traded.

Weekes would be traded.

DiPietro would be taken at No. 1.

And the hockey world was about to meet, for the first time, the irrepressible Mad Mike Milbury.

"This is it, this is my job," he announced when the day was done and DiPietro was, indeed, the first overall pick in the draft, Luongo and

Jokinen were dealt to the Panthers for Kvasha and Parrish, and Weekes was sent to Tampa Bay for the fifth overall pick that was parlayed into a fireplug banger named Raffi Torres. The final piece of work in the day was acquiring Hamrlik from the Edmonton Oilers for Brewer and Green.

"My job is squarely on the line," Mad Mike continued to a national media contingent that could hardly stifle its guffaws. "If we're not a better team immediately, if we're not a very good team over the long haul, then off with the head."

There was not as much criticism for the decision to take DiPietro, who at 18 was considered the top goalie available in the draft, as much as it was to give up on Luongo, who was 20 at the time and widely considered the next great goalie in the NHL. And to get what for him? Kvasha (a big, smooth-skating youngster with enigmatic flashes of talent) and Parrish (a purebred goal scorer in the mold of a Dino Ciccarelli without the mean streak), two players they could have had for Jonsson and Czerkawski in March, had Ed Milstein not pulled the plug.

Still, Milbury didn't flinch in the face of his detractors. Instead, he gave them more of his own words that they were expecting him to eat in the near future.

"We are rolling the dice a little bit here," Milbury said, before incredibly adding with a nod, "If we're wrong, boy, will we have made a mistake."

Somewhere in the background you could almost hear Homer Simpson slap his head and yell, "D'oh!"

But Milbury continued chattering excitedly. He then pulled out the label for all the world to use against him in the coming days, weeks, months and years.

"As dangerous as this may be," he said, "maybe Mad Mike maybe has something going for him."

D'oh!

In the draft pits, some GMs kept their thoughts respectfully quiet while others only tossed more fuel onto the fire.

"What does he know about goaltenders?" Sather said to a cluster of reporters who lined a wall that separated the pits from the media riser on the floor of the Saddledome. "He may have given up a better goaltender in Luongo. Remember, he didn't think Tommy Salo could play, either."

Salo had been an All-Star for Sather the previous season in Edmonton.

The following day, at his off-season home in the Czech Republic, Hamrlik didn't take well the news that he had been traded to the Islanders. This was evident shortly after Botta had called him to set up an interview with New York reporters in Calgary. Botta handed the phone to Hahn and stood in disbelief as Hahn showed him scribbled notes of the answer to the first question asked.

"They haven't been in the playoffs for as long as I can remember," Hamrlik said. "The team reminds me of Tampa and I was not happy there. So we'll see."

Hamrlik played six seasons with the Lightning, who drafted him No. 1 overall in 1992.

"I was six years in Tampa and we made the playoffs once," he continued. "It kind of stinks. . . . It's kind of like going to the worst team in the league."

Ouch. So much for good karma.

Botta quickly informed Milbury of Hamrlik's comments, and Milbury found his agent, Jiri Crha, in the Saddledome crowd and then called Hamrlik directly to straighten him out.

"I don't really care what your conversation was," a dismissive Milbury told *The Post*'s Barry Baum, who also spoke with Hamrlik over the phone. "Mine was a good one. I think you're making a mountain out of a molehill."

Milbury took veteran John Vanbiesbrouck from the Flyers in a minor trade the day after selecting DiPietro and called it "insurance." Over the summer, he then signed up more experience in defenseman Kevin Haller and forward Mike Stapleton. During training camp, another veteran, Garry Galley, was brought into the fold via free agency.

On paper, the Islanders appeared to be an improved team in both experience and talent. They actually had guys you've heard of playing for them. Some of them even had success once or twice in their careers. The team's payroll was still relatively cheap—$26 million—but it was a far cry from 1999-2000. And team charters were reinstated, along with a few other player quality-of-life amenities, including an upgraded and renovated locker room and weight room facility at the Coliseum.

But the arrival of Wang and Kumar didn't completely bring sunny skies back to the franchise. There were a few clouds hanging above that reminded everyone these were still the Islanders.

Milbury would later refer to it as a "culture of losing," an attitude that existed throughout the franchise and took time to flush from the system. After seven years of losing, it had become an epidemic. And that's why this team and all the newfound hope it brought with it was doomed from the start.

But that would later prove to be a blessing in disguise.

Goring finished the 1999-2000 season with a lot of personal momentum. Many of his young players praised how he handled the team during the latter part of the season and they spoke glowingly about playing for him. But the first day of training camp in Lake Placid, Goring got off on the wrong foot and never recovered.

Players woke up for the first day of practice expecting a schedule of times detailing when each group was to take the ice. Because camps are full of so many players from the organization's system, groups of three are usually made and rotated from on-ice to off-ice workouts and then scrimmages. But on the first day of the 2000-01 camp, Goring didn't make up a schedule. So at 9 A.M., players arrived at the Olympic Center wondering where they were supposed to be and when.

Goring said assistant GM Mike Santos was supposed to hand out the schedules to the players the night before at the team hotel. Santos said Goring never gave him any schedules.

That got a few veteran players such as Vanbiesbrouck into an ornery mood. Then they saw how loosely Goring handled the practices and the team. How he'd forget names of players or misidentify them and then be very standoffish. Associate coach Lorne Henning tried desperately to defuse problems, but it was clear that some of the new faces had already developed a negative opinion of Goring.

Another situation brewing during camp were the contract holdouts of restricted free agents Isbister and Zdeno Chara. Wang didn't tolerate such insubordination and therefore declared that any player who did not accept a contract by the first day of camp would be locked out for the entire season. No trade, no renegotiation and no compromise in any way.

A nervous Milbury called members of the media as well as the team to get the word to Isbister and Chara. But the agents that represented each respectively—Steve Reich for Isbister and Rich Winter for Chara—didn't budge. So on the second day, Milbury reluctantly told the 6'9", 250-pound Chara, an important piece of the defense that season, that he was done for the year. He then announced it to the media.

"This is the way the Islanders want to do business," Milbury explained. "This is a statement by the organization."

With Chara as the example, Isbister was given two days to come to terms or he was next. Despite scoring 22 goals in 1999-2000, second best on the team, Isbister, at 22 years old, was one of the lowest paid players at $350,000. The Islanders were offering a two-year contract at $385,000 and $423,500, which amounts to the mere 10-percent raises mandated by the collective bargaining agreement.

As restricted free agents without arbitration rights, both players were under complete control of the Islanders. This is where Wang was doing his homework, but was perhaps a bit overzealous. He read the collective bargaining agreement and noticed how incredibly it favors the player. This was a rare circumstance when it favored the owners, when a player doesn't have arbitration rights. So if a qualifying offer was all he was by rule under obligation to make, then a qualifying offer was what they'd get. The player's turn would come in arbitration, he felt. That's how the deal was supposed to work, though most teams didn't use this leverage to their advantage out of fear of upsetting a key player and the rest of the team.

In other words, other teams tend to avoid contract issues of smaller dollar amounts during training camp so as not to disrupt chemistry and attitude. Nickel-and-diming a good young player for contracts under $1 million per season doesn't go over well with players and fans.

Still, that's what Wang and the Islanders did. Until an appeal led by Vanbiesbrouck during a team meeting with Wang and Kumar—surreptitiously organized by an increasingly nervous Milbury—allowed Chara a second chance to accept a one-year qualifying deal at $660,000. Milbury, who gladly went back on his word that Chara was done for the season, said the owners allowed "a one-time exemption because this is a new policy" but warned that "next time, there will be no second chance."

With the gun now to his head, Isbister signed on as well.

And the only real message sent that weekend was that the Islanders, new owners and all, were still a cheapskate organization.

DiPietro turned 19 years old during training camp, and despite playing well, it seemed inevitable that he'd begin his career in the minors. A late groin injury in practice solidified it, but the brash, emotional DiPietro didn't want to hear it.

"Mike," he said when Milbury summoned him to deliver the news of his demotion, "we haven't won a game yet."

Milbury's affinity for the kid only intensified. He was right. The Islanders went through the preseason without a single victory in six games (0-5-1). Vanbiesbrouck looked ordinary, at best, and there was a gaping hole at No. 1 center, a role Connolly clearly wasn't ready to fill. Kvasha took the most criticism and was noticeably ineffective and practically invisible.

On the eve of the season opener in Tampa Bay, Hahn ran into Milbury outside the team hotel and got an impromptu interview. The first question was, is this a playoff team? Milbury carefully hedged, which was telling enough.

"I'm going to be disappointed if this team is not competing for a spot in March," he said. "I can't promise you that we'll get there, but if we're not hovering around a playoff spot then it will have not been a disappointment for me, but a failure."

That said, Hahn asked, would there be reason then for you to be concerned about your job?

"Fuck you, Alan," Milbury replied.

The team came away with a tie that night and—almost in spite of itself—got off to a relatively promising, though wildly inconsistent, 5-3-2 start. They were rolling with four straight wins—something the team hadn't done since April '98—and waltzed back to Tampa Bay on November 3 going up against an awful, but competitive, Lightning team. Everyone was sky high.

Except for Milbury.

"I'm scared to death about this one," he said before a game that would underscore the season for his team and be the night just about everyone points to as the beginning of the end for Goring.

It appeared that the Islanders would pull out their fifth straight win, if only barely. They held a 3-1 lead in the second period and it was sliced to 3-2 in the third. With under a minute left in regulation, Tampa pulled its goalie and Isbister charged toward the empty net. He was pulled down from behind by Tampa's star center Vincent Lecavalier and missed the open net just wide. Still, the Islanders were awarded a power play and had the puck deep in the Tampa zone with about a half-minute left. Victory seemed assured. The beat writers were already writing about the improbable position the Islanders were about to take in the Atlantic Division standings.

First place. First place!

The ensuing faceoff was won by Claude Lapointe. He sent a pass back to Kenny Jonsson at the blue line. But the puck took a skip in a rut on the ice and bounced over Jonsson's stick. Jonsson was frozen in the neutral zone as lightning bug Mike Johnson flew by him and broke in on Vanbiesbrouck, who flopped to the ice as the puck ripped the net cords behind him. The score was tied at 3 with 24.2 left in regulation.

The Islanders, however, were still on the power play and carried it into overtime. Late in OT they had a good scoring chance, but failed. During the ensuing rush, the players curiously started a line change. And when Czerkawski stood up to hop over the boards for his shift, Goring grabbed his shoulder and pulled him back. He then shoved a surprised

Parrish onto the ice, and by the time Parrish's skates hit ground, Craig Millar had finished what became an odd-man rush with a goal to win it for Tampa.

The Islanders were crushed. But more, they were angry.

Jonsson, who is normally friendly but mostly uncomfortable with the media, refused to talk after the game. Red-faced and sullen, he retreated to the team bus and did not move even after urging from the media relations staff. Milbury then blasted him for cowering.

But no one on the team was as upset with Jonsson's misplay and mind fuck as much as they were incensed with Goring for his antics on the bench. The explanation was that Czerkawski was dogging it, as he tends to do, and that Goring wanted to punish him by taking away his ice time in OT. But in doing so, many felt that he cost the Islanders the game.

Goring would find more trouble at the hands of Tampa Bay in the future.

Despite the loss, the Islanders were still above water, and following an election-night victory over the Nashville Predators, they joined the Devils atop the Atlantic. Though it was so early in the season, one would think the positioning—despite the team not playing well at all—would inspire the group somewhat.

It certainly had Goring feeling good about himself. After the morning skate before the team's next game, in Buffalo against the Sabres, he talked excitedly and at length about the team's position in the standings and the positive hope he held for the season. He seemed at ease and happy. It was very similar to his mood late in the 1999-2000 season, when he was very much in control of the young team.

Yet despite Goring's overflowing optimism, the Islanders that night in Buffalo went out and got shut out, 3-0, by Dominik Hasek and the Sabres. Goring kicked over a water cooler in the hallway outside the locker rooms after the game. The good mood was long gone. He called the flatline performance "our poorest effort in a long time."

This was 14 games into the season.

This was also the beginning of a losing streak that doubled over the season by the holidays. Eight straight defeats—including an overtime loss at home to the Rangers on the eve of Thanksgiving—sent the Islanders into a tailspin. The holes were too obvious. Vanbiesbrouck was mediocre. The defense was inconsistent. The power play was ineffective. And there was a major-league vacancy at No. 1 center, where Goring used everyone from Lindgren to Connolly to Kvasha to even Lapointe and Isbister. And when all else failed, a little-known minor-leaguer named Jeff Toms was given the job.

"There's only so much you can do with what you have," Toms said of his surprising promotion to the top line.

He didn't last, either.

During the streak, the Islanders continued to fall apart at the seams, and frustration was brewing. Following a bad loss in L.A., one fan leaned over the tunnel leading to the Islanders' locker room and yelled "You guys suck!" Czerkawski stopped in his tracks and shouted back at the fan.

Then, on the ensuing flight to San Jose, Goring spoke with Jonsson about the lack of leadership and accountability in the locker room. Jonsson, who seemed overwhelmed with the captaincy practically from the minute the "C" was sewn onto his sweater, agreed and told Goring he wanted to step down.

Milbury got word of this and immediately flew from New York to San Jose to meet with Goring and Jonsson. Bleary-eyed and slumped over a glass of wine at the hotel bar in the San Jose Hilton, Milbury growled.

"I smell a rat," he seethed.

He was referring to the leadership situation with the Islanders. Goring was a coach the team had praised only a year before. But those were the young players, who liked his leniency and goofiness. But the newcomers, especially the older types such as Vanbiesbrouck, Stapleton and Galley, weren't happy. And the room quickly turned on the coach. Jonsson had little control of the situation. He also struggled with the off-ice responsibilities of a captain, such as organizing events and player-related requests to the team. The aforementioned vets, it is believed, were basically giving Jonsson a hard time for every little thing, including the setup and rules in the wives' room.

Jonsson, true to his nature, kept it all to himself.

And like just about every coach he has played for, Goring loved Jonsson. He was a low-maintenance player. He was smart and talented and always showed up to play. But he was passive, and, to Goring's regret, he didn't want to be captain of this sinking ship any more.

Milbury was livid. After a handful of questions from the media the following morning, a red-faced Jonsson seemed to grow more and more uneasy. So Milbury put an end to it.

"That's enough," he said, breaking up the scrum. "He's got a game to play tonight."

The players were in shock, but all of them knew it was inevitable. No replacement was named, mostly because there wasn't one singularly dominant voice in the room. Vanbiesbrouck actually was, but goalies by league rules are not permitted to be designated as captains. And some suggest that the oft-capricious Beezer's influence wasn't always a constructive one, especially with a young core of players sitting around him. But he was the one symbol of success in the room. And compared to Goring, the players being well aware of their coach's penchant for hitting the late-night scene on road trips, the deeply religious Beezer was at least respectable.

But Milbury didn't want to hear about the absence of leadership as the team's greatest weakness or the reason why the team was losing. Simply put, he said, "our power play sucks," and he called for "all hands on deck" instead of waiting for the front office to shake up the team with a big trade.

Then he called out his team with some public ridicule to almost shame them out of the excuse that the team lacked the proper leadership necessary for success.

"For all the years I played," he said, "I never remember going to the rink and saying, 'Where's my leader? If I don't have my leader here, then I sure as hell can't play.' What the fuck is that all about?"

13

Butch Whacked

Talk of Goring's ouster started as a murmur as early as the days following the loss in Buffalo. As the losses mounted, so did the questions concerning his job. And when the Philadelphia Flyers fired Craig Ramsay in early December on the day the Islanders were in Philly for a game, Goring came face to face with the reality of his situation.

Suddenly, with Ramsay and, earlier in the season, Pat Burns (Boston Bruins) already out, Goring became the next likely coach to get gassed.

"It's obviously the easy way out for any team, to fire the coach," he said. "You can argue all day whether it's the right move or the wrong move."

If anything, he had to admit it was an inevitable one. At least Parrish said so when asked about it after the game, which saw the Isles pummeled 5-2 and outshot 40-18.

"When you're on a losing team in a losing organization," he said, "it's inevitable.

"I guess in some cases, it's not [the coach's] fault," Parrish continued. "But you've got to do something to change something and get the team to win."

The following day, Milbury called a meeting in the dressing room after practice. Every player was told to sit in his stall, and most of the coaching staff, too, was seated with the players.

Milbury then laced into them, calling out some individuals, but mostly as a group. He said he saw everything they were doing: ducking out of hits, not working hard for an entire shift and playing selfishly.

"Look, guys," he said to them, "I know we don't have a lot of talent on this team, but that doesn't excuse you from working hard every game."

He went into the meeting with two motives. One was to shake the team with a much-needed ass-kicking, the other was to get answers.

When his ire is up and the venom is flowing, at 6'1" and well over 200 pounds, Milbury is an imposing, intimidating figure. He went around the room, asking them one by one for suggestions. Galley, who has known Milbury since their days together with the Boston Bruins, mentioned a few things discussed in an earlier meeting among the players. Milbury was pleased with Galley's input, but frustrated that no others dared to speak up.

The fuming GM then focused on Goring, who stood quietly with his back against a wall—figuratively and literally. Slowly, as Milbury's rant continued, Goring went from standing against the wall to being slumped in the corner of the room "like a boxer who was waiting for the ref to step in," said one person in the room. Some believed that even the slightest show of defense might have won some respect from the players. Instead, they saw a beaten man take more of a beating.

Milbury then chastised the players, saying they talked about how much they loved Goring as a coach, yet they played as if they were trying to get him fired. Milbury told the players that he liked Goring personally, that the two had history and he did not want to fire him. But the team had to start winning some games for him.

Milbury then looked at Roman Hamrlik and Zdeno Chara sitting around the coach. Neither had anything to say. He then turned to Henning, standing nearby.

"What do you think, Lornie?"

Henning, in typical monotone, raised his eyebrows.

"I think you should back off a little, Mike."

Now Milbury had forced himself out of the focus of attention by staying away from the team. He did this knowing his past reputation as an overbearing manager that had undermined some of his previous coaches. He wanted Goring to have full control of the team.

And here was Henning telling him he's still forcing his will upon the team too much. The comment set Milbury off even more.

"Fuck you, Lornie!" he growled. "Fuck you!"

Milbury wheeled around and practically charged at Henning, who froze but did not back down. Many of the players sitting near Henning, however, did flinch at the sight of Milbury coming toward them with fire in his eyes and the words repeating from his mouth.

"Fuck you, Lornie!"

During the meeting, Milbury and Goring left the room for a while. One observer said it felt like an intermission during a play and wondered if the two had staged the whole thing just to spark the team. Milbury and Goring later both vehemently denied it.

Still, it had a major impact on all those who were present. Some players were reduced to tears while arguing their case.

"It was the most emotional meeting I have ever been a part of," one person said.

But the result of those emotions didn't turn into wins. Instead, if that meeting didn't serve as the final nail in the coffin, it certainly started the funeral. After that, the players figured Goring to be a goner and therefore tuned him out. Most didn't want to hear about it or talk about it.

"We felt like we've had to play for Butch the last little while," Dave Scatchard said. "We've got to play for each other, too. Everyone here is sick of losing."

Czerkawski, who had his best seasons as a pro under Goring with 35 goals and 70 points in 1999-2000 and 30 goals and 62 points in 2000-01, perhaps appreciated Goring the most. "If I had to end my hockey career right now," Czerkawski said, "he'd be the guy I most remember for being the nicest to me."

That might have been Goring's greatest downfall: he was too nice to his players. He didn't like confrontation and therefore left it up to assistant coach Greg Cronin, who was once a very successful coach at the University of Maine. A tough, musclebound New England-bred taskmaster with a fiery passion for the game, Cronin would do the yelling and screaming and challenging players who weren't playing up to par. He would be the bad guy, while Goring would remain the friend. Usually, it works the other way around.

But that's how Goring wanted it. He was a player in a coach's body. He often appeared to be one of the better skaters on the ice during practice and loved to take extra laps after practices to keep in shape.

He could break down the game as well as anyone and had a keen eye for assessing an opponent's strengths, weaknesses and tendencies. But his downfall was that he often had a difficult time getting his point across. Just as he stumbled at times when addressing the media, he would do the same with the team, often getting opponents' names mixed up or mixing his phrases to the point of incomprehension.

Following one ugly defeat, he attempted to explain the Islanders' inconsistencies to reporters. "We're a Heckle and Jeckle team right now," he said. Everyone in the room knew he'd meant to say "Jekyll and Hyde." But the notion of "Heckle and Jeckle"—the famous pair of goofy cartoon magpies—also seemed apropos of his team.

Still, what many afterward claimed to be Goring's greatest failure was his life off the ice, which often impacted his life on it. Goring is very much a friendly, likeable person. And he loves to have fun. Golf is one of his outlets. Alcohol, at least during his tumultuous tenure with the Islanders, admittedly became one, too.

On too many occasions, Goring, who was going through an emotional separation from his first wife, would arrive late for a morning skate and then not take the ice. The players noticed this, as well as noticing his rumpled clothes and other signs of a late-night excursion.

He didn't see much wrong with enjoying life on the road and even encouraged his team to go out on off days during road trips. He called it "letting them run," which is translated to mean go out, drink and have fun. Let off some steam. For a young team, that was as welcomed as an optional practice. For the 2000-01 team, however, with Bible thumpers such as Vanbiesbrouck and Kevin Haller on the team and veteran Garry Galley (who practically from the start wished he'd stuck with his decision to retire instead of agreeing to come to the Islanders), it didn't go over well at all. In fact, it was intolerable.

Some were concerned about the influence it had óver teenagers such as Connolly and Taylor Pyatt, who after one loss late in the 2000-01 season were seen at a Long Island club drinking and dancing on top of a bar.

Many players were upset with Goring for not holding Connolly, 18 and 19 years old during the two seasons Goring coached him, more accountable for his tendencies to go away from the system and freestyle with the puck. And, of course, his penchant for not getting his butt back in the defensive zone.

Still, Goring never sat Connolly and never criticized him, especially in front of the team. Some players felt it was called for on many occasions.

But Goring also had many supporters. Rivers, who later moved on to the Ottawa Senators, was one. As mouthy as Rivers can be, his word usually can be taken as honest opinion because of his candor. Case in point, at the end of the 1999-2000 season he was asked about the concern of leadership with the young team going into the next season.

"I'm not drunk enough to answer that," he replied.

The question was purposely loaded because Rivers was one of the few players who stood up after losses, while Jonsson would hide in the showers.

But when it came to Goring's situation with the Islanders during the 2000-01 season, Rivers, by then with the Ottawa Senators, said the blame was focused on the wrong individual.

"Coaching is not the problem with that team," he said. "I think you know what the problem is, and I don't know how he's kept his job."

Rivers, of course, was talking about Milbury.

A week after his locker room tirade, Milbury then publicly endorsed his coach for the umpteenth time by saying "I have no plans to make the coach the fall guy right now."

Coincidentally, the very next day, Wang came out and said that Milbury's job was safe, too, despite rumors surfacing that Wang was talking to Bill Torrey about a possible return to the Islanders.

A few days later, Wang met with the players the morning before a game against the Carolina Hurricanes and held an open discussion about the many gripes they had regarding the team. Wang went through each one like a checklist and met just about every request. He also offered them a little pep talk.

The team responded with a 2-1 win. It would be one of only three the team would see over the next month.

And almost a month after that, Wang met with fans in an open-forum setting to discuss matters concerning the team. As he often is, Wang was in full control and made it clear when he told one fan to "sit down and shut up."

That would be Craig Stanley, otherwise known as "Ziggy" or "Goldie." He's the guy you can see at practically every Islanders home game, somewhere along the boards, wearing a shiny gold pom-pom wig and an Islanders jersey. He also wears a Rangers jersey, which he designed himself with the word "Sucks" under the Rangers lettering on the front and the numbers 1940 on the back.

Stanley, too, was dominating the forum. In his own excitably boisterous way, Stanley shouted one question after another to Wang, offering suggestions for coaches and players. Finally, Wang had enough.

"Why don't you sit down and shut up?" he said, with a smirk. Other fans in the place roared. Even Stanley allowed a smile. Wang just wanted other fans to get a chance to speak.

But Stanley mentioned a name, former Buffalo Sabres coach Ted Nolan, that Wang acknowledged. And that was enough to touch off further controversy.

"I know who Ted Nolan is," he said.

He also addressed the continuous "Mike Must Go!" chants at the Coliseum, telling fans to "get a life" and get used to Milbury because he was coming back next season.

"It's a done deal," he said to the dismay of the fans. "So let's support the guy and make him feel loved."

As for Goring, there wasn't as much love.

"We don't know if Goring's going to stay or not," he said, with Goring down the hall preparing for a game against the Flyers. "Mike has to make that decision, ultimately. Really, the way I look at it is, if [Goring's] strategy doesn't work, the vision and all that, we'll know pretty quickly that Mike will have to change it."

Goring was advised of Wang's comments and just shrugged. "Anyone who knows me knows there's no quit in me," he said, "and I haven't changed my mind about wanting to coach the New York Islanders."

But apparently, Milbury and Wang already had made up their minds. Truth be told, Milbury had put a call in to the Boston Bruins around that time to see if he could get permission to speak with one of their assistant coaches, Peter Laviolette. Milbury knew of Laviolette from the latter's success with the Bruins' farm club in Providence. There was a lot about him that he liked, and what he didn't know, he heard and liked.

He also knew Laviolette was getting antsy. For two years, it was said he was being groomed for the Bruins' head job. But after Burns was fired early in the season, the organization decided to go for experience in Mike Keenan instead of promoting the 35-year-old Laviolette.

But after the abrasive Keenan quickly wore out his welcome in the Bs' mostly unhappy dressing room, the organization's brain trust was made aware that Laviolette and assistant Jacques Laperriere were keeping the team together. So Laviolette was too valuable. Plus, Keenan probably wouldn't be back after that season, so Laviolette would be a candidate for the job.

With all of that to digest, the Bruins denied Milbury access to Laviolette. So Milbury had to sit tight a little longer with a lame-duck coach and a plummeting team.

In the meantime, there were other notable happenings. First, there was the promotion of DiPietro, who'd been doing well enough with the

Chicago Wolves, a veteran-laden minor-league team in the International Hockey League.

DiPietro took his demotion after training camp hard, but it didn't take him much time to draw attention in the minors. In his very first game, he got into a fight with the opposing goalie—and got his ass kicked. The Wolves, full of journeymen types who were just hanging on for the paycheck, were an experience for the bouncy, effervescent 19-year-old.

And they did little to coddle him.

In a hilarious feature by *Sports Illustrated*'s Michael Farber, DiPietro was torn to shreds by his mates in Chicago. Kevin Dahl, who was a room-mate of DiPietro's on the road, reported that DiPietro was talking in his sleep the previous night.

Dahl then added, "He never shuts up."

The story followed DiPietro for his call-up in late January that would see his first NHL start and keep him with the team for the rest of the season.

When told DiPietro was packing for a flight to Buffalo, Chicago veteran goalie Wendel Young replied, "Ricky's going to need two seats on that plane: one in coach for his body and one in first class for his ego."

DiPietro's ego would take a bit of a beating, however. He lost his first start 2-1 at Buffalo on January 27 and actually went five games before finally earning his first NHL win. That came on February 16 in a 4-2 victory over the Edmonton Oilers.

A week later, the Islanders were hosting the equally pathetic Florida Panthers, and a DiPietro–Luongo battle gave a little luster to what would normally be a blip on the NHL screen. The Islanders had already once before defeated Luongo, 3-0 in Florida on November 1. But this time Luongo would meet, face to face, with the guy the Islanders replaced him with.

But Panthers coach Duane Sutter, the former Islander, didn't allow it. Instead, Luongo watched as DiPietro picked up his second career victory in a 5-4 win over Trevor Kidd. Luongo did get in for 51 seconds of the game as Sutter pulled Kidd to stop some momentum.

On March 11, the two went head to head for 60 minutes, and behind a Pavel Bure hat trick, Luongo and the Panthers won, 4-1.

"I felt it was just any other game," Luongo said afterward. "Sure, there was a little different emotion, but the win wasn't any more special than any other win. My time here is in the past. It's over."

With DiPietro around and the Islanders well out of contention, Vanbiesbrouck had little interest in playing the role of the mentor. He was already seeing the signs of what had happened the year before in Philadelphia, when a youngster named Brian Boucher unseated him in goal.

But this was a far different situation. Boucher led the Flyers to the Eastern Conference finals. DiPietro only posed a threat to Beezer's minutes and starts. He knew the team would be more inclined to get the kid experience since the games meant nothing anyway. Milbury was in love with a Russian prospect named Ilya Kovalchuk, who was undoubtedly the best player in the coming draft. So losing more games wouldn't be so bad in the long run. A top draft choice would reap rewards.

At about midseason, Vanbiesbrouck met with Milbury to discuss his future. He would stick around if they asked him. He liked living on Long Island and figured retirement was just around the corner anyway. But with veteran backup Wade Flaherty out for the season with a shoulder injury, Beezer knew that meant DiPietro was coming. And Vanbiesbrouck felt that if in time he would have to sit on the bench and watch someone else play, he'd much rather do it on a playoff team.

So he offered that to Milbury, who then looked around for takers.

The *Post*'s Baum got word through the grapevine that Vanbiesbrouck had thoughts of leaving. But his timing couldn't have been worse. A few days after Hahn did a sit-down interview with Vanbiesbrouck—in which the Beezer waxed nostalgic about his career and discussed his future by insisting he would be happy to stay an Islander—Baum ran a story based on hearsay from "confidants" who were saying Vanbiesbrouck wanted to be traded.

A livid Beezer sought Baum the morning of a home game against Ottawa and summoned the reporter into the locker room. He then gathered the team around them and asked Baum about the story, demanding to know where he got the information from. He then denied it and excused Baum.

Some were glad he did it, just to keep a member of the media accountable for his actions. But others felt the grandstand move was a bit over the top. As if Beezer wouldn't be elated if he was traded to a contender.

Embarrassing Baum in the locker room was just one of a few displays of the true character—or lack thereof—of some of the players on the team. Most of it can be chalked up to the growing frustration from losing and the cloud of negativity that hovered over the team. But that doesn't excuse the behavior.

One instance late in the season involved Galley, who had turned sour by this time, and the team's media relations director, Jason Lagnese. It took place in the hallway outside the locker room after a game-day morning skate. Galley called to Lagnese with ticket requests from a few players. Lagnese, who was tending to reporters' needs—that's his job— nodded to Galley and told him he'd get to it once he was finished with the media.

Galley grew suddenly enraged.

"Fuck the media!" he shouted with several reporters standing a few feet away. "Your responsibility is to the players on this team."

Lagnese fired back at Galley, who was quickly scratched off the list for the end-of-season "Good Guy" award given by members of the local press. When he arrived, Galley appeared to be a likely candidate. But it was evident by midseason that the 38-year-old Galley only wanted the year to end so he could retire to his house in Ottawa with his family. Stuck on the worst team in hockey was no way to close out a career.

As expected, just before the trade deadline, Vanbiesbrouck was moved. Milbury did him a solid by sending him to the defending Cup champion Devils in exchange for veteran backup Chris Terreri, who had to be furious with the Devils for shipping him to the worst team in the league.

"I'm just excited to play," he said, showing not a trace of bitterness. "If I can get into another three, four or five games, it would be fun."

There wasn't much fun to be had, however, but by the time Terreri had arrived, at least Goring was already gone.

It finally happened in early March on a night the Islanders would suffer perhaps their worst and most embarrassing defeat in years—perhaps ever. It came on a Saturday night home game against, who else, the Tampa Bay Lightning. But this time it wasn't a crazy bounce of the puck or a poor line change. It came in a hailstorm of goals in a 6-0 loss that literally brought the house down on the beleaguered coach.

Afterward, Goring was his usual resilient self, denying implications that the team had quit on him. He said it was simply a problem of the players motivating themselves to perform.

"Regardless of who the coach is here," he said, "if you're not playing hard as a player, your career is going to be fairly short."

Goring's ended that night. He was called into the coach's office and given the news. There was a press conference called early the next morning. A team meeting was also called, scheduled earlier than the press conference.

When a few beat reporters arrived early to get reaction from players, one of them, a pesky antagonist named Jason Blake who was one of the few players devoted to Goring, glared at them.

"What the fuck are you doing here?" he snapped.

Of all of his many coaching moves, this one seemed to hurt Milbury the most. He held sincere personal feelings for Goring. Milbury actually hired Goring's daughter, Kellie, to babysit for Milbury's two sons. His goal was to make it to the end of the season, then quietly let Goring go. But with 12 games to go and the team riding a four-game losing streak, he couldn't afford to wait any longer.

"Collectively, it got to the point where they embarrassed themselves," Milbury said of the team. "I let nobody off the hook here. It's a tough business and coaches probably have it toughest of all. I was not prepared to let this season go by without addressing that attitude change."

Then Milbury, who remained downcast throughout the press conference, was introspective.

"It would have been easier to fire the manager," he said, knowing full well that Wang had already endorsed his return for another season. "I would have rather that have happened than have to be here today."

Goring wanted to hear none of it.

"If I'm the problem," he said in a phone interview with *Newsday*, "I'm not the only problem. I think they've got some other issues to look at." He then pointed out the most obvious, that being the lack of leadership among the team.

"There was no leadership in that room," he said, "and there still isn't."

He said that during the season he held an open meeting to discuss problems. The complaints came back one by one. First off, there were too many meetings, too many video sessions. And the wives' room didn't have good food.

"They blamed everybody but themselves," he said. "I knew then that they didn't get it."

What burned him the most was players after his firing admitting they didn't work hard enough.

"I never needed anyone to tell me I had to work hard," he said. "It's beyond me to comprehend a team not playing hard."

Bottom line, he said, was that somewhere along the line, he lost the team. Then he paused and corrected himself.

"I don't think I ever had them," he said, "since training camp."

The Islanders might have been rid of Goring—Henning was tapped as the interim coach to finish out the season—but Goring wasn't rid of the Islanders. He actually kept coming back to the Coliseum for games and was even spotted at Madison Square Garden before an Islanders–Rangers game chatting up with his old friend, Rangers coach Ron Low.

He would slip into the press box before game time, and sometimes he sat with opposing general managers, as if begging to be seen. After games, he would appear in the halls near the team's locker room. As much as it upset some of the players and as odd as it seemed to everyone else, Goring saw nothing wrong with it.

"I wasn't embarrassed for what I did for the hockey club," he explained during a *Newsday* interview in Anchorage, where Goring coached a semipro team before he was fired in December 2001. "I worked my butt off. I gave them whatever I had. Because the New York Islanders didn't think it was good enough, for whatever reasons, I had no reason to be embarrassed. I didn't do anything wrong."

The reality of the situation was that Goring literally had nowhere else to go. He was struggling personally with a failing marriage and then had lost the job he dreamed of having since he first got into coaching.

"I was in disbelief," he said. "It was such an important part of me and I was on the outside with nowhere to go. The team was still playing and I was sitting there with nothing to do. You know, I was wondering, 'What did I do wrong?' And, 'What could I have done?' I was totally frustrated."

In the bitter end, it was the failure to fulfill the dream that pains Goring still to this day.

"I wanted to be the shining knight," he said, "to bring them back to where they were in the '80s."

He left knowing that his once-oh-so-glorious legacy of four Cups and a playoff MVP in 1981 was now and forever tainted in the franchise by one awful season as coach. And that might be the hardest of all to take.

14

Hey 19

Family squabbles. I hate my boss. From millionaire to bankruptcy. Unlikely suicide watches. Switching sides.

Next on Springer?

Hardly.

Bryan Trottier was arguably the greatest all-around player in Islanders history, although, in truth, there's not much of an argument. Mike Bossy got the glory, Billy Smith got the cheers and Denis Potvin got the ultimate respect of being hated by fans of every opposing team, most notably the rival Rangers. But from the day he showed up in 1975 as a 19-year-old small-town farmboy, it was Trottier who defined the heart and soul of the champion Islanders as one of the best two-way centers the NHL ever has known.

From the day he was run out of the organization by increasingly cheap management to the day in 2002 when he received his first NHL head coaching job with the hated Rangers, Trottier's saga, more than any other player in Islanders history, also played out like a bad TV talk show.

Over the years, the story has been twisted, the reputations tainted, the truth stretched and the emotions bent out of and back into shape. Perhaps only Trottier himself knows the truth about all of the bitterness, innuendo and mudslinging that developed between himself and the Islanders throughout much of the 1990s.

Trottier eventually made peace with his past and himself when he agreed to allow the organization, led by new owners Charles Wang and Sanjay Kumar, to retire his famed No. 19 sweater early in the 2001-02 season.

But he added another bizarre chapter to his post-Islanders life when he accepted Rangers president Glen Sather's offer to replace fired Ron Low as the head coach of Manhattan's hockey team in June of 2002.

"Loyalties switch quick," Trottier said at his Rangers press conference.

Especially when one's loyalty has been so often tested.

Growing up in Long Island during the late 1970s, and especially during the 1980s, many of us were convinced that Trottier was the best all-around player in hockey, better even than the great Gretzky.

"In my mind, Trottier is 100 percent better, defensively," former Rangers goalie John Davidson once said. "From what I've seen of Trottier, he's the best there is."

Trots was the man. He played with a snarl. He played Butch Cassidy to Bossy's Sundance. In a five-season span beginning in 1976, he won the NHL's Calder Trophy (best rookie), the Art Ross Trophy (leading scorer), the Hart Trophy (most valuable player) and the Conn Smythe Trophy (playoff MVP).

He is the all-time scoring leader in Islanders history, with 1,353 points (of 1,425 in his career) in a team-record 1,123 games. He scored exactly 500 of his 524 goals for them, second only to Bossy, his inseparable longtime shotgun. He was named to the All-Star team eight times over. He drove a Porsche every day to work.

From 1982-83 through 1989-90, in fact, Trottier was one of the five highest paid players in the NHL, albeit before hockey salaries escalated to a par with those of North America's three larger-revenue sports—baseball, football and basketball. Still, the nine-year, $6.62 million contract he signed in the summer of 1983 was considered a landmark deal in its time.

But Trottier's relationship with the Islanders soured in 1990, when the team's dynasty years were behind them and the winning well finally had dried up.

His original agreement included $170,000 in retroactive pay for the 1982-83 season, the closest thing to a signing bonus that the contract contained. And it called for Trottier to receive a $500,000 loan from the team. But the Isles also had included in his contract stipulations to defer

$1.315 million owed Trottier in installments over a 10-year period after the deal expired following the 1991-92 season.

For purposes of the NHL Players' Association's collective bargaining agreement (CBA) with the league, the deal he signed was a 1982 standard player's contract. It included a standard clause stipulating that if the contract was bought out, Trottier would be entitled to two-thirds of the remaining value.

But when the NHL and the NHLPA negotiated a new CBA in 1988—with Trottier serving as president of the Players' Association, no less—the sides agreed that a 1986 standard contract would supersede all previously signed deals. In the 1986 standard player's contract, buyouts were payable over twice the length of the remaining years, but at a rate of as little as $50,000 per year.

When Torrey and the Islanders decided to buy out the final two years of Trottier's deal on July 1, 1990, he was owed $900,000 in 1990-91, $1 million in 1991-92 and the $1.315 million 10-year deferment. His production declining, the Islanders didn't deem him worth that sort of cake, history be damned. And the team suddenly had the right to pay two-thirds of the total owed him, spread over 25 years. It was more than willing to wield the hammer with its once-signature player. He was offered $50,000 a year for 24 years.

Trottier had no choice but to accept it. He had numerous business commitments, many of which were failing, and he needed whatever cash had been promised him. The problem was, if you made plans expecting $1.9 million over two years, $100,000 over that time wasn't going to go very far.

If it could happen to superstar rapper MC Hammer, it could happen to Bryan Trottier.

But how did it happen to No. 19? He was not just any man, he was a well-paid NHL superstar, a champion, a Hall of Famer, the greatest Islander of them all.

A national group even named him as one of the top 10 Fathers of the Year in 1984—along with then-Congressman Al Gore and TV personality Willard Scott.

Yet Trottier ended up in a U.S. bankruptcy court in Pittsburgh 10 years later. On October 11, 1994, he filed for Chapter 7 bankruptcy protection while claiming debts of $9,498,897.04 and assets of just $141,629.05.

According to court documents, he listed 16 creditors, including the Internal Revenue Service and the Pennsylvania Department of Revenue. He listed eight lawsuits to which he was party within one year of his bankruptcy filing.

"Bryan was a victim of two things," said Marc Hamroff, the attorney who represented Trottier through the bankruptcy proceedings. "The [real estate] market at the time. And very, very bad professional advice."

Trottier, who was raised in Val Marie, Saskatchewan (pop. 250) where his sister graduated in a class of six, also was the victim of his own naïveté.

In one of many court motions and affidavits, Trottier claimed in 1992 that his former agent, business manager and friend Bob Thornton, "mismanaged me in such a manner that I have gone from substantial wealth to serious financial problems. . . . The financial ruin caused to me [by] my former agent and business manager has caused me to literally lose millions of dollars."

Trottier claimed he was the victim of incompetence perpetrated not only by Thornton but by others, including attorneys who represented him in other shady investments.

Trottier met Thornton in 1977, two years after the center broke into the NHL at 19 and captured the Calder Trophy.

Thornton then was employed by Andrews Management, a Long Island-based company that managed the finances of high-income clients. Thornton's job was to look for endorsement deals for high-profile people like Trottier.

By 1981, Thornton and Trottier had become good friends, and the established NHL star hired Thornton as his agent and business manager.

"I was not a financial manager," Thornton told *Daily News* reporter Barry Meisel in 1994. "I never said I was. I knew hockey. I knew hockey rinks. I negotiated his big contract, which at the time was state of the art. I didn't tell Bryan what to do with his money. I was in favor of him doing what he wanted to do."

Thornton was not a lawyer. He was not an accountant nor a financial planner. Yet for nearly 10 years, Trottier's paychecks were mailed directly to Thornton's new company, International Management Services. Until they parted ways in 1991, IMS paid Trottier's bills and collected his business income.

Not that there was much of it.

In 1984, with the U.S. economy booming and with President Ronald Reagan's new income tax laws giving incentives for real estate investments, Trottier paid $265,000 of his $500,000 Islanders loan for a parcel of land housing a tennis bubble in tiny Manhasset, Long Island.

When Trottier couldn't get zoning approval to build an ice rink on the property, Thornton solicited partners to erect a two-story office building under the corporate name, Plandome Road Associates, with Trottier listed as the president and general partner.

Trottier was one of the cosigners on the $2.5 million mortgage. By 1986, however, the commercial real estate market fell apart when the U.S. Tax Reform Act of '86 was enacted. Real estate laws changed drastically, making it less beneficial for individuals to invest.

To compound the problem, Trottier's company, Plandome, entered into a deal with Arnold M. Diamond, Inc., a contracting firm that owned half of the property and controlled the building's second floor, to convert the building into condominiums in 1990.

But the building didn't go condo, the deal never went through and Diamond sued Trottier, Thornton and others for an undisclosed seven-figure sum in 1992.

Still, this failed investment didn't deter Thornton and Trottier from entering into others.

In 1985, the Bryan Trottier Skating Academy opened in an industrial park in Port Washington, Long Island. It advertised the availability of a synthetic new skating surface, called Glice.

The plastic ice never caught on, so BT Skating Corp. borrowed roughly $900,000 to install the regular kind. Thornton, who years later ran the Long Island Skating Academy in Syosset where the Islanders sometimes trained, was in charge of running Trottier's ice rink and the Bryan Trottier Hockey School.

He did so until 1991, when Trottier fired him with the rink losing money hand over fist. By 1993, Trottier lost control of the building when the bank foreclosed on the $1.3-million mortgage.

"The damage was already done when I got my hand on the switch," Trottier said.

The damage was done, and there weren't many solutions for Trottier as his debts accumulated.

He had played a few more seasons after his break with the Islanders, winning two more Stanley Cup rings as a role player with Mario Lemieux and the Pittsburgh Penguins. He even returned briefly to the Islanders after Pickett's transfer of operating control went through to the Gang of Four management group. He was named an executive assistant to president Jerome Grossman in 1992, a nebulous title if there ever was one. Trottier, wanting to be involved in the hockey operations, never was happy to be simply a frontman for the organization's promotional arm.

By the end of the 1992-93 season, he was back playing for Pittsburgh before he finally retired after the 1993-94 campaign. He took a job as an assistant coach with the Penguins, but his $300,000 annual salary didn't come close to offsetting his ever-spiraling debts.

While filing for bankruptcy might seem a dramatic and embarrassing step, the process doesn't hold anywhere near the stigma it once did. Before filing, Trottier, a self-proclaimed "fixer," thought of drastic ways to fix the problem for his family.

Fighting exhaustion and depression as his life spun out of control, one of the alternatives Trottier admitted contemplating was suicide.

"I never thought I was suicidal, but apparently I was," Trottier told the *Daily News*'s Meisel in 1994. "There were days where I thought, 'If I could just run [my car] into a brick wall . . . '"

The 38-year-old husband and father of three senselessly believed one big tragedy would eliminate the constant consternation and pain that had enveloped him from several years of poor business acumen, leading to nearly $10 million in debts.

"There was no way I was ever going to do anything," he told Meisel. "I knew my insurance policy. In there is something that says if you commit suicide, you don't get your death benefit. But I was trying to think of ways it wouldn't screw up the life insurance. I couldn't think of the way, so it was completely out of the picture. Plus, I didn't want to hurt anybody.

"But I did think about it. I felt everything I was doing was affecting my family—either financially or emotionally. I said to myself, 'One big hit. One last tragedy.'"

Thankfully, on September 5, 1994—six weeks before he and his first wife, Nickie, officially filed for bankruptcy protection—Trottier visited a psychologist in his Pittsburgh-area neighborhood. In individual and group therapy sessions once a week, Trottier learned about clinical depression and learned how to become better equipped to cope with the problems.

"Sometimes there's no solution, and I have to accept there's no solution," Trottier said.

Nickie, who split with Trottier in the mid 1990s after their bankruptcy case was settled, was frank with Bryan, especially when he informed her he'd considered killing himself.

"I was angry, sad, very concerned," Nickie told Meisel. "It was like, 'How could you ever think about that and leave me with three kids to take care of? What kind of future would that be?' He said, 'Well, you get the insurance policy.'

"But what's that? That's not life. That's not your best friend, your lover, your husband. That's not what a person needs to go on. That would have been a quick fixer-upper. It wouldn't have been what I needed."

After he consulted for some time with bankruptcy attorneys, Trottier decided to file a Chapter 7 petition, which is a liquidation of assets, instead of a Chapter 11 petition, which would have required him to pay off his debts in the future.

"It's not so much that you're losing the battle, you want to win the war," Trottier said. "Everything that you do in your life is not necessarily a battle. You just find there are different forms of adversity. You have players like [former Islanders teammate] Bobby Bourne, whose son has spina bifida. You find support, you find strength you didn't realize you had."

Trottier was able to keep his beautiful suburban Pittsburgh home, make his mortgage payments and collect his salary from the Penguins. Within six months, Trottier's $141,000 in assets were liquidated by a court-appointed trustee and much of his $9.5 million in debts wiped out by a judge's order.

"After all the good things that have happened, well, something bad happened. Is it the worst thing? No. It's just one thing," Trottier told *Newsday*'s Mark Hermann in 1994. "You learn it's all right to make mistakes. I'm going to make a lot more mistakes in my life. They just won't be the same mistakes.

"I didn't create the image of Bryan Trottier. I don't feel like I had an empire. I never stood on a soapbox and preached. If someone asked me a question, I tried to be as honest as I could."

Trottier prided himself on usually trying to give honest answers to reporters' questions, although one of his favorite replies from his playing days frequently was "You saw it, you write it."

This portion of this chapter wasn't easy for us to write. But as Trottier once said, "It might help somebody else. If it can happen to me, it can happen to anybody—white-collar workers, professional athletes, blue-collar workers.

"But I promise," he added, "there's a story here and it will be a positive one."

Trottier's story turned out just as he'd predicted, even if his ascension to NHL head coach came nearly 10 years later and with the Islanders' most heated crosstown rivals.

Still, his story with the Islanders didn't reach the closure stage until the new millennium.

In a six-year span, the organization had retired jerseys of five of Trottier's brethren from its Stanley Cup dynasty: Potvin (5), Bossy (22), Smith (31), Nystrom (23) and Gillies (9). Banners later were raised for Arbour, noting his 739 victories for the Islanders, and for Torrey, whose banner included a trademark bow-tie and the fitting phrase "the architect."

When one looked to the rafters at Nassau Coliseum, Trottier's fabled No. 19 was oddly absent. Trottier and the Islanders rarely commented publicly on the rift.

In varying interviews, Trottier gave the impression he hadn't allowed his jersey to be retired because he was upset about having been bought out of the last two years of his contract in 1990 and because the team failed to provide meaningful front-office duties when he returned in 1992-93.

But in 1998, a representative for Trottier, New Jersey-based agent Tom Happle, revealed another reason to reporter Rich Chere for a story in the *Newark Star-Ledger*. To take part in a retirement ceremony (and to make future PR appearances for the team), Trottier wanted $3 million. Players typically receive airfare and gifts at such events, but not payment.

"I told [the Islanders] it would cost $3 million [to retire No. 19] and the price is going up," said Happle, who met Trottier through the sports memorabilia business. "I have been given legal rights from Bryan for the retirement of his uniform not to happen even if he dies. They can retire No. 19, but they can't put his name on it."

Nystrom, an active member of the Islanders alumni, was livid over the ransom and said so in a story by *Newsday*'s Hahn in the spring of 2001.

"I don't understand why someone wouldn't want their jersey retired," said Nystrom, whose No. 23 was retired in April 1995. "For me, it was the greatest privilege I ever received. And I was half the player [Trottier] was."

Trottier's financial concerns continued through the latter part of the decade. The information page on his official web site, www.BryanTrottier.com, included fees that Trottier charged for speaking engagements ($2,500 plus travel expenses), one-day ($2,500) and seven-day ($7,000) appearances at hockey clinics, autograph signings ($10 per signature with a minimum of 500) and appearances at birthday parties and executive luncheons ($2,500 per hour).

Happle contended that Trottier should be handsomely compensated because the Islanders would benefit financially from the publicity such a retirement ceremony would generate. Several former players believed the Islanders were interested in their past only when they saw an opportunity to fill the arena for a night.

"When you keep shooting tradition and finally kill it, it's hard when you want to bring it back," Trottier said in 1998.

"Bryan went through some hard times. He had some difficult times. I back him 100 percent," Mike Bossy told Chere. "I'll ask you a question: Why, with players making three, four, five, six or seven million dollars a year, do teams depend on bringing back former players to fill the building?"

So what took so long? Why wasn't Trottier's jersey retired immediately after his retirement in 1994, or at least after he was inducted into hockey's Hall of Fame in November, with Lemieux and Sather, in 1997?

"It's not always what it seems to everyone else," Trottier told *Newsday*'s Hahn in a strangely contentious interview while an assistant coach with the Colorado Avalanche in 1999. "But all the stupid people, hey, let them say what they want to say.

"It's almost like I'm tired of responding because every time I respond, it gets misunderstood or something like that. I just keep saying the same things, but the stupid people think what they want to think."

In the summer of 2001, with Milbury's Islanders searching for yet another new coach and with Trottier having won his seventh Stanley Cup ring as an assistant with Colorado, new Isles owner Charles Wang telephoned Trottier and arranged a meeting.

No. 19 finally found its rightful place in the Coliseum rafters on October 20, 2001, in a ceremony before a game against the San Jose Sharks.

Each Islanders player wore Trottier's No. 19 during pregame warmups in tribute. Alexei Yashin, forced to switch from the No.19 he wore in Ottawa to No. 79 with Isles (he felt it looked closest to 19 on the jersey), was spotted getting an autograph from Trottier before the game.

"I'm going to ride high on this emotion for a long time. This is going to carry me for probably the next hundred years," said Trottier, who, for the record, wasn't paid for his appearance. "This is the grandest moment I could ever have on Long Island and I won four Cups here.

"It's great to finally be home."

The homecoming didn't last for long. Trottier returned to Colorado, again serving as head coach Bob Hartley's chief assistant as the defending champion Avalanche fell one victory short of returning to the Stanley Cup Finals in 2002.

Throughout the playoffs, in which the Islanders participated for the first time since 1994, Sather had conducted a search to replace Low, who'd been fired after the Blueshirts missed the postseason for the fifth consecutive spring.

Former Dallas coach Ken Hitchcock came in for an interview, before he was hired by the Philadelphia Flyers. Former Buffalo coach Ted Nolan, who also had interviewed with the Islanders the previous summer, also was among those to talk about the job with Sather.

But Sather also had briefly gauged Trottier's interest before the playoffs began, and he wanted to speak with him in depth once the Avalanche's run had concluded. Shortly after they were eliminated by the eventual champions, the Detroit Red Wings, in the Western Conference finals, Sather sent Trottier a nine-page questionnaire regarding his coaching philosophy.

Sather remembered the gritty, hard-nosed superstar Trottier was in helping to dispatch his Edmonton Oilers in the 1983 Stanley Cup Finals. He'd also heard that stars in Pittsburgh and Colorado, such as Lemieux and Ron Francis with the Penguins and Joe Sakic with the Avalanche, had spoken highly of Trottier's coaching ability and his easiness in relating with players of all skill levels.

The Rangers—with Messier, Eric Lindros, Brian Leetch and Pavel Bure on their returning roster—certainly didn't lack for star power. Sather was intrigued, and didn't seem deterred by Trottier's Islander ties.

When Trottier faxed his questionnaire responses to Sather's Palm Springs home—90 pages of legible hand-written copy—Sather knew he had his man. "His enthusiasm was overwhelming," Sather said.

Trottier, the Islanders legend, was the first to be offered the position as the 30th coach in Rangers history. He quickly agreed to a three-year contract worth roughly $2 million to turn to the dark side.

"I haven't changed wherever I've been," Trottier said, with his second wife, Jennifer, by his side.

But, oh, what an interesting and eventful ride it was.

15

"Back in Business"

The 2000-01 season had hardly ended before Milbury began the search for his next coach. An interesting note about it is that of the six coaching changes made during Milbury's tenure as GM, this was the first time he actually performed an official search.

Henning didn't need to be told he wasn't a candidate, and Ted Nolan didn't need to be told he was. The flood of phone calls from reporters to Nolan's house in St. Catherine, Ontario was enough of a hint.

But Milbury all along had his man in Laviolette. The question was whether he would be able to get him. The Bruins hadn't yet made a decision on Keenan, and therefore, Laviolette wasn't available for interviews.

So Milbury spoke with a short list of typical candidates that was headlined by Nolan—who was clearly the fan and media favorite—and two other retreads in Kevin Constantine and Bryan Murray. By early May, it appeared as if Milbury had decided on Murray, an experienced and knowledgeable hockey man who was fired as GM of the Florida Panthers that previous December. But Milbury wouldn't commit until after the Bruins decided what they were doing with Keenan, and, subsequently, Laviolette.

Then word came out of Boston that Keenan would not be brought back. Soon after, the Bruins named Robbie Ftorek, a schoolboy hero in Massachusetts who also had interviewed with Milbury, as their next head coach.

The ink had hardly dried on Ftorek's contract with the Bruins when Milbury was already on the phone with Laviolette, who, because he was passed over a second time for the Boston head job, was given permission to interview elsewhere. The day Ftorek was introduced at a press conference in Boston, Laviolette was on a plane to Long Island.

Milbury then discussed the matter with Wang, who liked Murray and considered Nolan an intriguing second choice. But Milbury's endorsement of Laviolette, a young coach with an altar-boy image and a brief but impressive history of success in the minor leagues, convinced Wang to follow his GM's hunch to hire the unknown, inexperienced candidate. This despite the expected negative reaction from the media and fans and despite a desperate need to win now.

"It if doesn't work," Milbury said to Wang after they agreed, "I know what comes next."

Wang smiled knowingly.

"Right," he replied. "It was nice working with you."

Laviolette arrived at Long Island's MacArthur Airport—which is located in the suburbs and is half the size of New York's big-time LaGuardia and Kennedy airports—on a rainy Tuesday evening. He was flanked by his engaging wife, Kristen, and his parents, Peter and Helen. Barely out of the gate at the small, quiet airport, Laviolette was already met with well-wishers who recognized him from the back page of the previous day's *Newsday*.

"Welcome to New York," a woman said with a warm smile.

"No," a man corrected, looking around the airport. "Welcome to Long Island."

The group climbed into a limousine sent by Wang to take them to the Garden City Hotel. Laviolette looked out the window almost the entire time, as if searching for scenery. For most of the ride, all he saw was the tree-lined Long Island Expressway. At least traffic wasn't as bad as advertised.

On first impression, Peter and Kristen make a handsome young couple, yet very much down-to-earth types. Along the way to the hotel, actually just a block away, Kristen started feeling carsick.

A quick story about how they met: Kristen had plans to be a flight attendant, but had a problem with motion sickness. Therefore, the airline she worked for had to move her to gate attendant. And when Laviolette was playing for the Providence Bruins, he met her while checking in for a flight during a road trip.

So Peter was well aware of her problem, and when he noticed her turning green, he asked the limo driver to pull over. They were right by a green in the middle of the Garden City village. Peter whisked Kristen out of the limo and over to a bush, where she proceeded to vomit all over the greenery.

The following day, during the press conference that introduced Laviolette as coach, he told the story to the media and got a long, hearty laugh. Peter explained how this has happened regularly at his many stops along the way.

"I guess you could say Long Island has now officially been christened," he said.

It was his ease and everyman personality that won over the gathering of cynics, who were ready to torch Milbury and the Islanders for another bonehead move.

"With just a little tweaking here and there, Peter Laviolette could turn out to be an excellent coach," wrote *Newsday*'s Mark Herrmann. "All he needs is a superstar forward, a No. 1 line, a good second-line center, a captain, a couple of gritty, veteran defensemen and a goaltender."

In the coming months, the Islanders would collect just about all of the above.

There were many holes to be filled in the lineup, but the most important need the team had was a top-line centerman. Two were available for trade, Boston's Jason Allison and Ottawa's Alexei Yashin, and two were going to be available via free agency, Jeremy Roenick and former Islander Pierre Turgeon.

There was some thought about free agency, but Milbury was concerned about having to compete financially for players on the open market. If he was unable to land either, then he'd be right back where he started. And there were no guarantees an Allison or Yashin would still be available for trade.

So a deal at the NHL draft, that year hosted by the Florida Panthers and held at the National Car Rental Center in Sunrise, Florida, was the plan of action.

Laviolette suggested Allison, a player with whom he had developed a solid relationship with the Bruins. He's big, strong, puts up huge numbers, is still young and has leadership qualities. All the assets Milbury loves.

Boston was not going to make it a fair deal for Milbury, especially after seeing Laviolette join forces with the former Bruin on Long Island. They were asking a lot in return, including the second overall pick in the draft, which the Islanders earned after the Atlanta Thrashers won the lottery.

It seemed a given that Milbury would move the pick, since the Thrashers would undoubtedly take Kovalchuk at No. 1.

But a few scouts were pushing for Yashin, who completed his contract obligations with the Senators in 2000-01 and was heading toward restricted free agency. Ottawa clearly wanted to move him, and many felt he was a more talented player who could come for a lower price, considering Ottawa's need to move him.

Santos had been doing legwork on two deals that would have landed both Yashin and Buffalo Sabres captain Michael Peca, who sat out the entire 2000-01 season without a contract. Milbury had tried to acquire Peca at the trade deadline, but Buffalo GM Darcy Reiger—you remember, Milbury's rival with the Islanders all those years ago—wouldn't budge.

If the Islanders took the Allison deal, they wouldn't have enough assets to also acquire Peca, Santos said. If they went with Yashin, they could get two centers—both at 27 years old and just coming into their prime—instead of one.

Milbury wanted Allison. So did Laviolette, who had developed a strong relationship with the player during his time in the Bruins organization. But the pro scouts talked it over and sided with Santos. A miffed and ever-stubborn Milbury finally relented.

"Go make your fucking trade," he told Santos.

And for the second straight year, the Islanders were the center of attention at the NHL draft. But this time, no one was laughing.

That Saturday morning of the draft, the Islanders dealt the pick, Chara and forward Bill Muckalt to Ottawa for Yashin. The Senators then used the pick to select Jason Spezza, a blue-chip center prospect who didn't figure to be in the NHL in the coming year. Still, some in the national media—especially in Canada—felt the need to say Milbury and the Islanders were fleeced on the deal.

They also ripped him and the Islanders for taking Yashin, a player who sat out an entire season demanding that his existing contract be torn up and renegotiated for a higher salary. Yashin was ridiculed in Ottawa for every move he made. Some of it was justified—and the result of a misguided player following the instructions of a contentious agent—and some of it was outrageous.

"Mother Theresa would have a bad reputation in Ottawa," Milbury quipped, which the Ottawa writers ate up with giggles and guffaws and then furiously spat back at him in their copy.

As far as an analysis of the trade, only Chara, a towering defenseman who was just coming into his own, was considered an impact player and emerged as one of Ottawa's top defensemen that season. Muckalt wound up not even scoring a goal for the Senators in 2001-02. Spezza was sent back to junior hockey.

But despite the expected skewering he took in Ottawa and many points north of the border, Milbury noticed a change in the way he was being perceived by the general media. It was a good deal. Yashin, a bull on skates with a deadly wrist shot, is a hell of a player. And there were enough rumors about an impending deal for Peca that the buzz around the Islanders continued well after the Yashin trade was announced.

For Milbury, that weekend at the draft was the start of his own personal renaissance.

Finally, he was working for a team that was playing to win. And the pieces looked to be falling into place. The team would no longer be a laughingstock.

Maybe he wouldn't either.

"I want to shed my 'Mad Mike' title," he said.

On Sunday, Santos worked Regier for Peca and reported back to Milbury. Each offer, Milbury thought, was too much. Peca was the captain they needed and undeniably one of the best two-way centers in the game. Getting him and Yashin would be a coup and would solidify the Islanders down the middle, with Scatchard and Claude Lapointe already in place at the bottom of the lineup.

But both Yashin and Peca were restricted free agents; therefore both would cost money. Wang didn't hesitate. Go for it, he said. So Milbury waited until midafternoon and then left the draft to head back to Long Island. He didn't figure to have a deal.

Then he got a call around 4 P.M., just as the draft was wrapping up. Milbury was at the airport. He was told Regier would take Connolly and Pyatt, two 19-year-olds, for Peca. The deal was made.

And suddenly something was brewing with the long-lost Islanders. Even the reactions of the new players—you recall Roman Hamrlik the year before—was refreshing.

"I think the unfortunate thing nowadays in professional sports is you don't have players that want to go in and help make a difference," Peca said, when asked about leaving a perennial playoff contender to join a team that hadn't made the playoffs in seven years. "Players want to go into a situation where it is already a winning situation. I think there is a lot more pride and a lot more satisfaction when you can contribute to something and turn it around."

Yashin and Peca weren't the only key players the Islanders acquired that weekend. On the eve of the draft, Milbury sent another youngster, lanky defenseman Mathieu Biron, to the Tampa Bay Lightning in exchange for defenseman Adrian Aucoin and forward Alexander Kharitonov. It went mostly overlooked because of the deals that followed, but the coming season would reveal the acquisition of Aucoin as a crucial one, as well.

Satisfied with their work at the draft, the Islanders were then relatively quiet in free agency. They made one noteworthy signing—goalie Garth Snow, who replaced Vanbiesbrouck as the veteran insurance for DiPietro. Snow is one of those goalies who is better than your average backup and yet not quite established as a No. 1. Therefore, there remained a feeling that the Islanders were a vastly improved team, but their goaltending situation was definitely a concern as the season drew closer.

Another free agent signing that received little fanfare but, like the acquisition of Aucoin, later proved to be a terrific pickup was Shawn Bates. He was a little-used but versatile forward who got lost in the Boston Bruins system. But he was a favorite of Laviolette's from his Bruins days, and the Islanders' scouts liked his speed, versatility and ability to work on the penalty-killing unit. They also felt the former Boston University star had more offensive upside than the Bruins projected for him.

There were a few other minor additions for depth, but otherwise the Islanders' roster had taken shape. Milbury was not done, however. He still had to negotiate contracts for Yashin and Peca.

Peca's deal seemed pretty simple. He had asked for $4 million per year from the Sabres, who refused and offered under $3 million. Peca and his agent, Don Meehan, then agreed to lower their asking price, with hopes that the Sabres would raise their offer to meet them in the middle. But the Sabres didn't budge.

So Wang figured to make him an offer that averaged $4 million, but spread out the totals over a lengthy contract. Five years at $20 million was the clincher. The first-year salary was $3 million, but the contract ballooned to $5.25 million in the final year, 2005-06, which would eliminate Peca's first summer eligible for unrestricted free agency.

Yashin's contract, however, was not as simple. Rumors out of Ottawa all throughout the previous season had Yashin and Gandler wanting $8 million to $10 million a year on the next contract. That was one of the Senators' main reasons for trading him, along with the fact that he was Public Enemy No. 1 after the holdout season.

But as much of a bulldog as Gandler is as an agent, he is also a shrewd man. He likes a splash, just as much as Milbury and Wang. He also, most importantly, appreciates loyalty. The Senators, he always contended, weren't ever loyal to Yashin. They drafted him No. 2 overall in 1992 and said he'd be their superstar. But then they took right wing Alexandre Daigle at No. 1 the following year and proceeded to promote the handsome and more marketable French Canadian. Yashin was by far the better player, but he was shy and reserved. He wasn't very well-spoken in English or French. He didn't have the poster-boy looks Daigle had.

And so it infuriated Gandler when he saw the Senators promoting Daigle and pushing him for the Calder in his impressive rookie season of 16 goals and 37 points in 47 games during the 1994-95 lockout season.

Yashin's rookie year, on one of the worst teams in the history of hockey, produced 30 goals and 79 points in 83 games. He was named to the All-Star team, but he didn't win the Calder—Devils goalie Martin Brodeur did. He didn't even finish second in the voting—that went to Edmonton Oilers center Jason Arnott, who had 33 goals and 68 points in 78 games.

The bottom line, Gandler told Milbury, was not simply about a financial commitment to his client, but a show of loyalty. So Milbury and Wang both came up with an idea that the team—while still playing in the Coliseum—could afford and Yashin and Gandler couldn't afford to pass up.

It was another warm July morning and Gandler was sipping tea on a patio at the Southampton Inn, where he was to discuss Yashin's contract. Milbury excused himself to take a phone call and eventually returned after a half-hour with apologies. Milbury, who had just gotten off the phone with Wang, then slid a legal pad containing a series of numbers across the table.

The scribble was the basics of a 10-year contract offer for a record total of around $90 million. It would set a new salary precedent in hockey and brought a wide smile to Gandler's face. Not only was it big money, it was also a big commitment.

Early conversations started with the usual six-year contract, but Gandler didn't like the idea of Yashin being 33 years old when it ended. That was too young to retire but too old to be considered a big-money player on the unrestricted free-agent market.

So Gandler asked for a shorter-term deal for big money. Wang didn't want to give up big money only to see Yashin skip town in three years via free agency.

So the night before Milbury was to sit down with Gandler at the Southampton Inn to get serious about a contract, he phoned Wang to talk out their options. But Wang didn't return the call until that morning.

Milbury informed Wang that Gandler wanted the short-term deal. Milbury wasn't comfortable with that.

"Well," Wang then said, "what do you think about a 10-year deal?"

Milbury blinked. What? Is this guy serious?

He then explained to Wang that, despite what you see in the NBA, monster deals like that aren't done in the NHL. First of all, the league only guarantees contracts up to five years. After that, you're on your own to get it insured.

But Milbury, always up for causing a stir, convinced himself that it could be done.

"Let's go for it," he said. He then grabbed a pad and put down numbers, in no particular order, off the top of his head. He later said he used a player he considered a fair comparison to Yashin, Toronto Maple Leafs center Mats Sundin, and a six-year, $52.5-million contract he recently signed. Milbury used the $8.75 million average as a base number.

When Milbury returned with the outline of the deal, he handed it to Gandler, who then took one look at it and excused himself.

"I have to make a phone call," he said.

The finances of the deal were in place by the latter weeks of July. The 10-year contract amounted to exactly $90,174,972 and, to date, remains the richest deal in NHL history. It was structured so that Yashin would make low-end figures at the start and finish of the contract (about $6.5 million the first and last year) with incremental raises until the middle. Then, for five years in the heart of the deal, Yashin will earn over $10 million per season, with the apex hitting $10,402,304 in 2008-09.

To some surprise, there are no bonuses—statistical performance or postseason awards—or any no-trade clauses involved in the deal. It is strictly a what-you-see-is-what-you-get contract.

Out of his own pocket, Wang is paying the insurance premiums on the final five years of the contract.

The experience left Gandler in a rare moment of speechlessness.

"It's not possible to compare," he said.

Neither was the optimism felt at training camp that September in Lake Placid. But it was a week before the season opener when all the pieces appeared to come together.

· The Detroit Red Wings had traded for superstar goalie Dominik Hasek over the summer in an attempt to make another big-money run at the Stanley Cup. Their incumbent starter, Chris Osgood, was immediately put on the block by GM Ken Holland. But with the rest of the league knowing that Holland was stuck having to move Osgood, he received only a few weak offers. By summer's end, he had no takers.

Milbury spoke with Holland a few times, but refused to ante up anything big for Osgood, who had two years and $7.75 million left on his current contract. Milbury tried to get Holland to eat some of the cash, but he refused. So Milbury, like everyone else in the league, figured to wait for the preseason waiver draft.

The Islanders, by virtue of their dismal last-place finish in 2000-01, were set to pick first. They could scoop up Osgood for nothing then. All Milbury had to do was convince Wang to allow space on the payroll budget to accommodate it. The team was already over $30 million, which was double the payroll the team had when Wang took over.

About a week before the waiver draft, and knowing Osgood would be left unprotected (teams are only allowed to protect two goalies and therefore Hasek and backup Manny Legace would be the ones Detroit would protect), Rangers GM Glen Sather made a trade offer to Detroit for Osgood. Sather, who always has been quietly down on beloved Rangers goalie Mike Richter, wanted to pull a fast one.

He offered center Mike York for Osgood, and Holland accepted. But before the deal was sent to the league for approval, Sather incredibly demanded that Holland take some of Osgood's salary. Amazing that the filthy-rich Rangers would do such a thing.

Milbury exhaled when he heard that the deal had fallen through. The Islanders had their chance to get Osgood, a two-time Cup champion with Detroit, one of those as the starter. After some convincing, Wang gave Milbury the green light. And for one rare situation, the NHL preseason waiver draft was a headline event.

For the first time since anyone could remember, the Islanders also were doing everything right. Milbury made sure to give credit where credit was due.

"The owners are making a statement to fans on Long Island who have been abused for such a long time," he said. "The Islanders are back in business."

Osgood, who couldn't wait to get out of Detroit and away from the controversy that sparked since Hasek arrived, flew immediately to Atlanta to meet the team for the final preseason game.

"I believe this is an up-and-coming team," he said of joining the revamped Islanders. "We should look at bigger things than just making the playoffs."

Laviolette dared to take it a step further. Following one practice, he boldly announced his expectation to win a Stanley Cup, much to the guffaws of reporters who circled him.

"I've seen lesser teams get into the Finals," he said, mentioning examples such as the 1998-99 Buffalo Sabres, the 1997-98 Washington Capitals and the 1995-96 Florida Panthers—all low seeds that fell just short of the Cup. "I would be disappointed if every team in the National Hockey League didn't have the Stanley Cup as their goal. If you don't set that then you're selling yourself short.

"I don't want to tell you that I hope we just make the playoffs," he continued, realizing that not a single one of the people he was speaking to believed a word he said. "I hope we win the Stanley Cup. I hope we can stay injury-free, the guys come together and we get the lucky bounce. All the stars align and everything else.

"I'm not going to tell you that we can't play for the Stanley Cup or win a championship," he added. "If I think that, then I shouldn't have been hired."

The following day, after reading his words and the *Newsday* headline, "Laviolette: Let's Play for the Cup," Laviolette had settled down some.

"Look, it's not like I guaranteed we're going to win it," he said, rolling his eyes at the sight of his claims in print.

There was no mistaking that the arrival of Osgood was met with mutual anticipation. He stopped 26 shots in a 3-1 victory over the Thrashers, who, coincidentally, picked second in the waiver draft and likely would have taken him had the Islanders not.

But everyone on Long Island was glad the Islanders did. Well, just about everyone. DiPietro pulled aside a reporter a day after the Atlanta game and asked, "How was he? Is he that good?"

"Yeah, Rick," the reporter replied, "he is."

DiPietro then looked at the carpeted floor in the hallway outside the Islanders' locker room and knew what fate lay before him. It would be Bridgeport, the team's new American Hockey League affiliate owned by, of all people, the Islanders' first owner, Roy Boe.

"You gotta write that I'm playing really good," the desperate DiPietro then replied as he walked away.

Snow also wasn't pleased with the move, but in the long run it proved to be a blessing even for him. That month his older brother, Glenn, suffered a stroke while battling leukemia. By late October, Glenn Snow was gone. Snow spent most of September and October driving back and forth from his family's home in Wrentham, Mass. He later admitted that he would have put the Islanders in a tough spot had Osgood not been there to carry the load early on.

And carry the load, Ozzie did. Wearing his red and white equipment from his Detroit days along with his orange and blue Islanders uniform, Osgood put forth a dominating effort in the opening month of October. In 10 starts, he went 8-1-1 with a 1.85 goals-against average and a .936 save percentage. He earned NHL Player of the Month for his dynamic October. He became the first Islander player of the month since Mike Bossy earned the distinction in November of 1986.

Recalling history became a recurring theme that season.

"Right from the first game of the preseason, he has been a calming presence," Peca said of Osgood. "The way he has played has allowed us to be less apprehensive in our own end."

Less apprehensive, but still a bit shaky in the clutch. An incredible stat from the team's incredible start to the season was that they were just 14.5 seconds away from being 11-0 in the month of October. They blew a 4-3 lead against the Red Wings with 9.4 seconds left in regulation before losing, 5-4, in OT. Then a week later they blew a 2-1 lead with 5.1 seconds left in regulation to settle for a tie with San Jose.

A runner-up to Osgood in October was Mark Parrish, who was red-hot with 11 goals in the 11 games and was clearly rejuvenated on a line with Peca and Bates—a line radio announcer Chris King dubbed "the Lucky Sevens" because their jersey numbers each ended with a seven.

Laviolette drew rave reviews, as well, but did all that he could to deflect attention from himself. Milbury the same. It seemed everyone was as overwhelmed as they were psyched up about the fast start. Milbury, especially, was careful not to allow himself to boast too much too soon. He knew there was still plenty of season left.

But October would prove to be an undeniably crucial segment of the season.

16

9-11

It had to be some kind of eerie coincidence that brought the Islanders to visit Ground Zero on October 31, 2001, the final day of one of the most successful opening months in franchise history.

Consider that one night earlier they had defeated the Florida Panthers, 3-2, at the Coliseum for their ninth win of the season along with a tie and an overtime loss.

Their record, therefore, stood at 9-0-1-1.

Look at those numbers again.

Like many sports teams that year, most especially New York teams, the Islanders did their best to respectfully acknowledge the horrific events of September 11 and honor the heroes of that day. At the home opener on October 13 against Detroit, players from both teams, referees Kevin Maguire and Stephen Walkom and linesmen David Brisebois and Danny McCourt joined members of the NYPD, FDNY and EMT crews to unfurl a gigantic American flag at center ice during the singing of "God Bless America" and the national anthem. When the Islanders were introduced to the raucous home crowd by well-known "Let's Get Ready to Rumble!" announcer Michael Buffer, the players came out wearing hats representing the police, fire, port authority, paramedics and other service units who were part of the rescue effort in the wake of the attacks on the World Trade Center.

Peca, who suffered a concussion after taking a nasty hit earlier in the week against Mike Wilson of the Pittsburgh Penguins and did not play in the home opener, came out in the uniform of a port authority police officer.

Two Islanders that had a direct connection to the tragic events were Milbury and Laviolette. Milbury was friends with and a former neighbor of Garnett "Ace" Bailey, a former Bruin who was on one of the planes that slammed into the towers. Laviolette was friends with Mark Bavis, a former teammate with the Providence Bruins, who was also on that flight. Bailey and Bavis were scouts for the Los Angeles Kings.

"You try to think what was going on in the plane," Milbury said, "what was going on in his mind."

Laviolette, who twice represented Team U.S.A. in the Olympics, met with a group of reporters after practice and said his "stomach is in knots. It's a tragic thing. Everybody is sick about it. It makes me nauseous."

Other members of the team began to hear about friends and neighbors who were involved. Everyone was glued to cell phones and televisions the entire week.

Unlike the Rangers, who had planned to open training camp the week of September 10 at midtown Madison Square Garden, the Islanders were far away from the tragic events of September 11, tucked in the tranquil safety of the Adirondack Mountains at their training site in Lake Placid with the first group of players due on the Olympic Center ice by 9 A.M. That group was already dressed and warming up when the first airliner hit the tower of the World Trade Center. Laviolette had scolded minor-league goalie Stephen Valiquette and fellow minor-league prospect Juraj Kolnik for being late on the ice, and, at the time, a couple of beat writers sitting in the stands jotted notes about the obvious first-day story.

Of course, none of them, or anyone in the arena, knew anything about the tragic events that were unfolding at that time in lower Manhattan, Washington, D.C. and Pennsylvania.

The news quickly circulated as players from the second group arrived at the arena. Players filed in and out of a lounge where a television was on. Immediately, all conversation focused on the terrorist attacks. With phone lines and cellular signals overwhelmed, everyone scrambled to call home to check on family and friends. Security personnel at the Olympic Center closed the facility to visitors and tourists.

"Everybody was watching TV," Yashin said. "You never knew what would happen next."

"I couldn't stop watching," Claude Lapointe said. "I was up all night."

Yashin, who is Russian, and Lapointe, who is French-Canadian, were examples of the international interest in the attack on the United States. The Polish-born Czerkawski said the nightmarish images on the television screen didn't only affect Americans.

"I don't think it matters if you're American, Polish, Russian or Swedish," he said. "You feel the pain. It's just something that really hurts. So many people were affected by it. It's amazing."

Czerkawski was part of the third group that wasn't scheduled to take the ice until 1 P.M. That group witnessed the events as they happened after switching on the television. He and Isbister, his roommate, casually turned on the TV and saw the aftermath of the first plane that hit the first tower. Then, on live TV, they watched in horror along with millions of people as the second plane rammed the other tower.

"That was just sick," Czerkawski said. "It was like a movie."

DiPietro, one of six American-born players in camp for the Islanders, just shook his head.

"It's just crazy to see the World Trade Center isn't standing anymore," he said.

Milbury, a normally fiery personality on his own, was sitting in the stands watching the team practice when he was told of the horrible news.

"It's sickening," was all he could come up with as a reaction. "Just sickening."

Milbury considered canceling practice, but decided it was best to continue on with their business. "The team is kind of minor," he said, "compared with what's going on in the world."

But, as for most, life did go on. The season went on. And then the team revisited the horror and the sadness on a drizzly Halloween morning. That's when they saw the result of the destruction firsthand.

It was a scene, as many already know, that defied spoken or, in this case, written language. And even that doesn't pay it enough respect.

"How do you describe this?" one player asked reverently, as the team entered the Ground Zero viewing area.

The Islanders were just the umpteenth sports team or celebrity group to pay a visit, but the policemen, firemen, reservists and volunteers all greeted them with an appreciative warmth. The feeling was obviously mutual.

The team met at Nassau Coliseum at 9:30 A.M., less than 12 hours after another successful night on the ice, a win over the Florida Panthers. The players were still full of the usual post-win giddiness, chattering away and laughing easily as the Harran bus—which, as folks on the streets of Manhattan were quick to notice, has for years used a large logo that includes the skyline of the city with the Twin Towers the most prominent on the sides of all of its buses—followed the flow of traffic along the Long Island Expressway. The players noticed a huge billboard promoting the Islanders with the slogan "We're Back!" just outside the Midtown Tunnel.

The bus was stopped momentarily by National Guard soldiers at a checkpoint just before the entrance to the tunnel. When one soldier heard the bus was carrying the Islanders, his face lit up.

"Oh, the New York Islanders?" he chirped. "Heard you guys had a great game last night. Keep up the good work."

Then the soldiers stood at attention and saluted the bus as it drove by. Last season's last-place finish suddenly felt like 10 years ago.

The first stop was at the temporary headquarters of the Office of Emergency Management on the upper West Side. The entourage was met with smiles and handshakes and, when the team was announced as "the first-place New York Islanders," rousing applause. The group dispersed among the volunteers to sign autographs, take pictures and present autographed jerseys to the FDNY and NYPD areas. It was a genuine scene, with images such as Yashin and Kharitonov sitting at a computer terminal attentively listening to a worker describe what his responsibilities were. Peca signed anything and everything handed his way. Even Radek Martinek, a Czech-born rookie who at the time spoke and understood very little English, nodded politely and smiled at people who came up to him looking for an autograph or just to say hello.

Garth Snow spoke with a group of reservists from Long Island who were Islanders fans. One was a Coast Guard reservist from Long Island, who named a host of sports teams and dignitaries that had made their way through the center over the past month. He said it never got tiresome.

"It's good for morale," he said. "It's funny, you're in awe of them and they're in awe of you. It's like a mutual admiration society."

That part, of course, was upbeat. The mood was still light during the police-escorted bus ride down the West Side Highway toward the site. At one final checkpoint, a police officer heard that the bus was carrying the Islanders. He shook his head as if to decline permission for them to enter.

"Ranger fans only," he said in a thick New York accent. After all, the Islanders were deep in enemy territory.

The laughter subsided when an OEM officer who acted as the sort-of tour guide of the trip pointed out the window toward an obvious hole in the skyline.

"That's where the towers used to be," he said.

And with that, conversation immediately dropped to nothing more than a low murmur. When the bus pulled to a stop, another bus carrying the Panthers had just pulled away.

A short walk around Battery Park and past the moving makeshift memorial of flowers and pictures led to a construction entrance to the Ground Zero work site. Hard hats were distributed, and the group entered the site and gathered on a platform that served as a balcony to destruction. An OEM communications director and survivor of the tragedy—who made it a point to announce that he was a Long Islander and also an Islanders fan—answered questions about the site and told chilling first-person stories about the events of September 11. He had everyone's ear, but their eyes were on the incredible, smoldering crater of twisted iron, pulverized concrete and glass.

One would wonder if some of the European players, such as Czech-born Roman Hamrlik, were less affected by the images of devastation, considering what they have seen or even experienced in their own home countries.

The visit was over around 1:30 P.M., and the group exited the site. At the same time, a group of bereaved families entered carrying flowers and sobbing quietly. It was then that everyone among the Islanders, whether Russian, Czech, Swedish, Polish, Canadian or American, realized where they had just been.

Scatchard, for one, ducked his head to wipe tears from his eyes.

17

"White-Knuckle to the End"

The good times for the Islanders in 2001-02 rolled on for another week in November, when the team earned a 3-0 win over Tampa Bay at home for Osgood's third shutout of the season. The record stood at 11-1-1-1, which was the best in the Eastern Conference.

That was November 6. It would be 13 days before they claimed win No. 12, as a five-game winless streak finally put the brakes on the unbelievable start. Laviolette battled cynical reporters who continually pointed out to him that this was simply the typical holiday-season swoon for the Islanders. It was evident. Every season in recent history had seen a collapse in either November or December that pretty much ruined any hope for the playoffs. Despite the terrific opening, this team apparently wasn't safe from it either.

Laviolette, however, hated hearing such talk.

"I don't buy into it that 'Here we go again,'" he snapped. "I buy into the fact that all teams go through it and we'll be stronger when we come out of it. When we do, we're moving on and up. That's the way I feel about it."

Peca, who to no one's surprise was named captain at the start of the season, showed his usual awareness to the prevailing thought. Being a sports fan at heart and a guy who reads the papers, Peca knew exactly what this streak appeared to be to those who followed the downtrodden franchise. It was the other skate finally dropping. The real Islanders showing up.

So he used it as motivation.

"This is a perfect chance for us to prove that we're a different team," he then said, acknowledging the well-documented past failures of the franchise. "This is where the guys who were brought in and the guys who have stepped up in the past, this is the time to step up and show that we're a team to be reckoned with. We can't let this slide and just fall back into mediocrity. We've got to reestablish ourselves as a force in this conference and this league."

A day off in Dallas set up an opportunity for Laviolette to organize an impromptu billiards tournament with the players at a team hotel. This after coming off an embarrassing 6-1 loss at Phoenix. Laviolette knew the team needed to loosen up. The idea worked, as the streak ended against the Stars with a 3-2 win to kick off a six-game unbeaten streak. The team managed to escape November with a winning record (6-5-3) and a 15-5-4-1 mark overall.

December wouldn't be as lenient. Yashin practically carried the team through a dismal offensive slump. He exploded in November with eight goals and 16 points in 14 games and then followed it up in December with four goals and 12 points in 12 games.

But with his consistent scoring—all the while playing with a broken finger—Yashin was clearly not finding chemistry with Isbister and especially Czerkawski, who didn't score his first goal until the ninth game of the season and scored just 12 goals and 27 points in the first half of the season, well below his 30-goal pace from the previous two years.

Before the season started, Czerkawski was excited about playing with Yashin. He even dared to say that 40 goals was his target number. But while the streaky sniper thrived under the passive Goring and under the radar of a mostly overlooked losing team, he failed to gain the confidence of Laviolette and Yashin. At times he wouldn't see regular shifts on the power play, which was usually his specialty.

Laviolette learned quickly that Czerkawski was a high-maintenance player. He had to keep riding him, keep reminding him of his assignments and constantly talk with him after practices. Czerkawski, a very warm and friendly guy who loves the camera and attention and is adored in his native country, is simply a sniper, a goal scorer. But anything beyond that, Laviolette learned, especially if it involved decision making or back-checking, the player couldn't handle.

In late December, with Yashin clearly frustrated with the situation around him, Milbury made an attempt to acquire 40-goal winger Tony

Amonte from the Chicago Blackhawks. The deal would have included DiPietro going in return, but the Hawks decided against it at the last minute.

But Czerkawski wasn't the only forward not pulling his weight. Kvasha, after a decent start, went ice cold both in performance and in personality. Laviolette, by suggestion of Milbury, tried to get the big young Russian going. He moved an ineffective and practically invisible Isbister off the top line and put Kvasha at Yashin's left wing. Nothing.

Fans at the Coliseum got to a point where they booed Kvasha, who at 22 was the youngest player on the team, every time he touched the puck. When the Islanders held a pregame ceremony to honor the players selected for the Olympics, they announced Russian teammates Kvasha and Yashin together just to spare Kvasha anticipated abuse. Islanders fans wouldn't boo Alexei Yashin.

Especially not after his performance at Madison Square Garden on January 30, in what was one of the most dominating periods any recent Islanders player has ever had. He scored a hat trick in the first period, with two of the goals coming in a blazing 75-second span and a third coming off a spectacular stick-handling move by a stunned Mark Messier.

He also got involved in one of the many brawls of the night. He was aided by Czerkawski, who pinned down the arms of Rangers defenseman Tomas Kloucek. Moments before, Kloucek had swatted Yashin across the mouth. But Yashin, who earned the first fighting major of his career, raged back at the suddenly defenseless Kloucek with a flurry of shots.

"That," said tough guy Eric Cairns, "was awesome."

"He tried to pull my shirt off," Yashin said, explaining his surprising anger. "I had to fight back."

Laviolette tried hard not to smile when asked about his star center's sudden and rare display of emotion. "It's not something that happens a lot," he said. "But it's against the Rangers, so you never know what's going to pop up on a given night."

Yes, it is safe to say that if anything was accomplished during the 2001-02 season, it was that the Islanders–Rangers rivalry reignited. All of this thanks to Fleury (whose antics that season have already been documented in this book), an entertaining, bravado-filled rivalry between Cairns and Sandy McCarthy and, of course, the fact that both teams were in contention for a playoff spot.

The Rangers, however, failed to qualify in the end. What made it all the more delicious for Islanders fans was that one of the final blows to the Rangers' season came on March 25 at the Coliseum, with a rock solid

4-2 Islanders victory. In that game, Kvasha, who scored a pair of goals, including the game winner, became a hero and the Coliseum fans turned the boos from earlier in the season to cheers.

It got ridiculous from that point on with Kvasha, who inexplicably exploded for seven goals in the final 12 games of the season after scoring six in the first 70 (with three of them coming in the first nine games of the season). The guy was a cult hero by the time the playoffs began.

He did this after returning from a knee injury that required arthroscopic surgery. He played so well after it that Wang suggested the doctors work on other parts of his body. Reporters joked that the doctors might have also performed a heart transplant.

But before all of this, the Islanders were themselves teetering on the brink of disaster. They endured a few injury problems that thinned out the defense, with Martinek, an impressive rookie, out for the season with an ACL tear and Hamrlik out 11 games with a knee sprain.

The team also learned that Haller, who appeared in just one game—the season opener—before taking himself out of the lineup, was again done for the year because of a chronic groin problem that he has yet to solve. Haller was signed as an unrestricted free agent in the summer of 2000 and in his first two seasons played just 31 of 164 games. And the team still owed him another year on his contract at $1.7 million heading into 2002-03, though there was little hope he would return to the ice.

So for most of the rest of the season, Laviolette depended heavily on Jonsson and Aucoin, who, after being lost in the shuffle early on, was having a breakout season. Actually, Aucoin might not have enjoyed the season he had—12 goals and 34 points with a plus-23 rating—if it weren't for the injury to Martinek. Gordie Clark and Milbury had been urging Laviolette to use Aucoin more, and when Martinek went down, Aucoin stepped up and scored 11 goals and 22 points in the second half of the season. He also emerged as a leader on and off the ice, as he became one of Peca's most trusted lieutenants.

The Islanders headed into the February Olympic break on a high as they parlayed Yashin's big game against the Rangers in January to a 4-1-1 run that put them at 29-19-6-3. The final game was on February 12, and it was memorable. In Philadelphia, Snow out-dueled Roman Cechmanek in a scoreless tie through regulation. Then Peca won it on a shorthanded breakaway with 8.1 seconds left.

The victory gave the Islanders their first-ever season-series road sweep in Philly and moved them within seven points of the Atlantic Division-leading Flyers.

"It's huge," Aucoin said of the Islanders' run just before the break. "I mean, this is the time right now. There are so many teams piling up in the eighth spot, we want to get way ahead of them where we're not even worrying about it."

The worry came afterward.

Peca, who was Mr. Clutch many times during the season, provided more last-second heroics when he scored with 1.4 seconds left in regulation to earn a tie with Boston in the first game back from the break. Things couldn't have looked better as talk began of not just clinching a playoff spot, but going for a top four seed in the East and possibly catching the Flyers for the Atlantic.

The next block of seven games brought all opponents with losing records: a home-and-home with Atlanta, home games against Pittsburgh and Buffalo, at Columbus, again home against Atlanta and then at Buffalo. Piece of cake, right?

Wrong.

The team had hit a wall. Suddenly it had no legs, no chemistry on offense and no determination in the trenches. All the trademarks of their success early on and leading into the Olympic break were missing.

It appeared that the effects of a year off from his contract holdout in 2000–01 with Buffalo were wearing on Peca, who, despite being known as a hard-hitting, physical player, is hardly chiseled from stone at 5'11", 190 pounds.

He later revealed that he played the entire season with a very sore shoulder as a result of a hit in the season opener. Without knowing this, Milbury had quietly criticized his captain for not playing the style that became his trademark with the Sabres. The offense was certainly nice, Milbury said, but where was Captain Crunch?

Then Milbury focused his attention on the coaching staff, whom he felt had been soft on the team for the most part and unwilling to open up the lineup so others could get a chance. Examples included Scatchard, who scored 21 goals the season before but was relegated to being an extra for most of this season, and Cairns, who carried the burden of being labeled as a fighter though he wanted to be more of a complete player. Neither had much confidence in themselves during the early part of the season because of diminished ice time and diminished roles.

And, though he forced himself into the background for most of the season, Milbury felt it was time to speak up. Things had suddenly taken a turn for the worse and the attitude around the team was starting to slip. He knew opening his mouth might start trouble, as it often does, but with just over a month left in the season and a playoff spot far from being a lock, he just couldn't stand by idly any longer.

"It looked like the wheels were falling off the wagon," Milbury said in a *Newsday* interview. He went on to explain that when the team arrived in Columbus on March 8 to play the last-place Blue Jackets, the concerned GM met with the coaching staff to voice his displeasure. The trade deadline was less than two weeks away and he needed to know if major changes were necessary.

What he really wanted to know was if his 37-year-old rookie head coach had a grip on his team. He needed to know he had hired the right guy.

So he began with a tirade about the slumping power play—aimed at assistant coach Kelly Miller—and the team's dreadfully slow starts to games. And then, just as his infamous rage was building, Milbury was cut off.

"Hey," Laviolette calmly but sternly said, looking his boss right in the eye, "it's going to be all right."

For whatever reason, Milbury believed him. There was something about the confidence in Laviolette's eyes and voice. Milbury left the meeting satisfied.

That night, however, saw another bad loss, the team's third straight. But they were mostly done in by a nightmarish performance by Osgood, who was uncharacteristically shaky on three bad first-period goals. Milbury watched the game from the visiting coaches' suite and knew Laviolette was agonizing on the bench. But the defeat didn't shake his confidence after the reassurance the young coach had given him earlier in the day.

If anything, Milbury was impressed with Laviolette's fire. It made him root for the coach even more.

"At that point, I knew he could look me in the eye and tell me, 'No problem, I'm in charge,'" Milbury said. "And I think that's when he established himself with the team."

But there were still issues to address within the team. The seven-game stretch ended with an unacceptable 3-4 record. But a flatline effort in a loss to the Devils had Yashin concerned. He went to Peca before the team was to play the Senators in Ottawa and suggested a team meeting. But Peca, who after the loss in New Jersey ripped the team for a performance he dubbed "disgusting" and also referred to "babysitting" certain players, felt that enough had been said already.

There was little doubt that Peca's postgame comments were regarding inconsistent players such as Czerkawski and Hamrlik, who were always more concerned about their ice time instead of what they made of it.

"Just talking to the core players," Peca said, "you get fed up with not seeing everybody come to play every night. We said, 'If you can't come to play this time of year, you have to question your commitment to the team.'"

Peca's reasoning for declining the request from Yashin to have a pregame discussion with the team in Ottawa was, in his mind, simple.

"We can do and say what we like before a game," he said, "but unless you actually walk up and smack them upside the head, they won't be ready. And I'm not going to sacrifice my own preparation to make sure someone else is ready."

Yashin, despite his scoring prowess, was also known to occasionally take a shift off. That bothered a lot of the team, though many observers could see that Yashin was taking a beating on the ice, with two and three defenders hounding him. That has been the game plan against him since he first entered the league. Of course it works even better when you have players such as floaters Czerkawski and Kvasha and a struggling Isbister flanking him. So it might not have been as if Yashin gave up on plays as much as he simply wore down as the season went on.

Publicly, Yashin never complained and never allowed the public to see his frustration, despite a suggestion from one of his confidantes that by the latter stages of the season he had grown increasingly unhappy, considering that Milbury had not brought in better linemates for him as promised.

"I'm a professional hockey player. I can't be going around saying, 'I can't play with this guy,' you know what I mean?" Yashin said one morning, while tending to his stick preparation, a labor of love that was like a daily religion for him. It was usually the best time to catch him in a mood to talk, when most of the team had left and the hallways were quiet.

Yashin isn't an outwardly friendly person, but he is polite and can be engaging once he opens up. And he won't lie to you as much as he will hide the truth by avoiding questions he doesn't want to answer (such as those about injuries).

So in this conversation, Yashin decided to address the frustration of being double-teamed while his linemates did nothing to draw defensive attention away from him.

"It's what's happened to me the last four to five years I've played," he said of the shadows. "But it opens up so much space for other guys . . . It's part of the learning process to make scoring chances and then make them goals. That's the challenge."

But Yashin had more to contend with that night in Ottawa than a constant double-team or ineffective wingers. The score was 3-0 Senators by the 11:44 mark of the first period. It was 4-0 early in the second.

Coincidentally, Yashin's old linemate with the Sens, left wing Shawn McEachern, recorded an assist on all four goals. Yashin longed to have McEachern, a speedy, keep-it-simple forward with good hands, back on his side.

The game ended at 4-3, which, on paper, doesn't appear all that bad for the losing team. But the players and anyone watching knew better. Laviolette met with the media and offered terse, monosyllabic responses.

Did the comeback salvage anything for this game?

"No."

Are you concerned about your team?

"No."

Should you be?

"No."

(Pause)

"I don't know," Laviolette then said. "Maybe you should ask them."

To do that, members of the media had to wait around a while. Almost an hour, actually. The locker room door was locked shut, and inside, the players were airing it out.

Finally, Peca emerged. It was hard not to overlook that he was showered and dressed, suggesting that the meeting might not have lasted the entire 50-plus minutes the door stayed closed.

"We're all disappointed in one another," Peca said to a cluster of cameras and microphones that surrounded him. "It's sad. We've done some great things this year and, you know, we need to realize we haven't got a solid spot in the playoffs. In a blink of an eye, two and a half weeks pass by and we might be looking ahead to see if we can catch an eighth-place team. And it's sad. We've done way too many good things this season to possibly look back and have regrets."

Milbury applauded the meeting but downplayed any notion suggested by the players that a trade needed to be made. The deadline was looming and with the team in Toronto for two days, rumors were flying out of every corner of the city. Isbister was at the epicenter of a trade that involved the Edmonton Oilers sending soft but skilled defenseman Tom Poti in exchange. Milbury wanted more and mentioned Anson Carter, who was heading to restricted free agency (and therefore pricing himself out of tight-budgeted Edmonton) and would fit nicely at left wing next to Yashin. But Lowe hedged.

Eventually, Lowe accepted an offer of Mike York from the Rangers for Poti and Rem Murray and hung onto Carter for what became a failed playoff push.

Milbury had also made strong attempts to land Darius Kasparaitis from the Pittsburgh Penguins. He is the one player whom Milbury has long regretted trading and whom Wang quickly grew to appreciate because, like Wang, Kasparaitis is a devoted Long Island resident. He waited all season for the cost-conscious Pens to deal him and held out hope that it would be to the Islanders.

"I'll be happy to play for the Islanders," Kasparaitis said in January before a game at Nassau Coliseum. "I was always happy to play for them. I got traded. That was my first team, I have a lot of good memories. I would be happy to come back, I consider Long Island my home. I live here during the summer and I have a lot of friends. Every time I finish the season in Pittsburgh, I come to Long Island. It means a lot to me."

Milbury was outbid at the deadline by the Colorado Avalanche, who landed Kasparaitis mostly just so he wouldn't wind up on rival Detroit. Milbury would have to wait for the summer to try again to bring Kasparaitis back home, but the hard-hitting defenseman wound up yet another free agent to accept a lucrative contract from the blank-check Rangers.

Meanwhile, Milbury picked up another defenseman, Darren Van Impe, in a far more unheralded move to add depth at the trade deadline. Isbister was relieved when his cell phone didn't ring that afternoon.

Overall, there was some mild surprise that Milbury didn't try to pull something big to shake up his struggling team. But the truth is he wanted to, only he was cautious not to overspend just for the sake of making a trade.

Safe to say, Milbury learned from his own mistakes over the years.

"We made a ton of moves in the summer," he explained. "We have a team that is good enough to get there. We're not a perfect team, but we have enough to win games and make the playoffs.

"In some cases people were asking too much for what was offered. I can only do what I can do. We did the best we can with what we have. We're a team that finished dead last last year. We added tens of millions to the payroll. We're good enough to get there. We should be a playoff team."

No one could argue. And with a few days off to recharge, along with the fun of a bowling tournament Laviolette set up when the team arrived in Toronto, the Islanders were ready to get back to work.

"Too many meetings," Laviolette said. "It's time to shut up and put up."

That's exactly what they did. Following a hard-fought overtime loss to the Maple Leafs, a building-block game if there ever was one, the Islanders finally got it together and reeled off three straight wins and built an unstoppable momentum that carried them to 10 victories in the final 14 games of the season.

They seemed to get stronger and stronger and pull out gutsy performances in key moments, much like the start of the season. Yashin scored key goals and the power play was clicking. Kvasha stunningly emerged. Parrish caught fire again. Osgood was on top of his game. Jonsson and Aucoin were a brilliant tandem. Even Peca, despite the shoulder, was hitting people again. The penalty-killing unit, which included unsung hero Claude Lapointe throwing his body in front of shots, was dominant.

And, most importantly, the few setbacks along the way were never allowed to fester.

Finally, the goal was in sight. Sitting in the sixth spot in the East at the start of April, a playoff berth was just a few precious points away, with teams such as the Devils, Montreal, Washington and the Rangers nipping at their heels.

A tough stretch of games awaited. This is when, if you're an Islander, you look back at that seven-game run against losing teams and smack yourself in the head. Here it was April and the next four games were the oncoming Devils, the annoying Buffalo Sabres (who were still mathematically in it), the first-place Boston Bruins and then the desperate Washington Capitals, who were undefeated in 22 straight (19-0-3) against the Islanders and also fighting to stay alive in the playoff race.

Still, it didn't stop old-school television commentator Stan Fischler from announcing with confidence that the recent resurgence made it safe to say the playoffs were a lock for the Islanders.

Laviolette shook his head.

"I don't feel safe until someone puts an *X* next to our name in the newspaper," he said.

The Islanders pulled out a third-period comeback win over the Devils at home and then endured a clutch-and-grab, grind-it-out 1-1 tie with the Sabres to keep collecting points. The very next night, the team had to play the Bruins in Boston. It was a daunting task, considering the exhaustive defensive effort in Buffalo and the offensive firepower the Bruins possessed. So Laviolette had a plan.

The Islanders would play a stall. They'd sit back on D, keep three back at all times, and allow the Bruins to fire away from the perimeter. But nothing in the middle and take no chances offensively.

Basically, they'd trap. Something Milbury despises and Laviolette tries his best to avoid. But this game was important and both men knew it. So they bit the bullet and sold out to the monster many feel is killing the game.

The first period, as it goes with the trap, was an incredible bore. But the Bruins were caught off guard and the Islanders held a 1-0 lead— off a first-period goal by Czerkawski—for most of the game. The Bruins tied it late, but Kvasha—here he is again—won it in overtime.

Afterward, Snow, who was magnificent with 39 saves in the win, was told his team was now just one victory from clinching a playoff spot. More incredible than that, they were just four points behind Atlantic-leading Philly.

"Crazy, huh?" was Snow's reply.

Not as crazy as Nassau Coliseum was on April 6, 2002, the night the Islanders finally beat the Capitals and, more importantly, officially put an end to the seven-year glitch. At first the sellout crowd was tense. Before the start of the game, when one expected the arena to be bursting with energy, the crowd was instead overcome with an eerie nervousness.

Then the Caps scored first, which drew moans and groans. But such emotions were quickly dispersed when Kvasha—yeah, him again— and Cairns netted goals in the first, Jonsson and Blake in the second and Peca early in the third to give the Islanders a 5-1 lead and send the Coliseum into one huge exhale.

Milbury left the Coliseum at that point. He felt satisfied that a win was in the books and wanted to be home to celebrate with his family and especially his wife, Ginger, who with him had lived through all the past misery, depression and many countless sleepless nights. Being the former media relations director for the Islanders, Ginger also had a personal stake in the team that was more than just related to her husband. She had wanted to be there for the game, but at the last minute the babysitter for their two young boys had to cancel. So she stayed behind to watch on TV.

And when he arrived at the house, she greeted him with a surprised but tense look.

"What are you doing here?" she exclaimed.

Milbury then looked at the television. In the time it took him to exit the Coliseum, get in his car and drive the 15 minutes it took to get to his house, the lead had been cut to one. The two anxiously endured the final nail-biting seconds of what resulted in a gut-wrenching but euphoric 5-4 victory.

Milbury slumped in his couch. Nothing ever comes easy.

"It was typical of our season," he laughed. "White-knuckle to the end."

The three stars of the game were Steve Webb, Claude Lapointe and Kenny Jonsson—the three most tenured Islanders and therefore the most tortured.

"It's an awesome feeling," Jonsson beamed.

You had to imagine a majority of those countless former Islanders littered throughout the league wore a grin when they checked the newspaper the next morning and saw that *X* next to the Islanders in the standings.

"Finally!" was all that needed to be said on the cover of the Sunday *Newsday* sports section.

With a playoff berth finally in their pocket, the Islanders set their sights on the Flyers, who were struggling badly as the season wound down. If the games played out right, the season finale between the Islanders and Flyers at the Coliseum could decide the Atlantic winner (and also the No. 2 seed in the East).

But while the Islanders picked up more wins along the way, the Flyers knocked off the Rangers one game before the season finale to clinch the division.

Still, that last game did mean something for the Islanders. A loss would put them sixth in the East with what most considered a favorable first-round matchup against the Southeast Division champion Carolina Hurricanes, a solid but otherwise nondescript team that played in a non-traditional hockey market. A win moved the Isles to fifth place, which set up a first-round meeting with the more experienced and formidable Maple Leafs, who were located at the heart of the hockey universe in Toronto.

The confident Islanders wanted the Leafs. They said so before the game and said so after they beat Philly to finish the season 42-28-8-4 with 96 points, the best marks since the 1984–85 season. The Islanders were in search of the big-ticket matchup.

"It's not slighting Carolina or any other team, but if we go down there, that series would be off the map, compared to other series," Osgood said. "Now we go to Toronto, and it's the big spot. . . . It's going to give us a good chance to get exposure.

"Yeah, I'd say we wanted to go to Toronto before we wanted to go to Carolina."

They wanted 'em and they got 'em.

18

Playoffs!

"Wow," Yashin said as he emerged from the Islanders' locker room. "It must be playoff time."

He came out to address a horde of media that packed the hallway and requested his presence and wanted some answers regarding a strained groin that kept him out of the final week of the season—the first time in his career that he ever missed games due to an actual injury.

It happened, coincidentally, in the playoff clincher against Washington. Questions abounded as to whether he would be ready for the first-round series against the Leafs. The Canadian press was in a frenzy over Yashin, who with Ottawa had struggled for just one assist in his previous eight playoff games—both first-round sweeps at the hands of the Maple Leafs.

Yashin wouldn't discuss his injury. Laviolette, respecting the wishes of his star center, didn't either.

Laviolette's overall personality, especially during interviews, started to change. He was more direct and more entertaining. He even allowed for some repartee. He remained respectful of the Leafs, but stopped well short of being in awe of them and their coach, Pat Quinn, who through the press was already working officials before the series even started.

When told Quinn figured his somewhat hobbled team was the underdog in this matchup, Laviolette scoffed.

"Tell him nice try," he said.

Yashin did suit up for Game 1 of the series and set up the first goal of the series when Kenny Jonsson ripped a rebound of a Yashin shot by goalie Curtis Joseph to give the Islanders a 1-0 lead early in the first period. They carried it into the third and, with a 30-0-4-1 record during the regular season when leading after two, they seemed on their way to taking a 1-0 lead in the series.

But instead of attacking, the Islanders fell back into defensive mode, which Laviolette insists was "not by design." Clearly, it was nerves. The Leafs smelled the fear and jumped all over them in the third to take a 3-1 win, with two goals off deflections.

"We played," said Osgood, "pretty much awful."

In Game 2 the effort was much better, but the result was the same. Joseph stonewalled the Islanders—including an incredible point-blank save on Mark Parrish late in the game—in a 2-0 win.

The Leafs were in control of the series as it headed back to Long Island for Games 3 and 4, and if they didn't have the Islanders physically intimidated, they certainly had them frustrated. The first matter was regarding Leafs veteran nasty boy Shayne Corson, who in the waning moments of Game 1 had whacked Scatchard across the shoulder with his stick. Corson was given a penalty, but not suspended by the league.

The Leafs were getting away with a lot of physical action behind the play and sometimes even right in front of the action. Corson was doing his usual shadowing of Yashin, who had gotten to know him pretty well in the previous Ottawa–Toronto matchups, while Gary Roberts and Bryan McCabe used tactics of their own to muscle the Islanders off the puck.

Not much was being said about this in the papers, and that had Milbury frustrated. Instead, the media was concentrating on the fact that the Islanders were not fighting back.

The off day following the Game 2 loss, Milbury was roaming the hallways of the Coliseum while Laviolette met with the press. When one Toronto reporter asked Milbury if he would talk, the GM declined.

But as Laviolette was wrapping up his interviews, Milbury reemerged with a videotape in his hand. He made eye contact with a few of the New York writers and waved the tape.

"Follow me," he said.

As Milbury fumbled for the keys to the room, reporters sensed their day was picking up. Botte turned to first-year New York *Post* reporter Evan Grossman and veteran Toronto scribe Mike Zeisberger, who both just minutes before were groaning about the little they had to write about for the next day's paper.

"Your story for tomorrow," Botte smirked, "is whatever happens in the next five minutes."

Milbury led the small contingent of media—a collection of seven writers from Toronto and New York—into the Islanders' weight room facility at the Coliseum and popped the tape into a large TV/VCR setup hanging from the ceiling.

He then, in typical Milbury fashion, followed with a bitch session that became national news on what otherwise had began as a slow news day:

"We've got rules in this game and we've got to call them the way they're written," he began, as the television screen showed McCabe hugging Yashin in the corner and impeding his progress to the puck.

"You see, that's fucking. . . . Is that holding or is that fucking holding?" Milbury roared. "That's a joke. All week long I listen to Pat Quinn, that's a fucking hold. That's a fucking joke!"

The next clip is a penalty that was called against Hamrlik on Corson, and Milbury concedes the infraction by Hamrlik, but points out what the referees missed just before.

"At least recognize that the guy fucking spears him on his way in," he said, during a slow-motion replay of Corson charging at Hamrlik with his stick forward. "Watch his stick, right in the gut."

Milbury points to the official standing nearby, watching the play while Corson draws the penalty.

"OK, and look at him look," he said. "He knows [Corson's] diving. We knew he was going to dive when this series started. Even if it's a legit call [against Hamrlik], it's embellished. Which is supposed to be a [diving] call."

The next clip is of Peca being shoved and tripped to the ice by Mats Sundin off a faceoff.

"That's a trip!" Milbury growled. "But I was told that these guys had a hell of a game."

He was referring to what John D'Amico, the supervisor of officials for the series, told him after Game 2.

Perhaps the most priceless stuff from Milbury during this rant came at the expense of former Islander Bryan McCabe, who was using a move called "the can opener" against onrushing Islanders. The move is done when McCabe places his stick between the skates of an opponent and when the opponent gets close enough, McCabe twists the stick so that it locks the legs of the opponent. One shove and he falls.

Milbury showed a clip of McCabe pulling the move on Czerkawski.

"That's a fucking penalty!" Milbury yelled at the screen. "You cannot put your stick between a guy's legs. It's an illegal play, it's a fucking penalty. You'll see that happen ten times over. He did it when he was here and he shouldn't get away with it. That's obstruction tripping. Could it be any more clearer than that? It can't. And it results in a scoring opportunity at the other end of the ice.

"That's what we're trying to get out of the fucking game. We've been trying to get that out for years. We put it in the rule book because of that."

When Milbury pauses, the voice of announcer Harry Neale from the CBC broadcast is heard.

"His signature move," Neale says of McCabe, "the can opener."

"Signature move," Milbury growled, "it's fucking illegal. It's a fucking penalty. He can't fucking pivot that well, that's why he uses it."

A few clips later shows Bates hit from behind just before attempting a one-timer chance in the slot. No penalty was called on that one, either.

"This one is pretty amazing," Milbury said. "Is that interference or is that interference? It's fucking interference! He's telling me that they're calling a fucking good game, then I have some serious questions about judgment. I mean, fuck, if its not a cross-check it's interference. It's a scoring chance."

Van Impe is shown being whistled for a legitimate cross-checking penalty. But that's not what angered Milbury.

"Watch the vicious cross-check by Van Impe," he says sarcastically, "Ohh!"

He then turned to the entranced reporters, who weren't even bothering to scribble down anything he said. They all had tape recorders doing the work. This was too good a show to miss and Milbury didn't disappoint. By Botte's count, Milbury totaled 26 F-bombs in the tirade.

"If it goes one way it's gotta go the other way or we're getting jobbed here," he continued. "I listen to Pat Quinn fucking bitch about this for three days and now we get screwed. We go into Toronto and they can't fucking make calls when they're supposed to. They're under duress."

The video continued to roll, as did Milbury's anger. There was McCabe's can opener again, this time on Isbister, who pawed at McCabe afterward.

"Again, that's a fucking penalty!" Milbury said. "You can't put your stick between a guy's legs. If they don't have the courage to call it, then there's something wrong. I'm glad Isbister finally reacts to that. What the fuck is he supposed to do?"

A replay was shown.

"There it is, the stick between the legs," he said. "The can opener. It's fucking illegal."

To perhaps add some balance, Milbury included a clip of Lapointe pulling down Corson behind the net, an obvious obstruction penalty that went uncalled.

"It's not just all them," he said. "I mean, those are fucking penalties and they've gotta be called."

After a few more shots of the can opener, which became the buzzword of the series, Milbury finally clicked off the tape and faced his audience again.

"I think I've made my point," he said. "I just thought I'd share that with you."

A brief question and answer session followed, but there was really not much more Milbury could say.

"Hey, they're humans, they're going to make mistakes," he said of the officials. "But make 'em both ways. And at least respect the rules we work so hard to try to craft. They're there for a purpose. And we absolutely disagree with the judgment exercised yesterday. It was not right and I have the tapes to prove it. What good it will do, I don't know. I've seen it work for Pat Quinn when he bitched and moaned for three days before this series started."

He then removed the tape from the set and turned to the door.

"Have a nice day," he said.

Milbury was later fined $30,000 by the NHL, which released a statement saying they didn't find his actions amusing. But Milbury's rant, for the time being, certainly spiced up what had been a fairly lifeless series.

The question is, did he do it for that? Was he really that upset with the officiating?

Or did he do it to deflect some criticism from his wound-licking team?

Whatever the case, momentum had somehow shifted in the series even before Game 3. Islanders fans, already delirious from the fact that a playoff game was being held at the Coliseum for the first time in eight years, seemed to pick up Milbury's intensity and carry it through to the players, who responded with a wildly entertaining and desperately needed 6-1 victory. The old building rocked with a fever from an era long gone. They cheered as each goal flew by a shaky Joseph and roared with every explosive hit battering-ram forward Steve Webb laid on a Leafs player.

The crowd even called out McCabe when he attempted the can opener and applauded the officials for calling it a penalty.

In an incredible transformation from dormant to dominant, Nassau Coliseum actually provided the Islanders a useful weapon.

"I've never heard it this loud," Lapointe marveled. "It's like the last six years never happened."

If Game 3 was a long-awaited catharsis for Islanders fans, Game 4 practically put them into cardiac arrest.

The Islanders trailed 2-1 going into the third and were just 20 minutes from facing a daunting deficit of three games to one in the series.

In the dressing room during the second intermission, the Islanders kept their resolve.

"We knew," winger Kip Miller noted, "we had to go after them."

Miller started the eruption of three Islanders goals to spark the thrilling comeback. He scored on a wrap-around shot that deflected off McCabe's skate at 13:16 of the third to make it 2-2. One minute and forty seconds later, Hamrlik rifled a tricky point shot that deflected off the shaft of Joseph's stick and went in to make it a 3-2 Islanders lead at 14:56. The Coliseum exploded.

But the Leafs kept coming and Corson tied it with a broken-play goal at 16:34. Corson behind the net caught Osgood looking the wrong way when he deposited a wrap-around shot.

The building shook as it seemed the drama of playoff overtime was inevitable. No one was prepared for the real drama was about to take place just a minute later.

That's when Bates took a head-man pass up the left side and flew by the Toronto defense. He was heading toward Joseph when McCabe dove and swatted his long stick at Bates's feet, which tripped him. Referee Brad Watson immediately raised his arm to signal a penalty and then pointed emphatically to the center ice circle.

Penalty shot.

With 2:30 left in regulation.

The Leafs were incensed, but Watson's call stood. During the brief pause in action, Peca called Bates over to the sideboards a few feet away from the bench.

"I'm not going to tell you what to do," Peca said under the din of the buzzing Coliseum crowd. "I'm just going to tell you what to look for."

Peca, a true student of the sport, knew that Joseph—a superstar goalie who went by the nickname "CuJo"—was very tough to beat with a one-on-one move. Plus, at that late moment of the game, the ice was choppy.

"Take your best shot," Peca then said.

A few moments later, Bates was standing at the center-ice circle, feeling the emotions of every single one of the 16,000-plus patrons who couldn't take their eyes off him.

"I said, 'Oh man, what a feeling this is going to be,'" Bates said. "I thought I was gonna puke."

A few strides up the ice, Bates drifted toward the left side of the goal and started leaning into his right-handed shot. Joseph then started to shift toward Bates's right—his left—to counter, but he might have over-compensated. When Bates saw this, he snapped a hard rocket of a fore-hand shot over Joseph's right shoulder and into the top left portion of the net. The Islanders regained the lead at 4-3.

Bates coasted around the net and curled up the right boards. When he reached center ice, he fell into a bear hug from Scatchard and the rest of the Islanders players mobbed them.

It was the first converted penalty shot in Islanders playoff history and the first shot since Randy Wood failed on an attempt against Mike Richter of the Rangers on April 5, 1990. Denis Potvin had the only other attempt in franchise history, when he was stopped by Pat Riggin of the Washington Capitals on April 8, 1983.

Putting it in historical perspective, Bates's goal was just another magical moment in the fabled playoff lore of the franchise. It seemed if this team just got to the playoffs, something incredible always happened. Of course, for eight years the team couldn't get to the playoffs.

The series was tied heading back to Toronto for Game 5. Quinn, who spent most of the time in Games 3 and 4 shaking his head and wav-ing at officials, figured it was his turn to rant.

"I was asked the other day if there were some repercussions or in-fluence by Milbury's statements and I'm starting to wonder," Quinn said. "That was quite embarrassing for the league."

But the gamesmanship was only just beginning, and so was a volley of trash-talking between the two locker rooms. Reporters covering the event practically ran from one room to another like little kids in a schoolyard looking to start a fight.

"Did you hear what he said about you? What do you think of that?"
"Oooh!"

"He just said this about you for saying that about him."

The series was already nasty from the start, from the first whack Corson laid on Scatchard after Game 1. The end of Game 3 had more shenanigans, as Roberts jumped Czerkawski (later claiming that Webb was head-hunting the Leafs' skill players, so he was just doing the same to an Islander skill player) and Darcy Tucker and Corson took cheap shots at Osgood.

During Roberts's scrum with Czerkawski, Isbister stepped in and wrestled Roberts to the ground. In their ensuing scrap, Isbister sprained his wrist. He was lost for the rest of the series.

Osgood also suffered an injury, though it didn't take him out of the lineup. During a scuffle in the crease following a save, Osgood was twisted awkwardly under a pile and took a shot from Corson. He jumped up to go after Corson and rivets in his skate blade popped off. His ankle twisted and remained sore, along with his upper back.

The Leafs were also hurting. It was learned after Game 3 that Sundin suffered a broken wrist in Game 2, off a deflected shot. He tried to go in Game 3, but was ineffective. In Game 4 he didn't dress, but Quinn left the Leafs shorthanded because he failed to call up a player from the minors to replace Sundin, who didn't return for the rest of the series.

Toronto winger Alexander Mogilny was livid after the game.

"The last time I checked, you have to have fucking people around any time someone goes down," the Russian said, outwardly ripping Quinn to reporters. "You play with 19 guys back to back in a playoff game?

"You're not playing an exhibition game here. This is the Stanley Cup playoffs. It changed the whole scenario."

Quinn goofed again in Game 5 when he wrote the wrong name on the lineup card—crossing up injured Mikael Renberg with Robert Reichel. But there were other fireworks before the game that wound up being the bigger story afterward.

Peca and Tucker had a feud going on in the series, but nothing out of the ordinary. The two couldn't be any more different as personalities. While Peca tends to remain calm and do a lot of grinning in the face of pressure, Tucker is more maniacal. With his long, stringy hair whipping around his face and spitting sweat from his mouth, Tucker screamed at Peca during Game 4 from the penalty box after Peca continually avoided goading for a fight.

Tucker, a midsized professional agitator who also has some good offensive skills, hated the fact that Peca was running around the ice nailing people and not getting any in return.

"I'm going to kill you!" Tucker screamed as Peca glared at him with his dark eyes lowered under his helmet.

"I'm taking you out!"

During the off day before Game 5, Peca then took the opportunity to needle Tucker in the media.

"The thing is, they've got some guys that think they're bullies, you know?" he said, sitting casually in his dressing room stall with his trademark five o'clock shadow and youthful eyes. "And it's rare in this league that you're going to bully people around. People will try and try and say things, threaten you, whatever. It becomes ridiculous almost, where you hear the same things every day. 'I'm going to kill you' or 'Maybe next year.' I hear the same rhetoric over and over. It's comical.

"But you gotta deal with it. We just got to make sure physically that we don't get involved in this stuff."

He was asked about Tucker goading him and Peca helped himself to another helping of smack.

"It's not a good tradeoff for our team, myself for him," he said, regarding the coincidental minor for retaliating. "So I'm not going to get myself involved in something like that. The playoffs are about hard, physical hockey. If the only means to try to counter that is to fight all the time, then maybe you're not cut out for playoff hockey. Our team's been playing hard and physical and we're going to continue that way."

And, Michael, of the free-for-all scrums late in the recent games?

"People just feel that once two guys go, everybody's got to jump and make a pile out of it," he said of Toronto's bully tactics. "You shake your head sometimes. I know it's playoff hockey and everybody gets emotionally riled up, but I think it's comical."

Tucker had choice words for Peca in response, but his best line was about Peca being a good player.

"Just ask him," Tucker added sardonically.

Tucker and the Leafs then came out swinging in Game 5 and the Islanders, surprisingly, were caught on their heels. It was 2-0 in the first period, but the real damaging blows had yet to be delivered.

Late in the first, Jonsson went into the left corner of the Islanders' end to play the puck. His shoulders were square to the boards and his head was down as he tried to kick the puck free.

Suddenly, his legs gave out under him and his body crumpled to the ice. There isn't much Jonsson remembers after that.

Roberts had come screaming in from the opposite point and slammed into the unsuspecting Jonsson. The impact of the violet collision snapped Jonsson's neck back and his helmet cracked from the resulting whiplash into the glass.

After a few moments, he was able to get to his skates, but he needed help from Bates and Aucoin to make it to the locker room. It was the third concussion Jonsson had suffered in as many seasons. The Islanders' best defenseman was lost for the series.

Roberts was given a five-minute major for boarding, but because referee Paul Devorski supposedly didn't "see" a head injury to Jonsson, Roberts did not get a game misconduct. NHL Rule 47b states "when a major penalty's imposed (for charging), for a foul resulting in an injury to the face or head . . . a game misconduct shall be imposed."

"They told me there was no injury to the face or head," Laviolette barked incredulously. "Kenny lay unconscious on the ice, and I'm trying to figure out exactly what qualifies as a head injury. Kenny Jonsson is lost for the year now. . . . For [Roberts] to stay in the game is disgusting."

The Islanders managed one goal during the major power play, which carried over into the second period. Things turned terribly worse for them then.

Peca was in his own end and was set to outlet the puck when Tucker had him lined up from about mid-ice. Peca moved the puck up ice and out of the corner of his eye, he saw Tucker cruising in at the last second. He prepared himself for a heavy body-to-body hit by pushing off his feet to buffer the momentum.

But Tucker wasn't going body to body. He dipped at the waist and submarined Peca with a nasty hip check that sent Peca tumbling into the air. Replays show Tucker's hip made contact with Peca's thigh.

An MRI showed the anterior cruciate ligament in Peca's left knee was torn.

No penalty was called on Tucker.

But now Peca was out for the series, too. Later the team announced that Peca likely wouldn't be back until the middle of the 2002-03 season.

The Leafs won Game 5 with a 6-3 score and held a 3-2 lead in the series. The Islanders, without Jonsson and Peca, were clearly done. Afterward, they growled and grumbled about the two cheap shots delivered by notoriously dirty players. The Leafs, naturally, maintained a "Who, me?" innocence.

Tucker was asked if his hit on Peca was a premeditated dirty hit.

"That's ridiculous," he snapped.

The NHL's czar of discipline, Colin Campbell, sided with the Maple Leafs. Neither player was suspended for Game 6, which was back at the Coliseum.

"For me, it's disappointing. You have a guy [Tucker] who says he's going to take you out and then he goes through with it," Peca said. "You'd think a guy like that—that talks a good game like him—would go shoulder to shoulder, but he's come out on the wrong end of it so many times when he's gone shoulder to shoulder with me that he decided to go low."

Milbury also was pissed again, although his words were more G-rated than the ones he'd aimed at the officiating earlier in the series. Still, he lost it when informed by *Toronto Sun* reporter Terry Koshan that on-ice yapping is a common playoff occurrence.

"It's common stuff on the ice, but is it common to ram a guy's head face-first into the glass from a running start from the blue line in?" Milbury replied, referring to Roberts's charge on Jonsson. "Is it common to duck down on a late hit after a simple clearing play to aim at a guy's knees after you've talked about doing something like that?

"No, that's not playoff hockey," he snarled. "That's not hockey at all. That's thuggery."

The day before Game 6, with the mood somber and the media figuring the Islanders were through, *The Post*'s Grossman asked Milbury to reflect on the success the season had been for his team.

Milbury crinkled his brow.

"Wait a minute," he said, facing Grossman. "We're not doing any retrospectives here. We're playing Game 6 tomorrow. This is a game we can win. This is a game we need to focus on, have our game face ready and go out and win the damn game."

The Coliseum was packed again and it was an ornery bunch. Many fans got to the Coliseum early just to boo Tucker and Roberts during pregame warmups. Some fans outside the arena spotted a car with the Canadian flag on it. They ripped it off the car and burned it right in the parking lot.

And, despite criticism from everyone right up to Wang, a large portion of Islanders fans again embarrassed themselves by booing the Canadian national anthem, just like they did before Games 3 and 4.

But they got what they came to see, too. An emotionally charged Islanders team put a pounding on the Leafs, both on the scoreboard and on the ice. Laviolette inserted seldom-used tough guy Jim Cummins into the lineup for Peca. Cummins had one and only one assignment: shadow Roberts. And that he did from the moment the puck dropped.

Roberts just kept playing, taking the occasional whacks and swats from Cummins.

Milbury called up another well-known scrapper, defenseman Ray Schultz, from Bridgeport to replace Jonsson in the lineup. It was clear the Islanders felt the need to bulk up.

It was also clear that Webb was back to being a runaway train on the ice, as he blasted Roberts and Tucker with high, hard hits that certainly were out of the boundaries of clean, yet, in a clear sign from the officials that revenge would be permitted, went unpenalized.

The Coliseum crowd showered the Islander wrecking ball with chants of "Steve Webb! Steve Webb!"

Czerkawski, who had done nothing in the series up to that point, stepped up to score two goals in the 5-3 win to even the series and set up a decisive Game 7. Both of them weren't as much great shots by Czerkawski as they were terrible goals allowed by Joseph, who clearly was not as comfortable in the Coliseum nets as he was at Air Canada Centre.

And at the end of the game, with Tucker looking to fight anyone, Bates tackled him and wrestled him to the ice. At the same time, Cairns got a hold of Corson and put a world-class beating on the veteran Leafs forward that was memorable for the bloodthirsty Islanders fans who witnessed it.

But it was mostly forgettable for the NHL, who, from this series alone, took some heavy criticism for allowing two teams to get so out of control. Corson, after falling to the ice from a heavy barrage of punches, kicked at Cairns several times. Campbell had no choice but to suspend Corson for Game 7.

Campbell, who proved in this series that he is not comfortable with being in charge of disciplining players, explained his decision by saying he "took into consideration that there is nothing in playing the game that would justify kicking your opponent."

Well put.

Corson claimed that Cairns had pulled his hair in the fight. And with that said, the series had reached a point of ridiculousness.

The Islanders headed back to Toronto for the third time in this series and the fifth time within the span of a month since the trade deadline. In the past, the Islanders had rarely arrived there with much fanfare other than the usual media crunch in the hockey-mad city.

But now they were on everyone's radar. They were the sudden enemy in a region of rabid fans and proud Canadians who were livid over the booing of their national anthem by disrespectful Long Islanders. Never mind the fear that this upstart team was set to come in and eliminate the Cup-starved Leafs in the first round.

The Islanders took their usual chartered flight from Republic Airport in Farmingdale, Long Island to Toronto's Lester B. Pearson International Airport.

Now one of the main reasons—other than luxury—sports teams fly chartered flights is because they don't follow the same deplaning procedures as they do when they take commercial flights. The plane taxis to a separate terminal for private flights. Baggage is transferred to a waiting bus, onto which the players board directly from the tarmac. Especially in the days following the tragic events of 9/11, chartering is more convenient and usually hassle-free, even when crossing the national borders between U.S. and Canada. A customs agent greets the party and checks all IDs. Usually the process takes less than 10 minutes to clear customs and board the bus.

But on the eve of Game 7, when the Islanders arrived at Pearson, it wasn't the usual friendly faces awaiting them ready to help them make a smooth and quick transition to the hotel. It was then that the Islanders realized that they were going up against more than just the Maple Leafs in this series.

Kerry Gwydir is the team's travel manager and well-schooled in the customary process of arriving in Toronto via charter. For this particular flight he called ahead as usual to customs and the FBO in Toronto to check that all the right documentation concerning the charter had arrived to the proper offices. He received confirmation. In fact, the officials at Pearson were sent two copies of the Islanders' information because a team secretary, Joanne Holewa, had faxed the documents from the Islanders' offices earlier in the week.

Before the flight departed, Gwydir then made his rounds. He checked that each player, team staffer and a few members of the broadcast media that are invited on the charters each had the proper documentation to pass Canadian customs. All were said to be in compliance.

Around 2 P.M. the team's Midwest Express flight arrived at Pearson and was met by a group of customs officers. They boarded the plane and ordered everyone to remain seated. Outside, more officers surrounded the waiting team bus.

"I have never seen this in all my years of picking up sports teams," the surprised bus driver later said.

One officer walked down the aisle and checked off each passenger listed on the manifest, which was a typical procedure. However, as the officer came across two names not on the list—rookie Trent Hunter and call-up Ray Schultz—a problem arose. Gwydir noticed the officer was using a manifest from the team's first trip to Toronto for Games 1 and 2 of the series. Hunter and Schultz, who were added to the roster later in the series, weren't on that original trip.

So the officer started asking them questions. And another decided to make it known that Howie Rose, the team's television play-by-play broadcaster, would need a background check. It was a bizarre scene.

Then one of the officers asked for the team's travel director. Milbury was within earshot.

"I'm the general manager," he said.

"Are you the travel manager?" the agent replied.

"No," Milbury answered and then pointed to Gwydir. "He is."

"I need to speak with *him*," the agent said.

Milbury laughed. "I'm the manager of this team!" he exclaimed.

But the agent would only speak with Gwydir, who was taking calls from concerned players who were allowed to board the bus. Even they, however, were met with further hassles as the outside officers searched the players and their baggage extensively. "They might as well have been wearing DEA jackets," one of them said.

Eventually, everything checked out OK. An hour had passed before the bus was allowed to pull off the tarmac. Gwydir was then scolded by the officers.

"Because you haven't given us the proper paperwork," the person said, "you may lose your chartering privileges at Pearson."

Meanwhile, later that day, Botte and Hahn arrived via an American Airlines flight from LaGuardia. For sportswriters—especially those who cover hockey—entering Canada is usually met with a question of what one's business is in Canada. The reply, "Tomorrow's game between the Islanders and Maple Leafs," is often met with a smile and some small talk about the sport.

Hahn entered without a hitch, as the customs agent made a small joke about the Islanders on the verge of breaking Toronto's heart should they win. But Botte strangely was red-marked and asked to get on another line so that his personal items could be searched along with his background.

Did we already mention that the series had reached a point of ridiculousness?

Prior to Game 7, Botte approached Islanders legend (and current goalie coach) Billy Smith for an interview. Smith is generally approachable, but after that it's a crapshoot. True to his personality as one of the greatest money goalies in the history of the sport, Smitty can be as volatile as the stock market.

Botte barely got out a question about one of Smith's pet peeves as a player, the traditional handshake that follows every playoff series in hockey. Smith was notorious for refusing to participate in the handshake tradition.

So when it was brought up to him, Smith growled and tried to cut off the interview. Botte persisted and Smith, despite his growing anger, gave the reporter what he wanted.

"Are you telling me I should shake a guy's hand after someone runs somebody, or like Corson kicking Cairns, or a guy running Kenny Johnson (sic) from behind? That's my feeling on it," he said. "I don't shake hands with people that would run me from behind or would kick me with their skates on. Nor would I expect it vice versa, if I did something like that.

"But what I did in my career, I did it. It's been written probably 5,000 times. I know it hasn't been written this week, but the guys that should be heard from are the guys in there, not me. I had my time, it's their time."

He then explained himself one more time.

"I don't want to be a focal point," Smith said. "I'm better to be seen and not heard, but that's just the way I've always felt.

"This is not a game of fun. This is a game of livelihoods. If you go out and play golf, it's for fun. I just didn't because I don't believe in it. I believe a handshake is a thing that's done in a friendly game that livelihoods don't depend on it. Some guys, if you lose, some guys won't be here next year."

The slugfest of a first-round series finally came down not to who wasn't on the ice, but to who was. In Game 7, when it mattered most, those on the ice for the Leafs were simply better.

In the bitter end, however, when sticks stayed down, gloves stayed on and hits stayed clean, Toronto's experience and sheer determination won out—if barely—over the Islanders' youth and raw exuberance. Despite a rally to push the exhaustive series to practically the final seconds, the Islanders lost, 4-2.

Roberts set the tone by playing like a torpedo at the Islanders' net and tied the score at 1 on a play that essentially turned the game in favor of the Leafs.

Before that, Yashin, free from having to dance with the suspended Corson all night, had given the Islanders a 1-0 lead with his third goal of the series. (He finished with seven points in the seven games and put to rest the claims that he was not a playoff performer.)

But Roberts's goal was not as troubling as the Islanders' incredible Jekyll-and-Hyde act between the Coliseum and the Air Canada Centre. Webb was relatively ineffective and heard chants of "Steve Webb Sucks!" from the Toronto crowd. Cummins wasn't used against Roberts like he was in Game 6, even if for a few shifts. And Osgood appeared to be feeling the effects of a series of crease-crashing by the Leafs.

It took him a few moments to get up after Roberts ran him over for the tying goal. But it was a play many Islanders felt shouldn't have happened.

Czerkawski, after a rebound performance in Game 6, was back to circling and curling around the ice. It's something he tends to do, dance and spin. He also tends to avoid being hit. So with the puck on his stick in the neutral zone, Czerkawski went into his figure skating routine and lost the puck. A few Toronto players pinched to add pressure and Czerkawski, with the puck at his skates, appeared to tense up when he saw Roberts darting after him from the neutral zone.

In a flash, Roberts took the puck from a stationary Czerkawski and charged toward the Islanders' net. Osgood slid to make a stop, but Roberts stepped over the goalie and buried the puck into an open net.

That was the series in a nutshell.

In the locker room between periods, a few of the Islanders were furious with Czerkawski. The Leafs had built a 3-1 lead on goals by Mogilny and former Islander Travis Green heading into the third, but the Islanders were not dead yet. Miller capped a solid playoff for him with his team-leading fourth goal of the series to cut it to a 3-2 deficit. Yashin had a few chances late to tie it, but couldn't finish. Rookie Trent Hunter, who had been a pleasant surprise after he was called up to replace Isbister in the lineup for Game 4, also had a golden opportunity that was stopped by Joseph.

Mogilny's empty-netter with 40 seconds left finally—finally—put the Islanders away.

"I've been around this game for a long time and that was as tough, mean and dirty—whatever you want to call it—a series as I've seen in a long time," Quinn said afterward, as one of many Leafs who paid homage to the resilient Islanders. "They kept coming at us. It was almost like last man standing."

Laviolette didn't want to accept many pats on the back. He said it in early October, with the beat writers chuckling around him. He said it again in April, with not a soul laughing anymore.

"We didn't make the playoffs just to make them and gain experience like everyone else wanted us to do," Laviolette said. "Our goals were higher than that. Internally, I think we all thought that we could win the Stanley Cup."

Instead, it ended with the traditional handshake, despite Smith's aforementioned opinions. Even with the verbal and physical tête-à-têtes that marred the series, the Islanders and Maple Leafs lined up to make nice.

"Good series," Tucker said to Webb, patting him on the shoulder. "You made a name for yourself."

But for Webb and the Islanders, that wasn't enough.

19

How Soon Is Now?

They were paving over paradise with astroturf.

And while workers cleared away the ice at Nassau Coliseum for the last time during the spring of 2002 and laid the carpet for the arena football season, Milbury was sitting in the Islanders' offices fighting the devastation of what might have been.

The Coliseum that night would have been the stage for Game 1 of the Eastern Conference semifinals, had the Islanders won Game 7 against the Maple Leafs earlier that week in Toronto. They were so painfully close to advancing into the next round. Milbury thinks they were closer to even greater things. The Carolina Hurricanes' surprising run to the Stanley Cup Finals would later haunt him even more.

"It was wide open, just wide open," he said, with more frustration than disappointment in his tone. "We knew it coming in. Boston had established itself as the front-runner and then they went down. I thought that left it, as it is today, totally open for anybody. So nothing will surprise me in these series coming forward. Any one of those four teams has a very reasonable chance to advance to the Stanley Cup Finals. And yes, absolutely, we would have been relatively healthy, with the exception of Peca."

He then had to cut himself off.

"But, hey," he said, with a shrug and his eyes downcast, "you can drive yourself nuts thinking that way."

But that's what he would do over the next few weeks as the playoffs unfolded. Even when the Detroit Red Wings hoisted the Cup, Milbury knew his team had a shot at it. It took some time to fight the regret he felt as he forced himself to acknowledge his optimistic outlook for next season, which at the time seemed so far away. Of course the legacy of losing that clouded the franchise for so many years seemed just as distant.

It would be easy for most to take a year like the one the Islanders had in 2001-02, compared to those leading up to it, and feel satisfied. But Milbury, ever the tortured soul, just couldn't. Especially not with the Game 7 loss so fresh in his mind.

"It certainly was a season of progress and of building people up and of people maturing," he said. "But I can't let go of the fact that we lost in the first round. Yes, we made it. It's an improvement. We scored a lot more points. Great. But we lost Game 7 to the Toronto Maple Leafs and that, at least for a few days, will be first and foremost in my thoughts. And I don't want that to happen again. I want to go deeper, I want to go further. I want to go all the way sometime. The sooner the better. But it's nice to be thinking that way instead of, 'How can we survive next season?'"

The concentration instead is on how to, as Milbury likes to say, "advance the cause." He met with Wang to discuss preliminary plans for an off season that included attempts to upgrade the talent at the wings around Yashin and make his defense a bit deeper so that Jonsson and Aucoin aren't forced into playing 30 minutes a night. The payroll would inevitably go up again—for the third straight year under the ownership of Wang and Kumar. Naturally, so would ticket prices.

And then, too, expectations. Milbury more than anyone was aware of that. He entered the summer with one year left on his contract and therefore little time to bask in the afterglow of a rejuvenating season for his team and his career.

"We're all trying to coat this with sugar and it's not going down real good at this address right now," he said. "We were eliminated from the first round—Game 7 notwithstanding, the way we played notwithstanding—and that means that now the players go home, the coach goes home and the manager and his staff take a hard look at what we've done to get this far and find a way to make the team better from a personnel standpoint so that we're not out in the first round next year. So we have work to do, obviously."

Wang continued to work behind the scenes to get himself out of the SMG lease and into a new arena. Late in the spring Nassau County politicians were considering condemning the lease, parting ways with troublesome SMG and joining with the Islanders on an arena project.

And yet the old Coliseum was a rediscovery for Long Island sports fans, who raced to the box office to get an early jump on season tickets for 2002-03.

It even was a place Milbury had grown to love after, for many years, it had been a house of horrors for him. He said he'd never forget what the place was like for Game 3 against Toronto, which was the first playoff game at the old arena in eight years.

"There was as much electricity in a building that you can contain and still not have the roof blown off," he said, his eyes softening as if he was talking about an old friend. "That was a special feeling for everybody. For me, that sort of marked—no, stamped—that this has been a good season for Long Island hockey fans."

As for himself? Mad Mike will always be Mad Mike. He'll always be quick to dish out a smart-ass line, he'll never be shy to offer an opinion, and, no matter how hard he tries to avoid it, he won't be able to keep himself from being a lightning rod for controversy.

To paraphrase his own description of one of his prospects, what makes Milbury an asshole is what makes him good.

And what can't be denied is his very own claim in the worst of times running this comic-strip franchise: he's indeed an Islander. And considering all he's been through and survived, he's as tried and true blue as perhaps anyone in franchise history, including the dynasty era. Maybe even Denis Potvin would agree with that.

Then again, maybe not.

But of course, Milbury will continue to act as if he doesn't give a shit what Potvin or anyone else thinks of him. He also said in his final media address of the season that vindication was not his to savor. His point? Just like the Islanders' failures were supposedly not just about Milbury, neither are their successes.

Not a word of it is to be believed. Milbury's resolve and resiliency might not have been strictly motivated by selfishness—he truly holds deep emotions for the franchise in the way two soldiers do for each other after surviving a pummeled foxhole—but it certainly had a lot to do with a lifelong mission to somehow, some way become a person who earns the respect of the person who has been the harshest and most relentless of his many critics.

That, of course, would be himself. That would be the man whose self-evaluation of what in one breath he called a "renaissance season" was summed up the next breath in a simple, poignant and telling statement. The franchise's slogan might have been "We're Back," but considering all that the team had been through and all that Milbury had been through with it, he perhaps coined a more accurate phrase for this new era in New York Islanders history.

"It's nice," he says, "not to feel stupid anymore."